$\mathcal{M}$UTUAL $\mathcal{D}$

In the spring of 1978 I was attending a small Midwestern college. I was friends with a group of five young women who occupied a dormitory suite at the other end of our coed dorm. We were friends only, and I never felt any romantic interest in any of them.

One night I dreamt that I was in their suite, and I went from room to room and made love to each one. It wasn't passionate/lustful lovemaking; it was more like sharing a soulful experience, and communicating with each other our deepest thoughts and emotions. In fact, I clearly remember one of the women of the dream telling me how extremely unlovable she felt, while I reassured her. Later I learned that this woman had a very unhappy home life.

The next day I remembered the dream because it was so vivid. As I was walking to class that afternoon, someone in the dorm came up to me and said, "Hey, I heard you were quite a Romeo last night." I asked her what she meant by that. Then she told me that Nadine and Sheila both dreamt that I made love to them in their dorm rooms the night before. I was amazed! Three of us apparently recalled the same dream incident!

I was too shy to talk to them about it, and I was also concerned that they would interpret the dream on a physical level, instead of the deep emotional level that it was to me. Now I wish I had talked to them and gotten the details of their dream experience.

MUTUAL DREAMING

WHEN TWO OR MORE PEOPLE SHARE THE SAME DREAM

Linda Lane Magallón

POCKET BOOKS

New York   London   Toronto   Sydney   Tokyo   Singapore

An *Original* Publication of POCKET BOOKS

POCKET BOOKS, a division of Simon and Schuster Inc.
1230 Avenue of the Americas, New York, NY 10020

ISBN: 0-671-52684-7

First Pocket Books trade paperback printing June 1997

10   9   8   7   6   5   4   3   2   1

POCKET and colophon are registered trademarks of
Simon & Schuster Inc.

Cover design by Patrice Kaplan
Front cover photo by Ann Cutting/Photonica
Text design by Stanley S. Drate/Folio Graphics Co. Inc.

Printed in the U.S.A.

To the new heroes of dreaming.
Special thanks to my family
and to the members
of the Bay Area Dreamworkers Group.

CONTENTS

MUTUAL DREAMING

$\mathcal{P}$REFACE

$\mathcal{Y}$ou hold in your hands a key to the door of a
new reality: the domain of the social dream. Your
key is called mutual dreaming. This book allows you to turn
the key and go through the door. How far you will venture
is up to you. You can do it vicariously. Simply read about
what others have done; accompany them on a comfortable
voyage of imagination. As you read, you might come to recognize when your own dreams spontaneously resonate with
others. Perhaps then you'll realize that you are already on
the new heroes' journey. Or, you can join the growing ranks
of social dreamers who deliberately dream together.

This book introduces you to the idea of mutual dreaming
and tells you how to do it. You will have the opportunity to
consider the original concepts of what constitutes a successful result: "having the same dream" and "meeting in a
dream." But actual dream samples will allow you to expand
those concepts and journey even further into the wide field
of dreams.

1

What Can You Gain from this Journey?

- Recognize that you can have a mutual dream.
- Compare your motivation for mutual dreaming with others'.
- Consider the explanations for mutual dreaming.
- Discover how mutual dream language works.
- Learn how to dream together deliberately in the partnership model.

A Quest for the Mutual Dream

In 1982 I became fascinated by dreams. So that I might learn to understand their meaning and significance, I became an apprentice, not of individual psychology, but of community dreamwork.

A background in social science, education, communication, and business best suited me for this approach. In order to qualify for my MBA, I had to do a group project, not an individual thesis. This unusual requirement engaged me in that rare academic combination of theory plus applied experience in teamwork. The grade of our team and our ability to graduate were dependent upon the real-time results of our group's separate and combined abilities.

Within the dreamwork community, I became active as a dream group member, network coordinator, group founder, and board member. These waking-state connections were the testing ground to refine and develop mutual dreaming ideas and techniques. They were research and development for what did work, and what didn't.

But I am a dreamer, first. Not only do I study the subject, I do the deed. I know what lucid dreams, psychic dreams, and archetypal dreams are because I've "been there, done that." And when I do it in the company of others, it's what's called participant-observer behavior. This approach is fairly new to dream research. You'll read more about it in these pages.

As an in-dream researcher, I attempt to replicate others'

experiences in order to compare them with my own. I want to have firsthand knowledge so I can speak a communal language and compare notes and ideas with fellow dreamers. It's also extremely useful in order to weed out the flotsam and jetsam from real nighttime dreams.

Today I am a veteran of more than a dozen group dreaming projects and two dozen dream telepathy experiments. I've reviewed every book of dreams I could lay my hands on. I've exchanged information and worked firsthand with dreamwork colleagues and dreamers. I've distributed questionnaires, done surveys, and gone out to the hair salon, the workplace, and the cocktail party to ask, "Have you ever had a mutual dream?"

And I've dreamed—a lot. With family and friends, with colleagues and pen pals, with bare acquaintances and complete unknowns. Then I've used the information I gathered to analyze, study, and try to understand what happened when people dreamt together both spontaneously and with full conscious intent.

The effort generated thousands of dreams.

Structure of the Book

When I first began my research, there was no primer, no survey course, no owner's manual on mutual dreaming. So I had to write one. The first three parts are that basic text. It lays the groundwork for my own fieldwork as described in the latter two parts.

Part I, "Introduction to Mutual Dreams" defines the two classic mutual dreams and then compares those classics with the dreams that most folks actually experience with their friends, close colleagues, and family.

Part II, "Ways and Whys of Dreaming Together" expands the arena of twofold dreaming to group connections. We'll look at the big picture, today and throughout history. We'll also consider some of the explanations that have been offered for the occurrence of this unusual phenomenon and discover why people dream together with full conscious intent.

Part III, "How to Dream Together" is the nuts and bolts of deliberate dreaming in the partnership paradigm. We'll review how to induce mutual dreams and, even more important, how to understand and recognize the results of dreaming together.

Part IV, "New Field Research" describes the reciprocity of deliberate mutual dreaming. Step-by-step, we can track shared dreaming as it evolves into a dynamic social event.

Part V, "Results of Research" indicates that shared dreaming in the partnership model results in a shift from negative to positive dreams, which I call the Environmental Effect. Our hidden partners are unveiled, and their means of "meeting" hold some new surprises for us.

On to the Future

Someday the reality of mutual dreams may be proven in a scientific laboratory. But why wait? You can be part of the leading edge that lives the phenomenon in its natural habitat: your own comfortable bed. By dreaming with others from home base, you can learn to understand human connection, communication, cooperation, and collaboration from the inside out. You'll have no need to theorize about a holistic universe when you can have firsthand experience instead.

There's a strong vision in some quarters of dreamwork asserting that the wisdom of dreams can be used to change the outer world. But what's really going on in inner space? Perhaps we are already changing, in ways we've not suspected because we haven't bothered to compare notes, to compare dreams.

The dreams in this book come from the actual reports of real dreamers. Editing has been limited to the correction of spelling, grammar, and syntax to make them easier for you to read. But the information has not been altered.

Mutual Dreaming is a social collaboration. This book would not have come into existence without the cooperation of other dreamers and dreamworkers. Under the promise of full confidentiality, pseudonyms and initials are used. Real names are used with expressed written consent, or if the person referred to is on public record. In these cases, a bibliographic reference is used at the end of the book.

Dream sharing is the foundation of mutual dreaming. Opening the heart and mind to other people creates the communal field of dreams. I deeply appreciate the gift.

Part One

✦

Introduction
to
Mutual Dreams

CHAPTER 1

✦

THE VISION AND THE DREAM

✦

The picture was hanging a bit crooked, so I reached out to straighten the frame. Then I settled down into my easy chair, adjusted my eyeglasses, and looked up at the painting on the wall. The watercolor brushstrokes were vibrant, the pastel colors light and airy. Like a magic carpet, the watercolor painting lifted me into a reverie. I took an imaginative journey into the picture, making it my waking dream. It was like a glimpse of future promise and a taste of past glory. I remembered when artist Joanne Rochon told me the story of how she had come to paint the picture. I was a little in awe of her achievement. She'd had a mutual dream.

One night Joanne and her friend Toby participated in an extraordinary event. Spontaneously and together, they both experienced the fact that it is possible to connect with one another even while sleeping. Here is Joanne's version of their mutual dream.

I am inside an extremely large warehouse with a river rushing down the middle. It is a very long and narrow building—

several miles long. The left wall of the building has cross-iron beams. Through them, the sky can be seen. The ground outside is not in view, just the clouds below.

Thousands of people are running in the same direction. They are rushing, but not panicked. I see my friend Ellen, and we move side by side for a while. Then I see Toby. He is moving with both of us, until he says he has to go to the bathroom. He opens a big green barn-type door to what looks like a closet. When he comes out, he tells us to look at the room. It has changed into a miraculous place with black and white marble floors and gold fixtures. The light inside is beautiful.

Painting by Joanne Rochon

Then people begin to jump from the beams on the left. Some fly and some will fall. Toby says that we should try it, too. Ellen and I are afraid we'll fall and say so. Toby replies that we will fly because we can do whatever we want. He says he will go first and flies away. Ellen and I try flying. It works!

It was 1982. Both Joanne Rochon and Toby were working together at Eastern Michigan University. They discussed their corresponding dreams at work. Joanne would begin a thought and Toby would finish it. They switched back and forth to complete the story. Toby knew that another person was present in the dream besides Joanne but didn't perceive her to be a friend of Joanne's. He then added some information of his own. He recalled going to the bathroom in a dark basement on a second level of the warehouse. He also remembered getting up on a balcony before launching into a successful flight.

This was one of his first experiences of soaring through the sky. Toby told Joanne that the dream was very significant for him. But Joanne didn't think much about it at the time.

Years later Joanne was inspired to create the watercolor painting from her own imagery. The warehouse, the river, the iron railings, sky, and flying people appear in the scene, but Joanne's old friend Toby is not represented. Rather, Joanne changed his character to a boy in the foreground because it seemed more appropriate to the painting.

About two years afterward, Joanne was at a wedding where Toby was also a guest. In a separate room, where the showing wouldn't detract from the focus of the wedding, she had ten or fifteen of her paintings spread out on the floor. In walked Toby. He went right up to the watercolor and said, "I had that dream and you were in it."

By this time, Joanne had been observing her dreams on a regular basis. Now she realized just how remarkable a circumstance she and Toby had shared. Joanne Rochon and Toby had a **classic mutual dream.**

The Magical Mutual Dream

Now, how many mile-long buildings do you normally visit out here in waking reality? Especially ones with hallways that have rivers running through them? With rooms that change into castles? How often do you go flying into the stratosphere like Superman? Is your sky full of other flying folks? That's the power of a magic dream. And this one was a magical mutual dream. It was experienced by more than one person.

Joanne's story and her painting made a mutual dream real to my eyes and fingers and inner ears. Mutual dreaming seemed like a playground of the mind. I didn't know the rules for this new world, but as I drifted in reverie, I could feel them.

"I wish I could have a dream like that," I thought yet again. I wanted an experience in which I could discover the joy in friendship, where connection and communication could flower under magical circumstances. In a dream.

Then a tug of guilt grabbed at me. The lift of longing dissipated, and I returned to reality with a thud.

When I had first heard about mutual dreaming, I was very excited. I was going to be an extraordinary dreamer. Oh, yes. I was going to pass beyond the cellular wall of private dreams and escape into a mutual wonderland. Private space had been nightmare land for me. I thought mutual space would be much better. The new land was going to be as amazing as Oz and as intriguing as Alice's journey. I was going to meet folks on the level of their super dreaming selves.

Sure, I was.

For me, Joanne's watercolor held the promise of the dream I'd wished for, the one I had been trying so long to emulate. Yes, I'd had other sorts of mutual dreams. But not the magical mutual dream that was my heart's desire. After all, I was supposed to be the authority. I was the dream researcher that media people were calling to ask about mutual dreams.

Mutual Dream Visions

Now, where had I acquired such a fantastic vision of the mutual dream? Easy. From TV, movies, romance novels, out-of-body legend and lore.

In our culture, there are some very strong visions of a mutual dream. Often they don't even come from dreams! Rather, their origins might be visions, trance, hypnosis, or fanciful visualizations. Even if these pictures do come from real nighttime, asleep-in-bed dreams, the information is often funneled through those books, TV, and movies. They are edited and "smoothed" to make a good story.

Willful imagination fuels our common picture of how mutual dreaming should look and act. It's a case of placing the cart before the horse. And I'm not the only one to do it. There are other perpetrators: dreamers who try to have a mutual dream for a time or two, then give up in disgust or with a brooding sense of failure. Dreamers who dream of meeting other people, but don't try to verify their dreams with those other people (it would dispel the magic). Dream researchers who suggest experiments to prove the existence of mutual dreams, without studying the phenomenon first.

And the media! Hey, they'd call to ask, do you have a sample mutual dream? You know, one in which the dreamers (1) have an ecstatic love affair, or (2) heal their cancerous bodies, or (3) contact aliens or (4) meet the Christ. Or preferably all four. And, oh, yes, it'll run about fifteen minutes or less in prime time.

Sure, I do.

All of us lacked the same necessary element. A reality check. Not one of us really understood just how mutual dreaming works. Today, after thirteen years of research, I feel I'm only beginning to understand. Let me tell you, the reality of dreaming together does not equal expectation set up by imagination. But sometimes reality can be even more intriguing than fantasy.

We need to go back to the true source and observe dreams acting like the creatures they really are, both wild and domestic, spontaneous and intended. Let's look first at the classics.

CHAPTER 2

◆

$\mathcal{M}$EETING: I'LL SEE YOU IN MY DREAMS

A woman in England dreams she visits a friend who seems about to die. She takes his hand and comforts him, saying that he will live. As she speaks, she hears music fill the room. On his part, her male friend has been ill to the point of death. He dreams that he requests both his woman friend and a favorite sonata by Beethoven. While the music plays, he sees the woman enter his room and speak to him encouragingly. He lives.[1]

A girlfriend and boyfriend both dream of running inside a big stone building. Some menace is pursuing them. They rush through the hallways out into a field of mines and radar detection devices.[2]

◆

A woman in California and her friend in the Midwest dream about attending a party in honor of the woman's deceased grandmother. The grandmother is also present at the festivities.

◆

A young woman in central Florida dreams that her brother, a racecar driver, is working on his stock car when he forgets to rehook a rod and spring. She yells at him but is unable to make herself understood over the noise of the engine. The brother's wife dreams of seeing her sister-in-law's face over the bed and knows that something is wrong. She wakes the brother, and he reports he's just had a dream that his sister is yelling, but he can't understand her. After contacting his sister and hearing her dream, the brother checks out his car and finds that the cable connecting the brake pedal is broken. If driven in that condition, the car would surely have crashed.[3]

*H*ave you ever seen the movie *Dreamscape* or Counselor Troi's "directed dream" on the TV show *Star Trek: The Next Generation?* These are only two of the many media examples of the most common notion of mutual dreaming: the meeting dream.

In a **meeting dream,** two or more dreamers recognize or encounter one another in their dreams. The meeting dream seems to function just like waking life. I am I, you are you, we experience ourselves as separate personalities. Each of us seems to have the same appearance as our physical bodies. We often act like we do in waking life: walking around, seeing each other, talking to one another, perhaps even touching one another. In a classic meeting dream the dreamers use name or physical description to identify each other.

Out of 124 published classic mutual dream accounts, slightly more than a third (36%) are meeting dreams. Joanne and Toby's flying dream was just such a dream.

Dream Romance

To find just one example of a fictional story in which meeting dreams appear, go look up Rudyard Kipling's *The Brushwood Boy.* It tells a romantic tale that involves a young Englishwoman and a soldier in the Indian Army. In the story, both independently experience similar dreams before they meet, recognize one another, and finally wed. Actually, Kipling's twentieth-century story is a modern version of a twelfth-century novel, the *Kathasairtsayara.* Even back then, East Indian author Somadeva was using the fictional form to describe how a king and princess could meet in their dreams before being united in waking life.

This is one of those rare cases where the past efforts of fictional writers seem based on the actual experience of real dreamers. A dreamworker friend of mine, Peggy Specht, relates a similar tale.

> My friend Alison, on a business trip to Ottawa, lay down for a nap in her hotel room one afternoon. Dreaming, but in a very alert state of awareness, she seemed to see the door open and a totally strange but handsome young man entered. They greeted each other warmly, and were soon making passionate love. This dream was real and vivid; Alison was shaken by it. Within two weeks, at a dance she met this man. When they became better acquainted, each described the same vivid precognitive love dream. They are now married and proud parents of two beautiful daughters. I suspect this sort of preliminary meeting dream occurs rather frequently.[4]

Through such romantic stories we can come to realize that meeting dreams can reach forward in time, to an event yet to take place. However, other dream stories indicate that they can also reach backward in time and place the meeting in a house that no longer exists or with relatives that are no longer living.

Most often they reflect current circumstances. A pair of dreamers might dream of meeting at the bed of a sick friend or both see a dying relative at the moment of death. Or the two might awaken at the same moment to compare their similar dreams.

A Mutual Nightmare

The second most common meeting theme is the mutual nightmare. This might be a dream of shared contact with a fearful figure: a phantom, a devil, an alien, or simply an "intruder." But a waking-state fire, an automobile accident, a war injury might be foretold by dreams. Or a murder.

The following dream occurred at exactly twelve o'clock midnight in the year 1865. Henry Armitt Brown, a young law student living in New York City, lay down and dozed off, beginning a gruesome drama.

> Almost immediately he dreamed that a strong hand was clutching his throat while he lay on his back on a New York street. A bearded unkempt man of great strength was holding him down, one hand strangling him while the other held a hatchet over his head. Brown heard the anguished cries of friends who were running to his rescue, but before they could intervene, the hatchet split his forehead and he felt the blood spurt over his face. The dream ended with the sound of his friends' weeping in his ears.

The next day one of Henry's classmates excitedly related a dream he had also had at twelve o'clock the previous night.

> [The classmate] was passing by and heard the sound of scuffling and Brown's cries for help. He saw Brown on his back with the killer on top of him, but before he could rush over, the hatchet was buried in Brown's head. Other friends of Brown had also arrived but were too late to save him.

Despite the similarity of the nightmares, Henry refused to believe that there really was a burly man with a hatchet intent on doing him harm. Then the following week Henry visited friends in Burlington, New Jersey. The hostess was telling him about her husband's horrible dream of the week before.

> "He dreamed a man killed you in a street fight. He ran to help you, but before he reached the spot, your enemy had killed you with a great club."

At this point, her husband interrupted to say:

> "Oh, no, he killed you with a hatchet."[5]

As Henry Brown had believed, his particular dream murderer never appeared in waking life. Most mutual dreams do not seem to have any relation to a physical event. But do notice that this narrative story of a spontaneous dream event shows that mutual dreams can be shared by *more* than two people.

Hypnogogic Reveries and Out-of-Body Experiences

If you indulge in reverie as you drift into sleep, the last thoughts to occupy your mind may translate into imagery during the transitional period between waking and sleeping. These are known as **hypnogogic images.** They can be realistic or abstract, simple or complex. In the next situation, both man and woman were in the same state of dreamy consciousness.

> The informant, a twenty-five-year-old man, was lying on his bed thinking about a forthcoming visit to a young lady. In a dreamy reverie he imagined going up in the elevator, ringing her doorbell, and then sitting on the end of his girlfriend's bed. He came to again, looked at his watch, and saw it was 11:55. At the same time his girlfriend had been lying on her bed. She had seen a man come into the room, walk up to the bed, and sit on it. His breathing had been clearly audible. When she was properly awake again, she noticed it was 11:55.[6]

This dream report is part of a case study, solicited by a researcher who tried to gather information as specific as possible. It wasn't until the latter half of the 1800s that collecting case studies of dreams instead of narrative stories became the standard practice of researchers.

These sorts of dreams seem to involve what's been called **astral travel** or an **out-of-body experience.** In such cases, often occurring at the borderland of sleep, people view from a perspective not coincident with their physical bodies. They seem to leave their bodies temporarily, to journey away and then return to recount their experiences. To travel to another person in order to meet with him or her is the most common classic mutual meeting theme.

False Awakenings

When you believe yourself to be awake while you are actually in an altered state of consciousness, you experience what's called a **false awakening.**

Both dream researcher Ann Faraday and her husband have had mutual dreams. In this case it seemed to each that they awoke, but they really didn't. Concerning John's dream, Ann said, "In it I had shaken him awake because he was sleeping on the wrong side of the bed and he noticed a window on the wrong wall. As he pondered this discrepancy, he really woke up and wrote down his dream." Ann's dream also began similarly.

> I seemed to wake up, get out of bed, and wander around the room. Everything seemed perfectly normal, except that there was a large window on the inside wall, and this discrepancy made me aware that I was not really awake at all, but dreaming. . . .
>
> When at last I tore myself away from the window and turned around, my bedroom was exactly as it always is, and I wondered for a moment whether or not I really might be sleepwalking. Determining to make the most of my lucidity, I pummeled the bed in an attempt to discover whether it felt as substantial as it did in waking life—and it did. I then saw my husband asleep on my side on the bed, and wondered exactly what a human body might feel like in a dream. I shook him awake and found he felt quite normally warm and resilient. By this time, I was seriously wondering whether I was not actually awake and really waking him up, when I found myself curled up in bed alone knowing quite well that he had got up at least an hour before.[7]

Ann's false awakening shifted back and forth into a lucid dream.

Lucid Meetings

One important component of many mutual dreams is the presence of lucidity. A **lucid dream** is one in which the dreamer is aware that he or she is dreaming. Lucidity brings clarity to the dreaming experience. To be awake in your dream can help you identify a sense of connection while still dreaming. Or it allows you to take a more active role in the dream in order to contact fellow dreamers.

A mutual dream in which both dreamers are lucid is an uncommon phenomenon, but not an impossible one. In her records from the Institute of Psychophysical Research in England, Celia Green has such an example.

It seems that Green's dreamer had become aware she was dreaming and decided to try to communicate with her son, using the words, "I can't stay long; I am feeling muzzy." The dreamer met her son the next day. Before she had a chance to relate her dream, he repeated everything she had said. The son reported that he had received the message in a lucid dream.[8]

I was particularly interested to learn that mutual dreams can occur in many states of consciousness. It kept me alert for incidents in my own dream life. I came to understand that there is no such thing as a "mutual dream" level of awareness. Cross-connections can occur at any level of dreaming. So as developing mutual dreamers, we do ourselves a disservice to specialize too soon in just one level of dreaming consciousness, say, just regular dreams or just lucid dreams or just out-of-body experiences launched from the dream state. By not limiting ourselves, we can explore all the possibilities of our dreaming life and expand our entire repertoire of dreams.

Double Dream Reports

Most historical dream narratives are recorded from the perspective of a single dreamer. It's a rare treat to find more than one dream to compare contrasting viewpoints. Consider these husband and wife dreams from Susan M. Watkins's *Conversations with Seth.*[9] The first is from Ned Watkins's point of view. The second is the dream of his wife, Sue.

MEETING DREAM

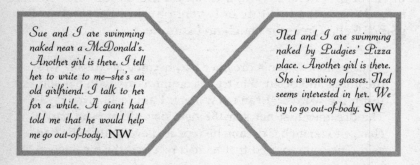

Sue and I are swimming naked near a McDonald's. Another girl is there. I tell her to write to me—she's an old girlfriend. I talk to her for a while. A giant had told me that he would help me go out-of-body. NW

Ned and I are swimming naked by Pudgies' Pizza place. Another girl is there. She is wearing glasses. Ned seems interested in her. We try to go out-of-body. SW

As can be seen, the actual dream reports are not exactly the same. As in waking situations, each dreamer reports a meeting from his or her own point of view. Given how individualistic dreamers can be, it's quite likely that dream reports will vary considerably.

It's only by looking at the raw material that we even begin to get an idea of how mutual dreams really work, instead of how we wish or imagine they should be. Imaginal fancies bear only marginal resemblance to the reality of meeting dreams. There is an all-too-human tendency either to embellish or censor facts in order to tell the tale. This proclivity has hindered the study of mutual dreams, which requires complete reports produced as soon after the dream occurs as is humanly possible.

Meeting dreams are by far the most recognized kind of dream mutuality. But they are not the only type, nor even the most frequent. The most common form of mutual dreaming is the meshing dream. The most common anecdote is about two or more people sharing the same dream.

CHAPTER 3

✦

$\mathcal{M}$ESHING: TAKE A WALK IN MY MOCCASINS

The same night, in the same hour, a pair of male and female friends each dream of leaves bursting into flames.[1]

✦

A man and his wife both have dreams of elephants with large human hands located at the ends of their forefeet.[2]

✦

A man and his daughter both have recurring "flying in church" dreams.[3]

✦

A woman dreams there is a needle in her bed, but wakes up to look for it in vain. Her mother, who has slept in another room, tells the woman she dreamt the same thing—only she woke up and really did find a needle in bed.[4]

✦

The meeting dream is important because it involves personal recognition and interrelationship in a shared dream space. It is knowledge by direct contact; a meeting of minds in which each of us retains our separate identities.

But there's a second type of mutual dream that involves a more empathic experience. Instead of seeing one another, dreamers share the same dream plot.

A **meshing dream** is virtually the same dream. It involves information interchange. Ideas, pictures, feelings, symbols, emotions, events, or the dreamscape can be shared between dreamers. When meshing is complete, dreamers will have the same dream. But in dreams that are *only* meshing occurrences, dreamers will not recognize separation between themselves.

The difference between the meeting dream and the meshing dream might be considered in this way. In a meeting dream, you would see me climb into the driver's seat of a Porsche, while I would dream of driving away in a sports car. Two points of view, just like in waking life.

In a meshing dream, I also dream of driving the Porsche. But instead of watching me, *you* dream of driving the sports car, too. You shift to the empathic point of view.

An empath is one who takes a vicarious journey in another's moccasins. When your dream meshes with my perspective, it's as if you see the world through my eyes. You usually aren't aware of me. And your dream has individual nuances of its own.

Let's take a look at dreams spontaneously shared by two sisters in Texas. The sisters reported that their dreams occurred at the same time, 6:30 in the morning on the 19th of September, 1987. The first was dreamt by Billie Petty.

I am at my grandparents' house even though it doesn't look like their house. Mom, Dad (deceased), my two sons, Greg and Chris, and I are there expecting a tornado. My (deceased) grandfather's essence is around, too. Mom and I get some mattresses out, and we sit on the floor around a coffee table, all except Daddy, who sits on the couch, not worried about a thing. He has an extremely white appearance. Mom sits next to my oldest son and pulls a mattress over them. I sit next to my youngest son. We are on the couch with Dad, and we pull the mattress over us.

We can see the tornado is enormous and coming our way. It takes up the whole view of the picture window. I can just imagine in my mind the grinding away at the house, and then I become frightened, for the first time, for our lives. Then the tornado is some distance from us, and I know it is going to pass by. I feel protected.

Here's the corresponding dream of her sister, Paula.

I am with Mom, Dad, and my two kids in a restaurant. I look out the window and see a huge tornado coming toward us. I get the kids under the table and try to shield them with my body. I feel I can get a better hold on my little boy than on my little girl. I say a prayer of protection and know I will be protected. Sure enough, the tornado moves away from us.

Each sister found herself with her family, at a table, frightened by the appearance of a tornado. Each protected her children from the tornado. In each case the tornado passed on by.

A meshing dream could involve the same dream environment. But this wasn't the case here. Paula was in a restaurant; Billie was in a house. Paula used her body as a shield; Billie used a mattress.

Most important, neither sister saw the other. It was as if Paula and Billie each experienced the event separately and singly. But did they really?

Historical Meshing Dreams

Meshing dreams have an even longer history than meeting dreams. There are published reports from Mesopotamia,

North Africa, Mexico, Corsica, and England, as well as the
United States.

It's clear from the reports that mutual dreams are not a
new idea. There is some speculation, which comes from
studies of native tribal practice and belief, that our primal
state of consciousness was very dreamlike and that this altered state was a mutual one. Thus, it's thought that we humans used to walk around in a sort of communal waking
dream that blurred the boundaries between physical and
imaginal existence.

What is certain is that by the time scribes were imprinting
hieroglyphics on clay tablets, the people of their time knew
about dream interpretation, dream incubation, *and* mutual
dreams.

For instance, during the early ninth century, B.C., the
great conquering Assyrian king Assurnasirpal recounted a
tale of how the goddess Ishtar let his entire army have the
same dream. In it she assured them that they could pass
through the raging torrents of the river Idid'e. The army re-
lied on this meshing dream and crossed the river safely.

Nebuchadnezzar's Dream

Another early recorded meshing dream is found in the
Old Testament. It is the famous story of the prophet Daniel
and the king of Babylon.

> In the second year of the reign of Nebuchadnezzar, Nebu-
> chadnezzar had a dream, and this spirit was terrified, and
> his dream went out of his mind.   DANIEL 2:1

Because the disturbing dream had such a tremendous impact on him, King Nebuchadnezzar called together his divin-
ers, wise men, and magicians. He asked not only that they
interpret the dream, but tell him what he had dreamt, for he
could not remember. Without knowing the dream, the
dream interpreters were unable to respond to the king's
command.

Daniel heard of the situation and told his companions. So that they all might not perish with the rest of the wise men of Babylon, he suggested they ask their god's mercy concerning the secret dream.

> Then was the mystery revealed to Daniel by a vision in the night.
>
> DANIEL 2:19

The line between "vision" and "dream" is not clearly defined in the Bible. Some people translate "night vision" as dream, others as trance; but clearly Daniel was in an altered state of consciousness. Afterward, Daniel went to the king and told him the dream and his interpretation of it. The king recognized the dream as his own.

> And the king spoke to Daniel, and said: Verily your God is the God of gods, and Lord of kings, and a revealer of hidden things: seeing thou couldst discover this secret.
>
> DANIEL 2:47

For dreaming the same dream, it is told that Daniel was presented with gifts and a position of honor and prestige in the king's palace.

Ironically, this story made no impression on the Babylonians. Instead, carved on a stele, is described how, after death, King Nebuchadnezzar appeared to his successor, King Nabu-naid, whereupon Nabu-naid related an astrological dream for Nebuchadnezzar himself to interpret.

More Meshing

Meshing occurs when dreamers decide to dive right into the communal pool of information. At times there may be the sharing of only a single symbol. At other times virtually an entire dream sequence will correspond with another dreamer's. The dream that two dreamers share in common may be related to a waking situation or be a fanciful event.

During this meshing of minds, you can be so immersed

in the shared field of dream information that there need be no realization of involvement with any other person. The recognition of correlation would occur upon waking, when dream reports are compared with your dream partner.

Meshing is a more common dream experience than meeting. It seems to be as natural for the dreaming mind to relax and spread itself throughout the dream as it is for the waking mind, to coalesce into a singular focus. Bathing in the field of preconsciousness, the dreaming mind has access to more information than is usually available to the waking mind.

Returning from the immersion, the mind tries to translate this information into symbols, pictures, and dramas, thus forming the remembered dream. The information gets ordered according to your own individual patterns, filtered through your individual perspective. Because every person is unique, each dream view will not be exactly the same as that of another.

On page 30 is a more elaborate example of present-day dream meshing by two dreamers.

What does it mean, to have the "same dream"? Does it mean that my dream will be a carbon copy of yours? No. Human beings are not Xerox machines! It means that the tone and flow in one dream are similar to that in another dream. Symbols are shared between dreamers. They can be literally identical, like "college" and "party" in these two examples. They can mean the same, like "dresses from the thirties" and "formal gowns with homemade lace." Or they can be metaphorically related, like the "spike-type" high heels and the long "crystal slabs."

These two dreams are a strict case of meshing because neither of the two dreamers saw or recognized one another. Instead, it's as if one dreamer walked in the "shoes" of the other, looking out the other's eyes. One dreamer saw the world from the other dreamer's perspective, but through the tinted glasses of her own perceptions. Her dream was filtered through her past associations and flavored with symbols from her own memory bank.

MESHING DREAM

I have one long dream which involves a formal dance or party. I am watching, not participating, in the dream, and I see two girls dressed in white formal gowns with handmade lace going inside to the affair with their escorts. I think I am one of these girls, really young women, and I admire the simple, yet elegant clothing, like a debutante might have worn in earlier times. I can hear the music coming from within an the sound of a party in the background. The dance seems to be part of an even larger event, such as a college weekend Homecoming event. I watch a nun whom I had as a college chemistry professor make hats out of live flowers, attaching them to the basic forms, such as wide-brimmed, cloche, or crown styles, etc.

I am leaving a building, like a college hall, and stop to pick up some shoes that I have left, it seems on the other occasions. They are in a pile with other shoes, apparently left by others, and I select a pair of tan sandals with a medium heel that I know are mine and begin to take a pair of burgundy-colored dressy sandals but discover that although they look just like mine, they have a higher heel, almost a spike-type, and I put them back.

ES, VIRGINIA

I'm back on the same campus as before or one very like it. There's an outdoor garden party, an afternoon tea in the women's college. As a result, there are a number of young women in garden party dresses from the thirties milling about, and a number of older women who are obviously faculty, with academic robes over their more staid dresses. I seem to be a guest, but feel a bit out of place in this setting, and I'm walking around looking at the beautifully tended gardens, with their old-fashioned plantings and herbaceous borders. In one of the borders something catches my eye, and when I bend down I see that it's a rather large rectangular slab of quartz crystal, about two feet long and two to three inches thick, with a perfectly clear window in it. Then I see that there are at least three or four more of these quite large crystal slabs, mostly buried in the black earth under the herbs.

TC, NEW YORK

Who was the primary dreamer and who took the empathic journey? At this juncture, it's still too early to tell.

Mutual dreams pop up in dream literature again and again down to the present day. If you'd like to read them yourself, the list is located in Appendix I at the back of this book. The majority of the published mutual dream accounts (64%) are meshing dreams. Out of these accounts, none contain dream reports that are *exact* copies of each other. Nor have I ever seen such an animal in all the dreams I've gathered. A meshing dream may indeed contain similar symbols, phraseology, themes, and emotions, but my dream isn't just the same as yours any more than I'm just the same as you.

Meshing and Meeting

Dreams can contain both meeting and meshing elements. The dreamer who experiences the meeting event may see the second dreamer. But the meshing dreamer usually has no awareness of the dreaming partner because he or she is too caught up in his or her own concerns, concentrating not on the partner, but on the drama of the dream.

I am crying because I know I am eight months pregnant. I stand by a window, gazing out into the distance, thinking sadly about my life.   ELIZABETH K.

Elizabeth awoke and pondered her dream, concerned about what it might mean for her. But before she had a chance to relate the dream to anyone, her grown daughter, Molly, came to visit.

"Oh, mother!" exclaimed Molly, "I had a dream about you this morning! You were crying in front of a mirror. And when I looked at you, I knew you were pregnant!"

Since Elizabeth was sixty years old, she was not literally pregnant. But she was in the process of transformation. After long, painful consideration, she had just made a major deci-

sion to leave a troubled marriage. Elizabeth was on the verge
of starting a new life for herself.

"Pregnant" and "crying" were the identical descriptions
used by both mother and daughter in their dreams. Elizabeth dreamt of looking out a "window," Molly translated
that idea into a "mirror." But the two objects are very similar
in both form and content.

Focused inward on her own concerns, Elizabeth had a
dream whose content meshed with that of her daughter's
dream. But Molly saw her mother. Her dream visit was more
of a meeting experience.

Once, a mother and daughter had dreams of the father
on the occasion of his death. The mother dreamt that she
was "awakened by a shadow in the doorway," which she
recognized as her ex-husband. She had the meeting experience with yet a third person.

But her daughter dreamt the following:

*My dream had no physical characteristics at all. It was
only a jumble of emotions and thoughts, not my own, but it
was as if my soul was touched by another's. And we joined
together in spirit and drifted through the darkness. In the
distance there was an odd light. Suddenly I was feeling an
indescribable feeling—fear and sadness and a great loneliness
that was almost unbearable.*

The daughter awoke at that moment and found herself
leaning over the bed gagging and choking and trying to cry
out. Two days later, her father's body was found in the apartment he had rented. From the spattered blood on the wall
beside his bed, it appeared that he had awakened in the
night choking on his blood and leaned over the bed as he
vomited the blood. The daughter believed she had actually
felt her father's experience of death.[5]

If dream partners are aware of the meshing experience
during their respective dreams, they can perceive it as a type
of merging—of bodies, spirit, mind, or identity. In its most

intimate form, the meshing dream can be a lover's union of the highest ecstasy.

In mutual dreaming, we can open up our personal boundaries to others and partake in theirs. We go beyond the limitations that we so often place upon ourselves in waking life and begin to realize our interdimensional connections. The dream is one of the most natural, spontaneous vehicles to encourage this. Our rigid boundaries melt, and commerce between us is much freer. Individual and group dreams overlap and intertwine, suggesting that we are in contact with one another through dreaming networks far wider than those we may realize in the conscious waking state.

Conflicted Dreams

My own idea of mutual dreaming had been to have a meeting dream, a magical positive dream encounter. Did I get it? No. The very first mutual dream I ever recorded was a mundane meshing dream.

It was May 9th, 1984. I had been deliberately dreaming with a group of people. We were trying to see if our dreams held anything in common. One night the leader decided to sleep outside in a tent on her back lawn in Virginia Beach, Virginia. At home in my bed in San Jose, California, I had the following dream:

I am digging the fingers of my right hand into the dark, rich loam of a lawn, trying to limit the spread of the banana slugs which are multiplying.

Banana slugs. Yuck. Squishy things in the dark. Awful icky creatures that hide like snakes in the grass, curled up just outside your tent, just inches from your face . . . lying in wait for you to stick a foot out of your warm sleeping bag. That's what I remembered about banana slugs from Girl

Scout days. And here's what my dream partner recorded the next morning:

This was a very short dream in which there were two small, transparent fish-like, snail-like creatures just outside the tent wall where my head was. I was aware of their presence for a while in the dream state.

"Then I woke up," her report continued, "I think to reassure myself that there were no creepy things inside the tent, and then went back to sleep. Interestingly enough, when I woke up the next morning, opening the tent door, there were two slugs immediately outside the tent door right where my head was."

In retrospect, I suppose it was inevitable that I would get a negative dream rather than a positive one. I had just emerged from thirty-eight years of nightmare. But it didn't make me feel one bit better to discover that the majority of spontaneous meshing dreams are about anxiety and conflict. Our slimy cocreation was just your average mutual dream.

CHAPTER 4

◆

OH, THE STORIES I'VE HEARD

◆

"No, I *never* have mutual dreams." That's what I would have told you before I started my search. I would have been utterly convinced of the truth of my statement. And I would have been completely wrong.

The problem was one of perception. I just wasn't that aware of the content of my own dreams and those of others. I hadn't begun sharing my dreams with enough people to uncover our cross-connections.

Like other neophytes, I had the mistaken notion that in the field of mutual dreaming, I could only score points if I participated in dreams that left my jaw hanging and popped out my eyeballs. That is, I thought they had to be epics that were virtual carbon copies of one another. Or they were only those dreams in which I meet you, you meet me, and we go off and share an adventure together. I didn't realize that in order to create World Series dreams, we might have to play a bunch of sandlot baseball first. Please take off the pressure to produce championship-quality dreams first time out of the batter's box. You might just discover, as I did, the fun of playing simple games of catch.

Stirring Up Interest

To warm up your interest, you might talk about mutual dreams with as many people as you feel comfortable. Relatives and friends are the most obvious choices. But coworkers, pen pals, and the folks that chat with you as you run errands might qualify. The gal at my local copy center, the fellow at the lecture, and the secretary at my office have all shared mutual dream examples with me. Talking about the subject often intrigues the people around you. Before you know it, they may chime in and tell a story of someone they know who had a similar experience. Just ask, "Have you ever heard of such a thing as a mutual dream?" Then be prepared to define it!

My survey definition of a **mutual dream** was "a dream with elements that correlate with another person's dream." But when I went out to ask the general populace if they'd ever had a mutual dream, I required only that "something in my dream corresponds with something in yours."

Sometimes individuals would respond incredulously, "Can you really do that?!" But usually, if I were in a group, at least one of the members would reply that they'd had such a dream experience, or knew of someone else who had.

When dream researcher David Ryback collected his psychic dreams, he commented, "So many people have told me their experience with shared dreams that I have to think it's a fairly common experience. When you consider that a shared dream goes unrecognized unless the dreamer happens to check with the person with whom he has shared the dream, there have probably been many more such dreams than anyone knows about."[1]

He's right. Just one study of a single American community by Susan M. Watkins, *Dreaming Myself, Dreaming a Town*, elicited mutual dream examples. The book demonstrated how the dreams and waking life of the citizens of Dundee, New York, would overlap and interweave with one another.

Collecting anecdotes has this benefit: The more samples you taste, the more likely it is that your dreaming mind will want still more. And if it can't be satisfied with outside sources, it just may come up with some of its own!

Anecdotes

These are the kinds of replies I'm likely to get when I ask people if they've ever had a mutual dream.

"My sister and I have had very similar dreams. The subject varies; usually about a relative, though."

LB, VERNON HILLS, IL

"My husband and I were both dreaming about Italy at the same time."

JM, RIVA, MD

"A friend and I once dreamed of being on an airplane and a bright yellow light, the same night."

AB, FLORENCE, AL

"Both of us dreamed about music performances with the same people present."

CC, TAMPA, FL

"I dreamed with a person who sensed the same thing as I did, involving her future."

AH, ELMIRA, NY

But sometimes the responses are more involved. Then the stories start to sound really intriguing.

"Sunday night, my maid dreamt of me and how happy I was, surrounded by a lot of people at something like a fair, and I was dancing and dancing. As for me, I dreamed of her, but this was a dream where all I did was complain and complain."

AM, MEXICO CITY, MEXICO

"The week before I moved to search for my natural mother, a friend who was in a dream group with me and I experienced a similar dream involving the symbol of a womb. In her dream, I was painting this symbol on a large wall. In my dream I had a painting (same symbol) wrapped as a gift that I was giving to my natural mother as we met."

AS, PITTSFORD, NY

"I work in a combined intensive care/coronary care unit. I had been under stressful conditions both at work and at home for a time and had begun to have palpitations.

"One night I noticed some disturbing disrhythmia on retiring for the night. During the night, I dreamed I saw my rhythm strip (electrocardiogram) slow and become a severe Bradycardic rhythm, and I thought to myself, 'I'm dying.' Strangely, I was very calm about it, and moments later I was fine and slept the rest of the night peacefully.

"The following morning a coworker rushed up to me. In some excitement she said, 'I had a dream about you last night.

"'I dreamed we were practicing CPR (cardiopulmonary resuscitation) and you were the patient, when suddenly you turned pale and looked funny. It was then I noticed your rhythm strip on the monitor. You were in severe Bradycardic. We gave you Atropine and everything.' (Atropine is the first drug of choice for symptomatic Bradycardia.)

"With an attempt at lightness, I asked if I made it. Her answer was, 'Yeah, we did a good job. But don't scare us again like that!'

"Of course after recovering from the shock, I laughed and told her what I had dreamed. And thanked her for saving my life."

MT, WAKEFIELD, VA

A fair number of mutual dream reports begin with the message, "We were sleeping together"—in the same bed, same room, same building. Proximity contributes to the discovery of mutual dreams, if not their production.

"My girlfriend Teela and I were sleeping together on the floor in a sleeping bag in the house where I lived. In the dream, there was a light, with beautiful colors, very bright, and we were walking together in darkness toward it, possibly holding hands. I mumbled something about, 'Can you see that?' Teela bolted up out of sleep and said, 'YES!' I sort of woke up and we realized we'd been dreaming the same dream."

UN, VIA E-MAIL

"In the spring of 1978 I was attending a small, Midwest college. I was friends with a group of five young women who occupied a dormitory suite on the other end of our co-ed dorm. We were friends, only, and I never felt any romantic interest in any of them.

"One night I dreamt that I was in their suite and I went from room to room, and made love to each one. It wasn't passionate/lustful lovemaking; it was more like sharing a soulful experience, and communicating with each other our deepest thoughts and emotions. In fact, I clearly remember one of the women in the dream, telling me how extremely unlovable she felt, while I reassured her. Later, I learned that this woman had a very unhappy home life.

"The next day I remembered the dream because it was so vivid. As I was walking to class that afternoon, someone in the dorm came up to me and said, "Hey, I heard you were quite a Romeo last night." I asked her what she meant by that. Then she told me that Nadine and Sheila both dreamt that I made love to them in their dorm rooms last night. I was amazed! Three of us apparently recalled the same dream incident!

"I was too shy to talk to them about it, and also I was concerned that they would interpret the dream on a physical level, instead of the deep emotional level that it was to me. Now I wish I had talked to them and gotten the details of their dream experience."

SY, FARGO, ND

I agree. Talking to the women could have helped establish both a deeper level of friendship and the reality of mutual dreams.

Negative Content

"What's a mutual dream?" the man asked.

I decided to use the most general definition.

"Oh, I've had a dream like that," he said and proceeded to tell me about the dream he had shared with his best friend.

"That's great!" I said and thanked him for yet another example to add to my growing file of mutual dreams. Then I walked away with mixed emotions.

On the one hand, I was elated to receive his gift of sharing—here was another person of slight acquaintance with no particular interest in dreams, yet one who had had a mutual dream. If so many folks had mutual dreams, it probably wasn't such a rare phenomenon after all.

On the other hand, there was the dream content. His mutual dream had been a nightmare. Why were so many of these spontaneous mutual dreams negative? It was consistent with what I'd discovered in the literature.

> "My girlfriend came to visit and we slept in the same bed. That night we both dreamed about older women wearing stretch pants who were nude from the waist up, and deformed."
>
> CL, SAN FRANCISCO, CA

> "I don't remember much about my dream except there was something about some son slugging his father in church and a few other similar events where members of the congregation were outdated and being judged. The same night, my girlfriend had a dream: something about being at church, seeing me and feeling very judgmental."
>
> CW, BEACONSFIELD, QUEBEC

> "It was a dream of me healing with others, possibly children. We were all Indians and the bandages were splotchy with blood. I was then awakened by my husband, who had a dream. A group of screaming high school students wear-

ing Indian headgear and costumes were running away from a black menacing cloud overhead."

MA, WOODLAND HILLS, CA

"While camping with a girlfriend in 1978, I dreamed of a rampant murder, which I never do. It shook me, so I related it. My girlfriend said it was a recurring nightmare for her."

MB, TULSA, OK

Some negative mutual dreams are recurring; some reach ahead of time to alert or warn. These dreams are **precognitive** in nature.

"In 1983, I was in a very serious car accident. Two of my friends seated next to me were killed. It's truly a miracle I survived. The night before the accident I had a dream of sinking in quicksand. As I was going down, gasping for air, a hand reached out of the darkness and pulled me into the light.

"Being a carefree lighthearted teenager at the time, I did not feel much of anything about the dream. It didn't really make any sense, even after the accident.

"When I did recover from my injuries, my aunt mentioned to me that she was happy to see me alive and that I must have an angel watching over me. Then she proceeded to tell me the terrible dream she had seen that night I had been in the accident. It was the same dream I had *before* the accident. I figure her dream was the exact time my accident occurred: 2:30 A.M."

CT, VANCOUVER, BRITISH COLUMBIA

"I had a dream about a friend who owns a motorcycle. He was sliding off the road into a ditch. At a party he was drinking too much, and I tried to persuade him to let someone else drive him home. He wouldn't listen until another friend spoke up and related the same dream as mine. He gave us his keys."

AA, CUPERTINO, CA

Mutual Dreams When One Partner Is Lucid

You stand a far better chance of experiencing a spontaneous positive mutual dream with your partner if at least one
of you happens to be aware of the fact that you dream.

Carole Dwight Russell seems to have shared two dreams
in a row with her youngest daughter. This is Carole's first
dream:

> My daughter, Ginger, and I are cleaning my mother's
> house. I am resting at the west side of the house on a porch
> that doesn't exist in waking life (symbolic of the fact that my
> mother is dead at the time of this dream). Ginger is carrying
> trash out to the alley. She passes a garage and grapevine
> (which existed before her birth but was afterwards torn down
> for a flower bed).

Carole reported, "The next day Ginger came over to visit,
and I said, 'I had a dream about Mother last night. . . .'
"Ginger interrupted and began telling me about the
dream she had the night before where she was in my mother's backyard by a grapevine and garage. She asked if there
used to be a grapevine and garage there. Then she said, 'I
was headed toward the back, but I don't know why.'
"I told her she was carrying trash out to the garbage cans.
I was teasing Ginger, for as yet I didn't really know that we
had shared a dream. I only knew they seemed remarkably
similar. I was as surprised as she was when Ginger looked
at her hands, and recognition lit her face. She replied, 'Why
yes, I was, but how did you know? I was talking about *my*
dream, wasn't I?'
"The next night the dream picked up where it left off, but
this time I recognized I was dreaming.

> I say to my mother, "You're dead!"

My mother laughs and says, "I know it."

Ginger comes back from emptying the trash and hears us both laughing. "Oo-ee-oo," she says in a singsong, making fun of the mystical nature of our talk.

There is a lot of laughter, and we discuss how Ginger and I are not in our bodies, but spirits also. Ginger says she bets the people who now live in my mother's house are going to have the house exorcised to get rid of us. We laugh and laugh after every remark each of us makes.

"The next morning I called Ginger to see if she dreamt the same dream as me again. Ginger said she couldn't recall dreaming, but that she had awakened laughing. So she must have had a good dream."

Peggy Specht reports that her most successful shared dream was with her son Andrew.

Becoming lucid and seeing Andrew beside me, I say, "I'm dreaming."

"Yeah," he replies, nonchalantly.

"What'll I do? What'll I do?" I exclaim, jumping up and down giddily, like a child. At this point I see a train approaching from the right, on a track just a short distance away.

"Shall I walk through the train?"

"Why not?" Still nonchalant.

Instantly, I teleport to the track and, standing still, allow the train to pass continually through me. This makes me so euphoric I blank out.

"Andrew, who remembered the dream, claimed it continued much longer, but I recall no more of it," said Peggy. "I had often speculated on whether I would have the nerve, becoming lucid, to stand still in the street and allow cars and streetcars to pass through me. Doing it with a train was even more satisfying."

Awareness and activity help change the content of mutual dreams from traumatic and distressing to enjoyable and adventurous and spiritually uplifting. And just plain fun.

Making Personal Contact

"Oh, I have mutual dreams all the time," I've been told.

"What do you mean?" I'll ask. Invariably, I'll be regaled with stories of meeting this, that, or the other person in a dream.

"But how did you know it was a mutual dream?" I ask. If I'm met with a blank stare, I know I'm in trouble. If pressed, some answer that they "just know." Or maybe they were told so by their Higher Self, guru, or local channeled entity.

Now, folks, it is understood that dream meetings with deceased relatives, extraterrestrials, and angels have to be taken on faith. But in mutual dreaming, we're dealing with live human beings who can provide feedback. So, at the very least, *ask the other person!*

And if that procedure is unwise or impractical, there are still other options. You might seek information from a third person who knows the dreamer.

Granted, many mutual dreams can't be corroborated for one reason or another. But in the game of mutual dreaming, we need to seek verification when we can, in order to learn the difference between perception and projection. Talking about how our dream does or does not relate to the other person is part of the ongoing dialogue. Mutual dreaming is an attempt to speak the same language. Engaging in mutual monologues offers no insight into the dreaming partner.

> "I was making love with a friend. It was so real, I asked him
> if he had the same dream. He gave me details of positions."
>
> CN, COLTON, CA

"I have friends that compare dreams. It happens most with my friend Ellie. Ellie and I meet in dreams and often call each other to confirm it."

BD, ELSBERRY, MO

These sorts of examples show us that "just folks" who pay attention to their dreams and those who don't both have mutual dreams. Chances are very good that you are having them, too. All it takes is developing recognition and comparison skills.

That you already dream with others may not be obvious to you because you haven't paid enough attention to your dreams. Or perhaps you haven't bothered to compare your dreams with anyone else's with an eye for similarities. I encourage you to do so.

Mutual dreams don't usually announce their presence openly. Ongoing exchange will increase the chance of discovering that you, too, are already having mutual dreams.

CHAPTER 5

✦

$\mathcal{F}$AMILY $\mathcal{D}$REAMS

A woman calls out from a scary dream and wakes her bed partner. She begins to relate the nightmare and he finishes it.

✦

A woman from South Dakota and her mother both have a dream of standing beside the hospital bed of the eldest brother, who is in Europe. They later discover that the brother had been in a jeep accident that injured his back and leg.[1]

✦

A mother and daughter in England are sleeping in the same bed. Each one dreams that the mother's brother-in-law requests a kiss as he dies. Later, they find out that the brother-in-law passed away on that very night.[2]

✦

The same night, an eighteen-year-old girl, her mother, and her best girlfriend all dream that a younger, dark-haired girl is pregnant, although none of them can identify her. Within a week, the girl's fourteen-year-old sister comes to her and admits that she, the sister is pregnant.[3]

Who has mutual dreams? Anecdotes and common sense tell us that spontaneous dreaming together most often happens between intimates, especially friends and family members. Sixty-eight percent of the published spontaneous dreams were in this category.

There seem to be two main reasons for this. First, the common emotional and psychological bond that forms between people is at the root of the mutual experience, and such a bond is more likely to congeal within a relationship that is constant over time. Mutual dreams most often occur between those who experience true empathy with one another: husband and wife, lovers, parent and child, close friends, and siblings. Second, people who are emotionally attached to one another are more likely to relate, feel more open to share, their dreams with one another. Thus, there is more data available to discover corresponding dreams.

Can you discover mutual dreams in your own family? Yes, if you can pass through the cultural resistance against the acknowledgment of strange and unusual phenomena. Your active attempt to reach out toward others ripples through the atmosphere of the family field of dreams and can find resonance there.

Perhaps you might hold a breakfast conversation like that of dreamworker Linda Reneau and her husband, Ben.

> BEN: "Boy, that was a nice dream I had. I was cuddled up with this sweet redhead. She just came over to me and cuddled up with me and kissed me all over my face, then said, 'It's time to wake up now.'"
>
> LINDA: "Ben! I was trying to tune in to your dreams last night to help you with your decision about the jobs, and this redheaded man came up to me and kissed me all over the face. I wondered if you were nearby and you weren't, so I just cuddled up with him!"

Linda also has discovered joint dreams with her son, Johannes. In one case, they both dreamt of going into a large building (he called it a castle). There they met a man and a woman working at a computer terminal who erased some data. The ceiling slid open, and a spaceship appeared. When Linda began to tell Johannes her dream, he got very excited and finished it for her. Johannes had seen the building from the outside, while Linda hadn't, but they both had experienced the other events.

Family Meeting

In the case of a mutual meeting dream, it is likely that one dreamer will recognize a family member in his dream, then go tell that member his own dream in the hopes it will spark recognition. Such as the case when Maureen Whitney related a dream to her mother, Rita, her brother, and other people in her family.

At eighteen years old, I told my mother of a dream I now call "The Reunion." It was a dream packed with people, strange and unknown, all engaged in a large dinner at my stepmother's house.

Surprised, Rita told me that she had dreamed it, too, and piece by piece, we found that our memories of details matched.

She recalled that I was over in the southern corner of the large room, cutting a cake set up on a smaller, separate table. I recalled cutting the cake, watching her argue with my father as they both sat at the dinner table near the northern wall. She remembered what the argument was about and told me. The dining table was small, but it seemed to hold all our family and their friends—a noisy reunion with food covering a long table.

Somewhere in my dream, my mother left the dinner through the double-glass doors near the northwest corner of the room, taking Sinbad, our German shepherd, with her. And she remembered leaving with Sinbad, and told me her personal dream adventures afterward.

Two days after our shared dream, my brother, Dan, told Rita of the same dream. He matched the details of it, and we were fascinated with the possible scope of a shared dream, as well as surprised that forty-eight hours had passed before Dan had his own experience of it.

By the end of the week, we found that of the five members of our family, four remembered the dream, leaving no doubt in our minds that dreams could be shared.[4]

Family Meshing

Most family members have mutual dreams of the meshing variety; that is, they share similar images and events in their dreams. Usually the dreams are one-time occurrences, such as when Billie Petty and her son Chris had dreams about a news event in their home state of Texas one evening:

I am putting a statue on top of a building, like the Statue of Liberty. A helicopter is lifting the statue and trying to swing it into place. I'm scared to death because I'm so high up. I'm holding on to the bottom of the statue and lose my footing. I'm swinging free, hanging on to the statue and losing my hold. I know I almost can't hang on. Then I'm viewing the scene, and I wonder at the workers who do not have any fears of danger.   BILLIE PETTY, 10/14/86

I am in a boat in the water, and pieces of the Statue of Liberty have fallen into the water. My mother is in the boat with me. I pick up the pieces of the statue so they can be put back together.   CHRIS PETTY, 10/14/86

At the time of these dreams, architects were removing a statue from the state capitol in Austin, Texas. Billie reports that the Austin statue is a lady who looks very much like the Statue of Liberty. Hence, it was easy for Billie and her son to make that substitution in their dreams.

Families often have dreams with repeating symbols. Dreamer Kevin Dole explained, "I have several scenes or situations that recur over and over in my dreams, and one of them is a large group of people in a big house. This group might best be described as a very large extended family."

I am in a large nursery; lots of children running around, and in the middle is a playpen with several toddlers playing. There are several mothers around chatting and watching. I have a bamboo pole perhaps eight feet long. There is a strong line tied to the end and a yellow ring tied to the other end of the line à la fishing pole. I lower the ring into the playpen, a child grabs it, and I hoist him out, let him down, and he waddles off to play with the other kids.

KEVIN DOLE, 4/19/86

This particular night Kevin's wife, Karen, joined him in his inner household:

I am a guest in a large, extended household. I am sitting at a table over the remains of a meal, discussing religion with a woman. The house is full of children and the sounds of activity. I am trying to control and feed a very lively infant. As I focus more intently on the child, I see it is really two tiny babies joined at the waist. I have swaddled them snugly to make the pair easier to hold. Their hands have worked free and they dabble and grab at everything within reach.

KAREN DOLE, 4/19/86

Dream Intimacy

Mutual dreaming opens the door to more intimate connections with the ones we love. It can also encourage the emergence in dreaming partners of advanced dreaming skills like telepathy, lucidity, and astral travel. One husband

and wife team actually used mutual dreams to help achieve deeper intimacy in their marriage.

Dreams helped bring Ted and Betty together in the first place. Betty reports that long before they had the respect, intimacy, and tools of a relationship, the two of them received deep and accurate insight into one another's psyches through the sharing of their dreams. That triggered the understanding and acceptance of what was going on "underneath," rather than concentrating on what was happening on the surface. Betty says that she never would have come together with Ted if she'd just looked at the outside events of their daily life.

Here's a pair of their dreams, which are spiced with sexual symbology.

BETTY: *Ted and I go to a participatory art show. There is a long white wall of wood standing in a meadow. People walk up and take a section upon which to make their own art. . . . They use tube lights which are flexible and can be bent into any shape. The tubes are a half inch thick and made of clear plastic. The insides are different colors. I especially notice the lavender color. . . .*

TED: *Betty and I are bartending a big party. On the wall is a four-by-six-foot piece of paper upon which people come along and draw funny cartoons with pens and pencils. Besides bartending, I also am selling my new invention, which is a solid mouth deodorant that is in the shape of a tongue. It is about a quarter inch thick and about two inches long and an inch and a half wide. The color is light yellow-green. It has a ring for a handle, and a leather cover that slides over that is the same shape as the tongue only a little bit larger . . . sort of like a sheath. A person sucks on it one* time, and it gives off a very strong flavor which completely deodorizes the mouth. The most popular flavor is "English Tongue." It is lavender-scented. There are also other flavors representing other nationalities such as "Danish Tongue," "French Tongue," and "Italian Tongue."

Later, Ted and Betty shared a particularly blatant waking and dream experience of intimacy.

BETTY: My dreams all seem to lead up to the awareness that there is a very large penis out there in the universe that wants union with a very large vagina. It's not that I became my vagina, but rather that the only thing that exists in my personal universe is me-as-vagina. I am aware of a very powerful attraction, as if between two poles of a very strong magnet. The energies of the vagina and the energies of the penis are equally balanced and equally powerful.

The presence of the penis and vagina erases all memory of previous dreams of the night. It is as if it is a birthing event. It's not that my mind decides for the event to happen, but rather that it is time for the event to occur. The event is so large and ready to happen that everything else is irrelevant or surrenders to it.

Betty commented, "While half awake and half asleep, my husband and I had one of the most unusual sexual experiences of our life. We had a very brief and very intense sexual union. Once his penis was inside of me, it seemed that there was no way again that it would ever not be inside of me. This joining was physically acted out as I crossed my legs so he would stay inside me. The decision, thought process, and coordination to carry out that physical movement were the only things that I had to fully awaken to do. Then I slipped back into my half-awake state.

"This unique experience was pure ecstasy and passion. It felt as though it were fated and ready to happen at just that time. I didn't want to move. I drifted back into sleep, but the power of the experience was so strong, I have no memory of subsequent dreams. When I awoke, I wondered if I had dreamt that it had happened or if it had really happened.

"Throughout the day, I noticed that my body felt very different. I had intermittent abdominal pain. I couldn't figure out what was happening or why until I said to myself, 'This pain feels like . . . I've lost my virginity.' Then I realized that I had been touched where I had never been touched before and that I was fighting it. That was the pain.

"As I walked on the college campus, I decided to go with the feeling and accept and embrace it, even though this didn't make conscious sense to me. As soon as I did, the pain abated and never came back. I almost called my husband at work to talk about the sexual experience—something I've never thought about doing before in my life. I held off, though.

"When he got home, one of the first things Ted said to me was, 'Let's talk about what happened last night. I've never felt anything like it before. It was a very weird experience.' As we talked, we pieced together the story of the experience."

This was Ted's dream of the night.

TED: *I am dreaming along, and this all leads up to me being a rod, or a very large and hard penis.*

Ted said further, "My physical erection had never been so hard in my life, not even when I was a teenager. I was consumed with desire for my wife. All social considerations were beside the point, but this was not an aggressive feeling, either. It was, for me, a taste of pure ecstasy. I wanted my penis to stay within Betty forever.

"I felt very different after the experience and couldn't remember any other dreams. I also wondered if it had been a dream."

Together Betty and Ted decided that a new era of intimacy in their relationship had been launched. Energies that had previously been tied up with their families of origin were now available to their marriage relationship.

This last in the series had a surprise ending for me.

TED: *I am going to the mountains with Betty. . . . We know the director and all talk together. Then we resume our traveling. We pick up a hitchhiker—a stranger who feels like an old dear friend of the family. As we drive, the road becomes quite steep, finally leveling out at the top with beautiful mountains and spectacular views. . . .*

Betty and I come back from the mountains to a motel, which has a room already rented for us. We sleep overnight. Betty gets up first, which is unusual, and takes a shower. Then I get up, go into the bathroom, and talk to her as she showers. I say, "Are we going to leave?"

"Yeah," replies Betty. I tell her that I agree, not wanting to stay here another night. I decide to shower.

BETTY: *I am with my husband, Ted, walking along a beautiful beach with pure white sand and bright blue water. . . . There are very few people, an occasional beach umbrella here or there, rather like being on a holiday while most people must work. To the left, we see a white mobile home or trailer parked on the sand. Ted and I both agree that we wish to check it out.*

We enter a door on the side away from the beach. A man joins us who is a stranger but who feels comfortably intimate with us. He is being our guide. He takes us to a bathroom. Ted sits on the toilet. I climb into the shower, which is a typical cheap molded plastic and aluminum con-

trivance with rickety sliding plastic doors. When I stand under the showerhead, it automatically begins spraying me with very warm water. As the water streams down my body, my clothes vanish, and I begin feeling and moving sensually with the spray. The guide is standing next to Ted and is watching me.

Feeling erotic, I begin to dance an ancient sexual dance, caressing my body, swaying my hips, winking at the men, flaring my nostrils, rubbing my breasts, and licking my lips. Boy! I am really getting aroused! I feel powerful, womanly, happy, playful, and very connected to women of ancient cultures. Both men are enjoying my dance.

I put my right hand between my thighs and rub my crotch. A phallus three feet long and three or four inches wide appears. Holding it with both hands, I stroke it, bring it to my lips, and lick it, continuing with my dance. I am so sexually aroused that I must stay with expressing it. The guide senses my puzzlement at having a penis and explains to us both that the shower was designed by Moses for the purpose of arousing individuals' eroticism and passion. I look at the tacky shower and wonder what makes it produce erotic responses.

"Wow! Moses was really a genius," I think to myself. My dancing gets more passionate and excited. I am really throwing myself into it. Vigorously stroking and squeezing my penis, I look at its glorious circumcised head. I look foward to an ecstatic orgasm since I know I am dreaming and move consistently towards that moment.

Instead, I find myself and Ted walking down a hall in a small motel towards a room which apparently has been reserved for us. We pass one room and enter the next. The rooms are on the right side of the hall, and instead of doors, there are hanging beads like the hippies popularized in the sixties. As we climb onto the bed, it switches from a double to a single bed. I am amused, assuming that it happened to emphasize the closeness of our connection. We wouldn't need separate space for our bodies to lie down since we will be on top of one another. As soon as our bodies touch the bedspread, the giant phallus is on Ted instead of me.

I caress, stretch, pull, lick, and suck the phallus energetically. Ted is in bliss. I get more and more excited, knowing that since this is a dream penis, I needn't worry about hurting it by getting carried away with passion. I also know that despite its huge proportions, it will fit me perfectly.

Ted reported, "After hearing Betty tell me her dream and sharing my dream with her, I tried to reenter my dream."

TED: I find myself in a hotel room with a lady about forty-five years old who looks like Lauren Bacall. She has a nice body. She lives in this room. She has never had a baby and wants me to get her pregnant. She immediately climbs onto the bed and lies down on her back with her legs spread, naked and ready for intercourse. I have a giant penis. In fact, it is so huge, that I want to wake up and see if I am dreaming!

I wake up in the dream, thinking that I really have awoken. I have sex with the lady, rather mechanically, just thinking about my own climax. I have a great orgasm, although I am puzzled that the lady wants me to ejaculate on her pubic hair, which I do.

I meet another woman, and she and I have sex also.

Again, I orgasm, feeling both pleased and surprised that I am finally having orgasmic dreams, twice in one night! It is so realistic and vivid, that I look for signs of ejaculation when I actually do awaken.

I feel tired and happy. I snuggle with Betty and do not want to go to work.

When Betty and Ted sent me their dreams, I did not read them dispassionately, but had a very intense emotional reaction, instead. My reactions probably formed an emotional gestalt in my own family field. I did not show Betty's and Ted's dreams to my husband, Manny, but given the similarity of symbols (shower and body parts), it appears that that night he did some "psychic snooping" in the dream state. An erotic gestalt would be just the thing that Manny would be likely to tune in to.

MANNY: *I am inside a house with several rooms. There are nude men and women standing around. At one point I see Linda standing in a shower.*

Then I'm looking at a room that looks like a combination morgue and bedroom; there are beds instead of slabs. A couple of cartoonlike skeletons are lying on their backs with arms on top of the covers, straight and still.

A cartoonlike woman says, "Look what I can do!" She jumps up into the air and twists around, heading for a toilet that's flush with the wall, rather than the floor. As she comes down, she starts changing into a skeleton (her skin starts shrinking to her bones). She goes through the opening, hits the bottom of the toilet, and breaks through onto the floor. When she hits the floor, there are big pieces of toilet bowl flying all over the place. Bones and all of her internal organs (kidneys, lungs, heart, intestines, etc.) flop on the floor as if all of a sudden there is no skin to hold them.

Although this dream is amusing to me and causes me to smile when I awake, later I wonder why I don't laugh out loud, in or out of the dream.

Part Two

✦

WAYS AND WHYS
OF
DREAMING TOGETHER

CHAPTER 6

✦

ARE WE PSYCHIC OR IS IT MEMOREX®?

✦

When it came to dreaming with my own family, I began from ground zero. No one else in our family foursome was very interested in dreams. As time passed and I began relating some of my nighttime experiences, one or two of them would chime in, too. For the family, the telling of a dream has always been a rare treat. We did so intermittently, when the mood struck us, not under any predetermined circumstances. Dreams never became a main means of bonding.

I occasionally did dreamwork with my family, especially when my children were bothered by a nightmare, by using the techniques of interpretation and conflict resolution. I have personally discovered that doing intensive dreamwork with family members or groups actually inhibits the emergence of mutual dreams. On the other hand, simply enjoying dreams with a light touch of dreamwork provides a more supportive atmosphere for their emergence. In this way the sharing of the dream becomes a gift to the family group rather than a task to be accomplished.

Family Connections

My husband, Manny, and I were sometimes able to catch the last vestiges of mutuality as we emerged from the dream state.

Once, as I began to awake from sleep, I had the sense that someone had thrown a pillow at me and hit me full in the face. Waking fully, I realized it had been only a false awakening.

But then Manny stirred and grumped, "Did something just fly by you?"

This dream pair is far more typical:

LINDA: *A boy toddler is defecating in the living room.*

MANNY: *I am baby-sitting a toddler who turns into a Cabbage Patch Kid and goes to the bathroom on his hand and arm.*

In such a case, it's hard to discover any cause and effect. Other times, it's more obvious. For example, once my artist husband spent the day drawing rock formations on the computer. I came in to watch over his shoulder for a while. That night I dreamt of rock formations. But so did our daughter, Teresa, who hadn't seen them at all.

With my son, Victor, mutuality occurred most often around themes of family health. Like the rest of our family, Vic incorporates symbols from the science fiction shows he sees on TV.

LINDA: *I feel like I have long, dark, straight hair and am East Indian. I walk into a building and sit on a bench seat next to a pregnant blond woman. She is groaning, clutching her stomach. I say, "My dear friend, can I help* *you?" She replies, "Ohhh, I have a stomach ache. . . ." I hold her briefly, wondering if I should take some of her pain upon myself.*

I awoke to discover that I actually had a slight stomach ache.

I was writing out my dream on the kitchen table when Vic looked up from his homework and said that he had had a dream last night, too.

VICTOR: *We are in a room. The surroundings are like a hospital; there is a doctor and a nurse. The whole family is there with my mom, but my mom is pregnant, and clutching her stomach. I look at the woman on the table, and she looks like the alien on TV. Then I look back at my mom, and she looks like the woman on V that was pregnant by the alien.*

Obviously, Victor had tuned in to my physical predicament.

Are We Psychic or Not?

Before we get too far afield, let me say that I thoroughly endorse the concept that not all mutual dreams are psychic. When you're talking about sharing dreams with folks in close proximity, the possibility looms large that your similar dreams will be the result of a similar response to waking-state events.

In other words, they are parallel day residue.

Day residue is the explanation, suggested by Sigmund Freud, that dreamers are responding to a daytime event. The notion is that our dreaming minds take whatever information, ideas, or feelings are "left over" from the previous day and turn them into a nighttime drama in order to complete the psyche's processing activity. Freud described "these residues of the day's waking life" as having five components:

1. Thoughts and impulses that, owing to some accidental cause, have not been completed during the day.
2. Harassing cares and problems left unsolved.
3. Impulses and thoughts that have been turned back and suppressed during the day.
4. Unconscious elements that have been excited by psychic processing of the mind.
5. The overwhelming and unsettled impressions of the day.[1]

People having similar dreams would thus be responding to the same daytime occurrence. The dreams might include quite literal descriptions of the elements in waking life.

One day my husband and I witnessed a confrontation between our elderly black cat, Charcoal, and an opossum that had wandered up from a nearby creek. Charcoal raised herself out of her usual lethargy to stalk the opossum and defend her food. That night both Manny and I translated the day incident into dreams about a group of black kittens playfully hopping back and forth.

A "leftover" response to the unusual energy of the cat incident would account for the fact that both of us had incorporated the same kitten symbol into our dreams. Day residue does not explain why, out of all the events we had shared during the previous day, both Manny and I would have dreams that chose to comment on that particular personal incident.

Sometimes the "day residue" is due to related physiology. Our body positions in bed can produce falling experiences.

LINDA: *In the astral state, I feel light in my upper torso and sense myself starting to rise. I think, "Finally, I'm really levitating."*

When I "open my eyes," I'm a foot off the bed. I make a big effort and "push" so I rise up, seeing the bed and Manny sprawled in it. I realize this is an out-of-body experience. Then I start falling back down off the end of the bed. I try to stop myself but wake.

MANNY: *I am lucid, flying with a young man. The dreams ends with both of us falling out of the sky.*

Both of us awoke abruptly at the same moment. Our feet were hanging over the end of the bed!

Waking in the early morning can provide opportunity for stimulus that incubates the dreams upon return to sleep. On one occasion I was awakened by a woodpecker tapping on the roof and by Manny hitting the wall in return. Imagining the woodpecker poking holes in the shingles and cracking them in two, I moved slowly back into the dream state. I was able to retain a low-level awareness of the fact that I dreamt. Eventually, Manny attained lucidity, too.

LINDA: *I am on the roof with Manny. There's a party going on in our house, and we've come outside to escape the crowd, although a few others do follow. I imagine us next to a balustrade, first on a small wooden porch just outside our bedroom window. After the guests come outside, we leave them to move to the edge of the roof, where I construct another waist-level balustrade with my mind.*

Finally I take off flying from the roof. I wind up flying over a field with a chain link fence, yelling, "I'm lucid!" and wondering why the dream is still so two-dimensional.

MANNY: *The four of us (Victor, Teresa, Linda, and I) are in this structure made of large blocks of stone stacked one on top of another. We are located up in a corner where* *the vertical wall comes in contact with the roof, except there's one large piece of stone that's missing. I'm sitting on the second stone with Teresa. Linda and Victor are off to the side.*

We're back from the inside wall, inside the structure. Linda and Victor are standing by an opening that goes up. I don't see any top to it. In the back is an open space.

We're trying to get down. There're people down there— men and women—inside the structure, and I'm yelling at them. Somehow they get a really tall ladder made out of metal. . . .

All of a sudden the stones behind me start to move. They're on a slope and stacked one on top of the other. As they're moving, they start to crack because they're very large. I'm scrambling up, as they're moving down.

I start to yell for Vic. I yell "Victor!" several times. When I really start yelling loudly, somehow I'm aware that this is a dream, that I'm in bed, and Linda's next to me, and that if I yell too loud, I'll wake her up.

So I'm still scrambling, and I'm still moving toward the opening, and all of a sudden the dream goes.

Shared psychological history means that, over time, people will develop a mutual bank of symbols from which they withdraw in order to create their dreams. The shared experience of powerful emotional, sensory, mental, and intuitive events will produce ideas and feelings that translate into similar symbols for each person involved. These mutual dream images will be the effect of parallel histories.

More often than not, waking stimulus translates into a symbolic, rather than literal, dream event. For instance, I once heard of a psychologist husband and wife team who had had an argument one day. That night, they both dreamt of houses burning down. Now, there wasn't any physical home on fire. Their anger painted the same picture. They both had accessed their individual data banks of dream imagery and retrieved the same images to describe the actual waking-state event.

Here are two dreams from our family that both contained the shared symbol of a mutilated child.

TERESA: *I am in a school-hospital building, in a room full of grown-ups. A man rushes in with a blanket bundle—a baby boy with dark hair. The mother is trailing behind. I instinctively know something awful has happened to the child, and I want to leave the building before seeing it. Someone rushes out to call 911.*

The man sets the baby down. Its eyes are wide open and look glazed. Its left arm is spread out with the blanket partly covering. The arm is almost completely cut at the joint; the skin in back is still attached. Although it's open, I see no bone but red blood, which is not running out.

I turn away feeling sad for the baby because it is so out of it.

MANNY: *In a field, I see a wheat thresher coming. After it passes, I see a child lying there on the ground. Its left side is mutilated. It has dark hair and is a baby or toddler.*

The mother runs up and straightens out its arm and leg. The left leg and arm are bent at weird angles.

Where did such a disturbing symbol originate? It came from the previous night. Both Manny and Teresa had been watching a TV newscast of the Los Angeles riots after the Rodney King verdict. Teresa went to bed feeling lousy.

This is one of many instances that point up the fact that

the strongest incubator of mutual dreams is what happens right before you go to sleep. That's why I ask, when you intentionally incubate a mutual dream with a partner, do you really *have* to watch the eleven o'clock news?

Common intent becomes a factor in mutual dreaming whenever shared dreamers successfully create and execute a plan to program a dream about a certain symbol or topic.

It is a sure sign of the strength of programming skills to intend to dream about a subject, then actually to dream about it. If the goal is to have a lucid dream and one occurs, if the target is "vacation in the mountains" and folks do dream of being in the mountains, if the intent is to dream about a best friend and this happens, then dreamers have consciously programmed their dreams.

On one occasion, in the middle of summer, I requested that my husband, Manny, dream with me about the funding of an upcoming project. We both had dreams of school settings with large groups of people.

But the real surprise came the next morning when our children, who were unaware of our intentions, both reported dreams involving the first day of school.

> **VICTOR:** *There are about twenty people in front of the school. It's the beginning of school and basketball practice. I have a paper due. Mom drives me to class. I am doing the paper when the library bell rings. The classrooms are open and my classmates are laughing at me. I give the paper to the teacher. "What should I do with this?" she asks. The teacher wipes around my eye. "Why are you doing this?" I ask her. "I'm wiping off the pressure," she says.*

> **TERESA:** *It is the first day of school. I'm afraid because I've never been to this school before. I have a new schedule of classes. I go to my first class, which lasts about two*

seconds. *Then I go to my second and so on to my fourth. It's lunchtime when I realize I had nothing to be afraid of because it was easy going to different classrooms. I look on my schedule to see when my P.E. class is.*

The phenomenon of response dreaming to someone else's intention is one I am quite familiar with. On several occasions I have programmed dreams, only to have friends spontaneously dream a related theme or an answer to my question. This same reaction occurs within our family unit. After I incubated three dreams about the color orange, my husband dreamt of seeing me under an orange tree. Are such cases only coincidence?

Coincidence is defined as "an accidental and remarkable occurrence of related or identical events, ideas, etc. at the same time with no apparent causal relationship." The operative words here are *apparent* and *causal.*

The appearance of mutual dreams can seem to be a coincidence without awareness of all the elements of the events involved. This could be because most people aren't in the habit of looking for them. The solution is to become more sensitive to the subtle clues in dream reports and to seek relationships between dreams and waking lives.

Waking perception of reality looks at experience as the result of cause and effect, involving linear or clock time. But dreams don't seem to conform to such laws. They float freely in regard to both time and space. Thus it can be difficult to decipher which waking or dreaming events are the cause and which are the effect, or if indeed there is such a relationship.

Programming a dream *is* a causal action, whether it results in your dream or somebody else's. Another causal action is to intensely focus on a particular subject, with the result that you dream in response, whether you intend to or not. When the focus is strong enough to program your dream, it might just as well incubate the dream of someone else who resonates with you through the bond of familiarity.

One afternoon I reviewed my first dream journal, which included two nightmares from my childhood. They occurred between ages eight and twelve. Both involved my parents and our old blue Plymouth station wagon. My parents were either trying to get me to drive the car (when I was much too young to do so) or they were driving off and leaving me behind to run after them in vain. In both cases I had awoken in terror. These two emotionally disturbing dreams became prime incubators of yet another dream for me that night:

LINDA: *The children and I are being driven north in a white station wagon (similar to my parents' when I was a teenager). I open the back right-hand door to look out with the intention to disembark while the station wagon is in motion. When I see a metal guardrail approaching, I quickly pull the door closed so it won't impact.*

Afterward, I reopen the door, while the car is still moving, and jump out with a child in my arms as if I am going to "save" this child. I run up the hill into a parking lot with multi-sized buildings that seem to be under construction.

As I look back, I see my children, Vic and Teresa, walking along a meridian of grass and trees. They are stopped by a man who hassles them, but they are able to get past him and come along towards me.

After I awoke, I guessed that the "child" I was rescuing was my "child-self" who had experienced those childhood nightmares. But before I had a chance to develop this line of interpretive reasoning further, Teresa related her dream of the night at breakfast. Teresa was nine years old (Vic was thirteen). I had never mentioned my nightmares to either of them. Teresa's dream had the same "leaving while the car is still moving" theme. But that's not all.

TERESA: *Vic, Dad, and I got into two cars: our old (blue and white) Mustang and Dad's blue Honda. Vic got into the Mustang, and so did I, and Dad got into the Honda Accord. So Vic started driving the car, and I was curious—how he was doing it—and why.*

Then we took off. I suggested to Victor that we wait for Dad, but he said, "No," so we kept on going. Then I heard an engine start—it was Dad in the Honda. I said, "Vic, stop!" and he's all "No."

Then finally we came up to a construction site—the building was almost done. There was a desert in front of it, like sand. I opened up the door, got on the curb, and was running. Then he stopped, and I closed the door.

Soon Dad came up, and he stopped and got out of the car. He scolded Victor for driving off without Dad, and he scolded me for getting out of the car while it was still going.

So Teresa identified the "hassle man" from my dream as my husband! It made sense in terms of our family dynamics at the time: no major problems but a lot of minor hassles.

I was gratified that neither Teresa nor I had experienced nightmares. My own growth in controlling the inner vehicle of self was reflected in an improved dream scenario. Perhaps my children were benefiting from that fact, too, in both the dream and waking states. Both Teresa and I seemed to be able to jump from our moving vehicles and hit the ground running.[2]

Was it simply a matter of synchronicity?

Synchronicity is a term coined by Carl Jung. Jung described synchronicity as a "meaningful coincidence of two or more events, where something other than the probability of chance is involved."[3]

In Jung's view, events occur simultaneously to demonstrate that the universe is interconnected and unified by a central point of meaning. The common elements, the shared images, in dreams are clues to the significance of the universe.

In this understanding, there is an acausal, rather than cause-and-effect, relationship between dreams and any waking-state event. But some mutual dreams seem to bear no literal relation to a waking event. Like the flying pillow, toddler, and lucid out-of-body incidents, they are dream-to-dream correspondences only.

Synchronicity might apply to spontaneous mutual dreaming, but such an explanation doesn't relate well to intentional incubation of dreams in which cause precedes a definite effect. Common elements that seem random at first may prove to be sequential. Using a large body of dreams to track them over time might eventually provide clues to the true nature of the associative process.

Dream ESP can be considered as an explanation for the mutuality in dreams, after the other possibilities for spontaneous or intended mutual dreaming have been exhausted. If one person can experience clairvoyance, remote viewing, and telepathy, so can two. If precognition or retrocognition can apply to a single dreamer, such phenomena can certainly apply to more than one.

I once thought I heard someone knock sharply three times on the bedroom door. But shifting to waking focus, I realized that this had been an audio dream. Two hours later, Vic knocked three times on the bathroom door down the hall. At the sound, Manny turned over sleepily and asked, "What? Who is it? Come in." It was so loud, he thought the knock was on our bedroom door.

Later, Teresa shared her dream of the night. In it, Victor knocked sharply on a door.

You can call this incident synchronicity or coincidence if you want. I call it parallel precognition. The dreams of both

Teresa and me recognized an event before it occurred in the waking state.

Putting Clues to Work

One night in late December of 1985, Victor went to bed with a cold and fever. That night he reported the following dream:

VICTOR: *I start off in a room filled with electronic equipment and all these high-tech gadgets. I'm flashing to different parts of the room real fast.*

Then I come to a big room with eight people in it that say there is a mystery going on between all of them. Two people are working together. . . .

Around the same time of night I dreamt this:

LINDA: *A young boy has developed some sort of electronic equipment involving communication (a tape recorder?), which isn't working correctly. . . .*

There is going to be a presentation to a group of us seated in rows of folding chairs, but the speaker has not yet arrived. Maude Cardwell gets up to make a short introductory statement about the speaker and begins a discussion on the presentation topic. A woman with long, light hair seated toward the front turns and says to the group, "Dis-ease . . . that's what we're here for." I think she means that this is the "life lesson" that all of us have in common.

"NO!" I yell. Then, surprised at the force of the statement, I continue, "I apologize for the vehemence . . . or enthusiasm in my voice, but I must insist that the emphasis

*be not on sickness but rather on the positive—our good
health."*

Are these examples of dream ESP? When I analyze
dreams for signs of psychic resonance, I take into account
the other possibilities, too.

Common intent? Victor and I had not made a decision to
dream together.

Day residue? It's obvious that some of our dream similarity was the result of common waking stimuli. I was certainly
concerned about returning the health of my son to its usual
positive stance.

Shared psychological symbolism? The "electronic equipment" was probably our computer. Both of us enjoyed its
use, I for recording dreams, Vic for playing adventure
games. Due to his ill health, neither Vic nor I had been on
the computer that day. Instead the "electronic equipment"
served as an example of a symbol that we share in both the
waking and dream states.

However, the electronic dreams contained a clue that indicated they might not be concerned just with Vic and me. I
sent copies to the person mentioned in my dream: Maude
Cardwell, who was the executive director of the Austin Seth
Center. She responded that around the time of the dreams
she had been preparing some course notes for an upcoming
presentation.

"As I read your dream of December 22," Maude wrote,
"I was amazed at how well it fit my present situation. 'Dis-
ease' is surely a topic in my mind right now.

"My preparation of the Course Notes was done on an
electronic gadget, my computer. Also, we have had a fair
amount of difficulty with the tape-recording of the presentations. Finally, like Vic, I have a cold and fever."

It is possible to have mutual dreams between people who
are connected by shared emotion or interest, or are involved
in life experiences that are substantially or symbolically similar. Like ripples in a pond, our own dreams reach out to

include many people and events in our waking lives, even those beyond our private circle of friends and family.

On another occasion that same year, I was lying on my bed trying to meditate when my (then blond) daughter Teresa came in and interrupted me, twice. "What are you doing, Mom?" she asked, and, "Can we go see *Baby* at the movies?" This last was a request to see a movie about a small brontosaurus.

Finally, I gave up trying to relax and suggested that she come lie down next to me. On impulse, I asked Teresa if she wanted to be hypnotized. This was the first time I'd ever tried it. When Teresa assented, I suggested that her left arm rise. After an initial false start, it did. And its apex, the arm and hand reminded me of the head of some long-necked animal. We were both happy that we were able to accomplish this. Teresa gave me a broad grin.

That night the day residue made a terrific translation into my dream.

LINDA: *A young blond person is going somewhere, wading waist-deep through the still, green, phosphorescent waters of a pond. She comes upon what at first looks to be a large, overhanging tree branch that extends out over the water. At closer view, the "branch" seems to be a long serpent neck, with head just barely touching the water, as if this serpent were getting ready to take a drink.*

I begin to feel alarm, but neither the head nor neck moves. Maybe it is a branch after all. Then my focus moves back, to take in the entire scene. Across the pond, in the distance, are several other graceful, serpentine heads arching out of the water. The whole scene is motionless, like the intake of a breath, or a photo taken by a still camera. The setting is a dark night, illuminated only by the glow within the water.

Suddenly, the serpent head moves, pulling up and back to contract into the body of a small brontosaurus. The young person exclaims in surprise and delight, "Ohhh! A dinosaur!" The baby brontosaurus closes his eyes and grins in satisfaction.

But that wasn't the end of it. At the time, I was facilitating a shared dreaming group called the *Lucidity Project*. On the very same night, Mitch Elrod has his own dream version of the event.

MITCH: *I'm walking with some man on the ocean floor, about one hundred yards from shore. It's fairly light down here. I see some creature under a rock. This creature is long with big eyes and seems to reside upside down while under this rock. It waits for prey to come by, then shoots out and gets it.*

I see several of these. The first one is only a few feet long, but the other two are much longer and more fierce. I don't seem to be afraid. This is like some scientific exploration.

Mitch and I had only corresponded by letter, and the amount and quality of information we had exchanged about each other was purposely minimal. At the time of these dreams, we had never met in the waking state. That makes dream ESP the most compelling hypothesis for the emergence of his half of our mutual dreaming pair.

Family Unit

My experiences have convinced me, in agreement with other researchers, that the best environment for the emergence of spontaneous connective dreams is the family unit.

However, the fact that my family was able to produce what it did is, in my mind, a minor miracle.

My daughter, Teresa, has reported the most psychic dreams (clairvoyant, telepathic, and precognitive). Manny is my bed partner. I had about an equal number of mutual dreams with each of them.

My son, Victor, has been aware of dreaming while dreaming only a few times in his life. Once they discovered they could dream lucidly, Teresa's and Manny's lucid dreams averaged from two times a year to semimonthly. My own lucid dream frequency depends on intention. It can peak at three times a week, or I can have none for months on end.

The only other person in my family who tried dreaming intentionally was my husband, Manny. I could persuade him to do so about once a year. Victor hardly ever shares a dream; Manny and Teresa talk about their dreams with me, on average, about once a month.

So there has not been a large selection of dreams to compare. Yet, mutual dreams have been found among them. We just had to be alert to the possibility.

We were able to discover a smattering of wild meshing dreams and a few nonclassic mutual events. But the woodpecker-inspired "roof" dreams of Manny and me were the closest we came to a classic dream meeting.

That's why I was motivated to share dreams beyond my family circle.

CHAPTER 7

◆

WHY DREAM TOGETHER DELIBERATELY?

◆

*U*ntil I began the quest for the magical mutual dream, my dreams were my own to claim, to possess, to experience, to live. Good or bad, simple or complex, inspirational or mundane, nightmarish, troublesome, anxiety-prone, or flights of wondrous fantasy, they were mine, all mine. And now I was choosing to open the door marked "private" in large, bold letters and venture outward into the unknown. The challenge of human interaction under the surface of public courtesy was the riskiest journey I could possibly imagine.

Joanne Rochon, who painted the magical mutual dream I so desired, had what I didn't—a fellow dreamer. I realized that the game of mutual dreaming requires at least a pitcher and catcher. At first I knew no other dreamers. No one who was keeping a dream journal. No one who was doing dream-work to unlock the secrets of symbols.

So I had to expand my search beyond my local area. I began by subscribing to magazines and newsletters and by buying books, then writing to the editors or authors in hopes that I might find a dreaming connection. Not everyone responded; I had to be persistent.

Eventually, I made contact with several folks who were willing to correspond with me. I began sharing dreams by mail. Then those connections led to others, and I heard about some dream groups. None were close at hand; I had to drive up to seventy miles to attend an evening meeting in the Bay Area. Some groups were in other parts of the country, and I became a long-distance member. I shared with Jungian dreamworkers and whose of the Gestalt persuasion, with followers of Edgar Cayce and Jane Roberts's Seth, and lucid and nonlucid dreamers.

During this time my interest in dreamwork grew; I joined several organizations as a volunteer, then was promoted to officer. In such situations, dreams could reflect not only the separate lives of the members, but the communal life of the organization. For instance, during my first year on the board of the Association for the Study of Dreams (ASD), we began each meeting by sharing dreams. Not personal dreams; dreams about ASD, about the process that we were going through to incorporate as a legal entity.

The dreams were only vaguely mutual in classic terms. But they did have some common themes. They did reflect the social side of the dreamers.

I was doing plenty of meeting in the waking state. Although I would bring up the subject of mutual dreaming wherever I went, not everyone took me up on it. Dreamwork, dream research, dream community came first. The magic waited patiently, in the wings.

In the meantime, I began to dream deliberately with others, through dream sharing and group dreaming.

In **dream sharing,** people intentionally report their dreams to others. Dream sharing can occur one-on-one or in a group. Dream-sharing groups may center around a particular skill or dreamwork method. The recognition that dreams have mutual elements may emerge in the exchange of information.

In **group dreaming,** intentional dreaming moves up a notch. Now the intent is for a group to dream together on the *same theme.* A group goal like "Let's dream for peace" can produce meshing dreams. In that case, all or part of one person's dream will be the same as the dream of at least one other person in the group. Several people might have dreams with common elements like symbols, feelings, and events.

Single samples of spontaneous dreaming don't provide a lot of clues to the underlying nature of the process of mutual dreaming. That requires tracking many cases over time. That requires intentional dreaming.

The Advantages of Dream Sharing and Group Dreaming

Group dreaming and dream sharing are a good place to start. When it comes to dreaming with unknown partners, dreaming about a topic is far less troublesome than dreaming with or about other people. By focusing on an objective theme, we can maintain an arm's-length relationship with any individuals in the group. This makes group dreaming more of an intellectual experience as contrasted with the emotional reactions that can characterize some types of telepathic and shared dreaming. But the very act of sharing dreams can help move us and our fellow dreamers toward a more personal level of intimacy.

Reviewing the dreams of a dreaming group can indicate possible mutual dreaming partners. For example, when members of the Seth Dream Network shared dreams about Jane Roberts after her death, three dreamers reported dreams of Jane that also involved their mothers. The three later became group members of a dreaming project, and two of them engaged in individual sharing between themselves.

Group dreaming and dream sharing provide practice in being the individual in the midst of group diversity. Seeing how other people deal with issues through their dreams, the difficulties they face, the solutions they come up with, their successful and unsuccessful attitudes and activities, can be a source of information for your own journey.

Group dreaming can be the first experience of social dream dynamics: communication, collaboration, and cooperation. We begin to become aware of how the social environment impinges on the feelings of us all.

Finally, group dreaming gives us the opportunity to practice "incubation" or the deliberate "hatching" of a dream. This practice can involve multiple intentions to recall a dream *and* to connect with other dreamers *and* to dream to a goal. The more complex the incubation, the more likelihood there is for a complete meshing dream.

Why Intend to Dream Together?

What reasons have been offered for people to deliberately try to mutual dream? Those who try the experience today suggest a potpourri of reasons why mutual dreaming can be beneficial: for information gathering, to assist in the operational dynamics of a group and its members, for healing, to track cultural change, and to achieve a psychic experience.

Information Gathering

Dreaming in groups has been sought to improve the quality of the life of the group members, to help in decision making, and to glean information about past, present, and future.

In 1980, thirty-five members of a group from Malvern, England, called the Atlanteans attended a weekend dream workshop. After all had slept under the same roof, twenty members reported dreams about the same historical time period. The setting was the Tudor London of Henry VIII; the theme was the river Thames.

During the late seventies, in Sausalito, California, houseboat residents gathered dreams of their current life situation in a community dream journal called *Gates*. The journal was formed in response to investment development that threatened to change the composition of the free and easy community to a more formal marina. *Gates* also spawned a flurry of journals in other California communities.

Couple dreams have been incubated to depict future events such as a new job, a prospective pregnancy, or heightened creativity. Dreamworker Joan Windsor cites several instances where mutual dreaming gave her information on a proposed journey. In one case, she deliberately dreamt about the upcoming trip with her husband.

Dreamworker Marcia Rose Emery has demonstrated that dreamers in a group can intentionally induce precognitive dreams. The goal of her dream group at a January 25, 1988, meeting was, "Show me the scene of the next immobilizing environmental situation." Three group members responded with dreams depicting the devastating Rio de Janeiro floods and mudslides that forced the mayor to declare the city a disaster area. The words "mud," "erosion," and "slide" were mentioned in the dream reports that clustered around this actual waking event.

Some dream researchers claim that group energy actually helps increase the probability of identifying mutual events. For example, researcher Alan Vaughan suggests that the best way to encourage success of intentional precognition is to solicit the testimony from several independent psychic sources. These could be waking sources, but they might just as well be dreams. The predictions are culled to see where they create consensus. Vaughan found the strongest "consensus predictions" to be the most accurate.

Researcher Jule Eisenbud says about extrasensory perception, "The goals psi serves are primarily not those of the individual at all, but of an ascending hierarchy of interrelated systems."[1] This view makes **psi** or ESP, a field effect and each of us, each of our dreams, pieces of the whole. Whereas a single individual might have trouble getting the entire puzzle assembled, a group can go further to achieve that result, just by the sheer volume of information they generate.

Conflict Diagnosis and Resolution

Mutual dreaming has been promoted to get several viewpoints about an individual and to provide the keys to his or her unresolved problems. When previously unspoken fears and frustrations are conveyed through the medium of the dream, comparing one person's dream to those of other dream-sharing members can help make the distinction between which concerns are common to the group and which are particular to the individual.

Dreamworker Adrienne Quinn and her student in Tacoma, Washington, had similar dreams about a red-haired woman. The student's woman was very agitated; Adrienne dreamt of escaping out a window trying to get away from her woman. Earlier that evening both had attended a prayer circle at a friend's house. There a newcomer had talked nonstop about her problems and complaints. The newcomer had red hair.

Given the propensity to concentrate on the psychology of the individual, it's delightful to discover that mutual dreams can even be found in therapy. Yet, mutuality is just as true there as well as in any other setting. E. B. Taub-Bynum reports an instance in which two sisters in family counseling both reported to him that they had dreamt of a man running around in a strange or threatening manner. One of the dreams was a recurring nightmare. The therapist had judged that the girls' father was a manic-depressive.

On the other hand, Jule Eisenbud has contributed a case in which two patients had strikingly similar dreams, though they had never met. Their only common connection had been that Dr. Eisenbud was their analyst. The two dreams, occurring a day apart, both contained a shared event in which the dreamers were caught in a heavy downpour. One sought shelter in a shack; the other in a mansion. In addition, the first names of each patient were practically the same. When Eisenbud told the second patient of the first patient's dream, the second woman was able to use a symbol from the first woman's dream to break through a long-standing block involving her ex-husband's impotence.

This is a rather amazing use of problem-solving techniques. The currently most popular dream interpretation methods are based on theories that direct the spotlight on a single dreamer. Such approaches do serve the purpose of making either the dream interpreter or the dreamer responsible for understanding the dream. But they don't make room for the idea that a mature, responsible dreamer might also be able to correctly perceive what is true, what applies to *another* person.

Group Issues

Dreamworker Barbara Shor states that in a small group, mutual dreams "can be used right now to sort through conflicting or confusing issues, to clarify the strengths and weaknesses, to hone in on shared ideas, ideals, and goals, and ways of implementing them. It can be used for incubating individual and group healings. It can bind together distant friends or defuse family tensions. It can be invaluable in the search for creative solutions to personal, business, and governmental conflicts before they escalate into open warfare."[2]

The following dreams were shared the morning after an overnight dream workshop consisting only of women. They were recorded at various times throughout the same night. Four dreamers had correspondences that ranged from very similar to very slight.

I'm in a room with some other people. A black-and-brown German shepherd runs up excitedly and jumps on me, licking my face. I think to myself that the dog should be sent to obedience school.

I'm in a room with Brenda [the first dreamer]. A black-and-brown German shepherd runs up to me and jumps on me. It is wagging its tail and licking my face. I turn to Brenda and say, "There's nothing wrong with this dog, he just needs to go to obedience school to learn where to lick!"

A gray German shepherd runs in and jumps on me. . . .

A gray lamb runs into the room and jumps on me. . . .[3]

It is not reported whether either an actual dog or lamb spent the night with the dreamers!

In the same workshop, over half of the women had dreams in which the entire group was being held captive by a mob of men who were plotting to rape and kill them. A discussion of the dreams involved sharing their feelings about their own sexuality. They reaped the benefit of reduced anxiety in the workshop's safe, supportive atmosphere.

A private spiritual retreat in a religious community also resulted in recognition and discussion of common elements in the participants' dreams. These included themes of sexuality, death, and spirituality. And the shared themes of dreams occurring at the beginning of a series of conferences facilitated by dreamworker Robin Shohet contained elements of anxiety about being at the conference. With the appearance of such emotions, one wonders what the content of the conference might have been.

On the other hand, in 1986 Kent Smith and a group of dreamworkers undertook a project with a group of top managers of a secular business corporation. Using a form of group dreamwork called "dream consulting," Kent and his colleagues used the managers' dreams to focus on the organization as a whole. The intent of the project was to improve the decision-making process of its members. The methods of dream consulting emphasized the "family" nature of an organization of employees working together daily to solve organizational problems.

Healing and Problem Solving

There is a firm belief in many cultures that dreams are themselves a healing mechanism. Group dreaming had been observed to be diagnostic of psychological conflict and physiological problems. It remains to be demonstrated how and to what extent a group influences a dreamer through member dreams and whether or not such healing is reciprocal.

The Dream Helper Ceremony is a group project created by dreamworkers Henry Reed and Robert Van de Castle to explore how telepathic dreams can be used in a group to facilitate problem solving. A member of the group who has some sort of personal dilemma in his or her life volunteers to step forward as a target person and, without revealing the nature of the problem, asks for help.

The remainder of the participants agree to serve as Dream Helpers. They form a circle around the target person and engage in some activity to create a feeling of bonding such as holding hands, mediation, prayer, or singing aloud. That night they attempt to dream about the nature of the target individual's problem and to offer some solution for the problem or help the individual toward some form of growth experience. The dreams are then brought back in the morning as gifts to the target person.

Over time, Henry and Bob have found that the issues that obtain the best input from their groups usually deal with a person's past or relationships, something of deep emotional significance, and not what they consider "frivolous" surface concerns.

The target person writes out a statement of his or her question or problem to place under a pillow. If more than one person volunteers, their names are written on pieces of paper and selected from a hat. The target person loans each Helper some personal item such as a watch, piece of jewelry, or article of clothing that might serve as a "linking" object for the Helper. After returning to their bedrooms, each Dream Helper sleeps with the target person's "linking" object under the pillow or wears it on the body. An equally effective alternative is for the target person to sign pieces of paper for the Helpers to bring away with them.

Bob Van de Castle and Henry Reed suggest to the Dream Helpers that their recall will be very good because they don't want to let the target person down. For some, the person will appear in the dream. Others will have a dream that will give them a feeling that they connected with the person and found something of value. But many can feel that they've failed the person. They might expect that if they were successful they would have a dream in which they see into the past or have voices describing what is wrong, but that type of dream is found to be a rarity.

Some people, like Bob, awake every few minutes and write down notes. Henry seems to wake up only with a sentence or two. Others have epic dreams.

The Helpers write down their dreams so that they will be able to give them to the target people to read at their leisure or refer to them later. The reports also enable the dreams to be documented ahead of time. This helps the dreamers avoid subjective judgments or influence from one another's stories. There can be a tendency on the part of some dreamers to prejudge whether the dream might have anything to do with the target person or whether it informs fellow dreamers of issues too personal to share. Also, without some sort of written record, after the problem is revealed there can be a proclivity for people to start giving advice and ignore what the dreams are saying.

Henry and Bob caution the Dream Helpers not to withhold anything; all dreams whether X-rated, violent, or bizarre, are encouraged. By dedicating their dreams to another person, they don't embarrass themselves. With this disowning process, the Helpers are enabled to be much freer to let whatever is pressing for expression come through.

Bob describes the Dream Helper process this way: "One

dream is like a point on a blackboard. It doesn't go anywhere until we get other dreams and start to see whether we've actually got a square, a triangle, or parallelogram."

Henry adds, "Invariably, however, when we start hearing everybody's dreams, by the time we're around the circle, people will be exclaiming about how there's so much in common. For example, if one person dreamt of finding an orange on the sidewalk, we'd think nothing of it. But when someone else reports a dream of an orange banner and still another person reports finding an apple on the sidewalk and somebody else dreams about a beautiful orange sunset, all of a sudden the orange in the dream starts to feel significant."

Social Commentary and Cultural Change

Cultural anthropologists have long used dreams to examine the underside of the social order of society. Dreams paint a picture of individual and collective values and mores. They can also reflect a shift in values through the expression of new images that will combine with old ones to create new stories and myths. Mutual dreaming has been used to get mass input on issues of a particular cultural group or for the entire planetary body.

In 1982, Bill Stimson, as editor of the *Dream Network Bulletin*, suggested that people dream in a global form. On Saturday, December 18th, groups of dream networkers in the United States and Europe held Winter Solstice gatherings to share dreams they had been incubating on the topic of a World Dream. One dream apiece was selected from among members of each networking group. Nine dream network centers from France to California hooked up by telephone to share their dreams, each relaying the dreams they'd received to the next center. The similarity of images in the networking process was impressive. Themes included a recognition of the importance of the era in which they lived, a realization of the choices they faced, and great hope for the future. There were three mentions of animal and intercultural themes; four references to water, five to transformations or new beginnings, and five to flight or upward movement.

As editor of the Guild of Asaph's newsletter, Robert William Krajenke was involved in several dream projects, including the Vision Quest for America on July 4, 1981, and the year-long (1984) Mt. Rushmore Full Moon Medicine Wheel Dream Quest. But the strongest correlation seems to have come during the 1982 Full Moon Dream Conference. Bob Krajenke had intuitively chosen Mt. Rushmore as the "meeting place." Thus the focus was on a specific time, date, and location. Almost half of the people who responded dreamt of groups of people; many dreamt of traveling; there were often symbols of cleansing and balance. Plus, some dreamers actually did dream of Mt. Rushmore.

In 1987, Charles Upton created a dream group called the Gate of Horn. That group's most notable achievement was the U.S.-Soviet Dream Bridge. Upton managed to persuade two dozen dreamers from the United States and Russia to dream to a common goal. He suggested incubation should begin at the new moon during the last three months of 1988. The intention was to dream about how lasting peace could be established between the two countries and how to deal with "other pressing global problems." Perhaps taking his words literally, two dreamers dreamt of the Armenian earthquake!

Dream Bridge included dreams with topics appropriate to the stated goal, like Americans talking with Russians or visiting Russia. But there were also themes of incomplete attempts to connect or communicate. The status of U.S.-Russian relations was described akin to that of cats and dogs, with either possible conflict or friendship. Dreams demonstrated a need for red, yellow, and golden fire energy to melt the ice of the cold Russian winter. The sharing of food was a connecting motif, as well as sitting around a table with others. Travel themes included trains, underground railways, tours, and boots made for walking. There also were moon and spacecraft dreams as a response to the "New Moon" incubation suggestion.

The closest correlations occurred among three dreamers. The correlations clustered around the subject of a *shared activity* at a particular *meeting place*. These will turn out to be two crucial elements in successful mutual dreaming incubation.

Dreamworker Linda Reneau observes, "Mutual dreams occur for the same reasons that mutual daily experiences occur. We seek out a particular person because we like that person; being around him makes us feel good. Or we need his services, what he has to offer us that we can't do on our own. Another person seeks us out because of what we can do for him or her. And we enjoy the company of colleagues. We like to discuss our interests with people who are interested in listening to us and listen to people who have ideas we're interested in hearing. Even when we're among strangers, we're all in the same place at the same time because of similar needs or desires."[4]

Psychic Motivation

"Just to have a mutual dream . . ." is why most dreamers tell me they want to experience mutual dreaming. The unspoken ending of the phrase is ". . . to see if we're psychic." These dreamers usually mean they want to have one of the classics: a meshing or meeting dream. They have an intrinsic interest in the social state itself.

Montague Ullman is especially interested in communal dreaming. He was one of the scientists involved in dream telepathy experimentation during the 1960s. Since then he has lead many dream groups, both formal and informal. One of his groups, which met in the late 1970s, shared their dreams with a particular eye for correspondences among them.

The meetings occurred weekly for approximately one and a half hours. There was a nucleus of five members, although at times as many as seven or eight participated. Each member's dreams for the week were typed, copied, and distributed at each meeting. Members reviewed and compared the dreams of others looking for three types of correlations: 1) correspondences among the dreams of the group members; 2) correspondences between a dream and the lives of one or more members of the group other than the dreamer; 3) correspondences, telepathic or precognitive, between the dream and events in the life of the dreamer.

Judgments of correspondences were purely subjective and, as in many dream groups, a light and informal spirit prevailed. The group did not stipulate a target or goal in advance; neither did they suggest a particular person as objective target or subjective dreamer. Rather, they simply added their dreams to a communal pot for review.

Over time, Ullman reported several correspondences with one particular group member, Barbara Shelp. Here are their two dreams from April 9, 1978. First is Monte's, then Barbara's:

There were preparations for a large-scale dinner meal for one hundred and fifty people. Some people felt the meal would be stereotyped and wanted more variety than could be arranged for so many.

Food is laid out on several tables—varied gourmet foods. It seems as though this has been done in Tom's honor. I am there as his guest. I am sampling foods, and they are delicious. It occurs to me that this is wasted as far as Tom is concerned, as he is a picky eater.[5]

Both dreams involve or imply a large-scale meal and a problem of selection among the dishes. Like the great bulk of dreams gathered in groups, these mutual dreams are not so much alike as reflective of the same themes.

The results that James J. Donahoe obtained were far more vivid. Donahoe was the first to use the term "mutual dream" and the first to publish accounts of deliberate group induction. His own definition is based on the results he obtained from such research, as well as from spontaneous first-hand experience. "In a 'mutual dream,' two or more people shared an identical dream environment," he wrote. "There are two types of mutual dreaming. In the first, two or more people have the same dream, but without each being present in the other's dream plot. In the second type, at least two people participate in the same dream and are aware of each other's presence."[6]

Lucid-dream researcher Stephen LaBerge also wrote about the subject of mutual dreams. "These are the perplexing experiences in which two or more people report having had similar if not identical dreams," LaBerge said. "In some of these cases, the reports are so remarkably alike that one is almost compelled to conclude that the dream sharers have been present together in the same dream environment. . . . On the other hand, we may only share dream plots in mutual dreams, not the dreams themselves."[7]

The published definitions of "mutual dreams" vary according to the authors' knowledge and experience of the subject. Contrast the preceding ideas with that of the leaders of the "jumping dogs" workshop. Phyllis R. Koch-Sheras, E. Ann Hollier, and Brooke Jones wrote, "A mutual dream is a telepathic experience in which two or more persons have the same or similar dream." For these three authors, mutual dreams were primarily psychic experiences.[8]

Mutual Dreams in the Lab

Bob Van de Castle and Allan Rechtschaffen have reported mutual dreams in the laboratory that happened on a spontaneous basis in the depths of sleep. But I know of only one occasion when two dreamers went into a sleep lab, both having the specific intention to incubate mutual dreams. They then brought their dream reports to me for analysis. Unfortunately, these dreamers had to do this on the q.t. Because of their standing in the scientific community, the researchers at the lab were not themselves willing to sponsor the idea that dreams could display psychic overtones.

These dreamers slept under laboratory conditions during the two nights of June 12 and 13, 1988. One had spent enough time in the lab to become acclimatized to the situation. For the other, it was a first-time experience. Both were trying for lucid dreams, as well as mutual ones. Both had several false awakenings, but only one achieved lucidity long enough to seek out the other partner. (And it wasn't the old-timer!)

Each night there were several cases of shared symbols and many common themes as well as evidence of a similar thinking process.

BLANCHE: *Comparing different colors of sweater . . . at first I think the young man who is showing me the sweaters intends to wear them himself.*

ELIOT: *I lend him a scarf and also a sweatshirt . . . the clothes I give him transform to matching plaids.*

BLANCHE: *Then I imagine Eliot and I are doing something he would consider coming for, in my opinion, sensual sexual play.*

ELIOT: *[I was] thinking if it were possible to be in a lover relationship with her.*

However, their weekend of dreaming together didn't make its full impact until more than a week later. On June 22, after they had returned to their own comfy beds in their separate homes, Blanche and Eliot finally had their complete **meeting dream.**

"When Blanche told me her dream," said Eliot, "I excitedly told her about my dream double. He is just like me except he is from Russia!" Eliot dreamt of Blanche, but Blanche didn't dream of Eliot. Instead she dreamt of an aspect of Eliot, a creative variation on his waking self.

MEETING A PARTNER'S ASPECT

I am with three lovers, all male, one of whom I feel very close to . . . the man from Russia. He just escaped and is still wearing a shirt covered with Russian Communist emblems and insignias. Hand grenades blast around us occasionally as I steer him through Santa Fe streets. I feel protective of him and am very sexually desirous of him.

I kiss him impulsively and passionately all over his neck, face, and shoulders. I tell him, "I can't wait to get you out of that shirt," referring to its dangers for designating him a Communist in our country.

We meet three women who will live with us in a commune in Santa Fe. They are lovers with the three men and with each other. The men are lovers with each other as well. We arrive at our home. It has a rambling long hall with rooms along it on either side. We choose our rooms, first come, first serve. I get the last room and find it quite nice. Hanging curtains serve as doors.

We all feel happy together, though our circumstances are simple.

BLANCHE

I am with Blanche and desire her sexually. I kiss her passionately all over her face, neck, and shoulders.

Blanche and I give a dream presentation together and it goes very well! Feels great!

ELIOT

Laboratory and Field

If I had been a scientist, perhaps I would have been drawn to the dream laboratory. But there have already been results from laboratory experimentation in telepathic and precognitive dreams that demonstrate a need to cultivate dreams in as natural a setting as possible. For one thing, the decision to go public with dream material is best motivated by a genuine desire to share and explore rather than a demand to comply. A gamelike atmosphere makes available a level of comfort and sharing not available in a formal laboratory setting. It relaxes us and allows emotion to flow freely. The atmosphere shifts the goal from demanding proof of psychic phenomena to allowing it to emerge as a fragile plant nurtured by plentiful water and encouraging sunshine. For most people, this is best accomplished through dream sharing and dreaming at home.

The field approach means less control of definable variables as demanded by laboratory protocol, but focusing just on discrete elements loses sight of the big picture. As anthropologist Margaret Mead has noted, "Most people prefer to carry out the kinds of experiments that allow the scientist to feel that he is in full control of the situation rather than surrendering himself to the situation, as one must in studying human beings as they actually live."[9]

Mutual dreaming is a *social* science. I don't think you can fully appreciate the relational aspects of a monkey caged or dissected on the laboratory table. So I chose to take a Jane Goodall/Dian Fossey approach and live with the dreaming monkeys. Then, in the process, I was able to realize how much I was a monkey, myself.

CHAPTER 8

✦

THE HOLISTIC DREAM UNIVERSE

*W*hen Michael Talbot described the view of our world as a hologram, an image projection from a reality beyond space and time, he tapped into a picture that, for some time now, has been gathering energy at the leading edge of conscious thought. In *The Holographic Universe*, Talbot illustrated the communal aspects of this holographic reality by using examples of shared visions and mutual hypnotic trances.

Then he stated, "In a holographic universe, a universe in which separateness ceases to exist and the innermost processes of the psyche can spill over and become as much a part of the objective landscape as the flowers and the trees, reality itself becomes little more than a *mass shared dream* [emphasis added]."[1] He believed that to make connections with other human beings via the medium of the dream might just unlock the secrets to the challenges that beset humankind.

The idea of the world as a shared dream is as fresh as

future tech and quantum physics. It's as ancient as shamanic ritual and epic journeys through the netherworld.

Out-of-body folks and lucid dreamers have been especially attracted to the idea. They resonated with the experiences of Oliver Fox, Carlos Castaneda, Jane Roberts, and Robert Monroe, as well as the research of Charles Tart and James J. Donahoe.

On the other hand, community dreamworkers have been influenced by Carl Jung's theory of the collective unconscious. Jung proposed the belief that myths, hallucinations, religious visions, and dreams all spring from the same source shared by all people. Jung conceived the collective unconscious to be a level where the individual mind merges with the unconscious mind of the entire race of humanity.

Although Jung's concept of the collective unconscious has had an enormous impact on the field of dreams, he did not conceive of a mechanism for realizing its existence first-hand. Secondhand, yes. Through recording, analyzing, and processing dreams, dreamwork attempts to make the unconscious conscious. By interpreting the meaning behind your dream imagery, you can procure information that Jung believed to come from a common pot of symbolic material. Generally, the information is considered to be provided for your own personal use.

Yet, in the holographic model of the universe, the dream is reflected in waking life as much as our waking lives are reflected in the dream. Unless we are literal hermits, our waking lives include a social component. The holographic model insists that our dreaming life must also. This makes the unconscious universe both collective and distinct.

We resist the reality of the holographic universe while we hold on to the illusion that a dream is but a fortress of solitude lined with mirrors. When, like Talbot, we follow the path of logic to its conclusion, we will find ourselves at the edge of our personal dream space. There, we can peer closely at our images in the self-reflecting glass and see them begin to shimmer. When the silvered prejudice of privacy slips off

the back of our mirrors, we will find ourselves gazing
through the looking glass to see what lies beyond. In a holographic universe, there is room for precognition, clairvoyance, psychokinesis, and telepathy. Talbot reminds us that
certain axioms of quantum physics infer that these psychic
elements *must* be present for such a universe to exist.

Why We Don't Mutual Dream

Perhaps it would be advantageous at this juncture to ask,
"Why *don't* we dream together?" If, as the newly emerging
holographic world view suggests, we are truly droplets in
a whole sea of unconsciousness, then why not experience
spontaneous mutual dreams on a regular basis? Why might
we need to use intention to produce the experience?

The most obvious answer is that the new world view is
still in its infancy and that traditional scientific and philosophical perspectives deem our waking selves and our
dreaming worlds to be separate one from the other. With
such an attitude, any evidence that falls outside this belief
structure serves as a troublesome irritant and can be intensely rejected or ignored. For example, the psychoanalytic
field has had a continuous struggle with the emergence of
telepathy in the therapeutic setting. Psi just doesn't fit the
"facts."

Second, mutual dreaming takes more than just a mastery
of dream manipulation and understanding. It takes social
skill. The dreamer who is essentially a solitary soul in his
own world will not venture far into shared reality. Others
who may want to do so will hesitate out of a realization born
by waking experience: that overlapping intentions, perceptions, and expectations can breed dispute. In fact, the greater
focus of traditional dreamwork is geared to resolve just such
problems. Those who view dreams from this therapeutic
perspective may conclude that dreams are inherently disruptive and any attempt to "meet" another must involve a bat-
tle. The attempts to hold fear and the accompanying sense

of powerlessness at bay will command the majority of the dreamer's time and resources. A potential partner may avoid such a person, aware that the urgent push to avoid fear distorts the fearful dreamer's perceptions, thus producing conflict dreams and nightmares.

Third, there is often a reluctance to share oneself for fear of being overwhelmed by the experience. In some people, this is a legitimate concern. Their personal boundaries are ill-defined. They are not able to clearly sense where they "begin" and where they "end"; what is internal and what is external.

Common agreement is necessary to sustain a common world view. But to hold the belief that common agreement *demands* self-modification, that we dreamers must leave our individual minds behind in order to participate in a group mind, is a sure source of conflict.

Successful mutual dreamers learn to tell the difference between their energy and that of others and between waking and dreaming life. They are also likely to have frequent encounters with the "borderlands" between dreaming and waking. In addition to mutual dreams, they report experiences with false awakenings, astral projection, lucidity, hypnogogia, trance, and other altered states, which are not quite waking and not quite dream.

Fourth, dreams reflect the current status of human perception and communication skills. Through the process of acculturation, our waking views of reality have been skewed to emphasize what we have in common, at the expense of our individuality. Our commonalities are important to enable social interaction. They form the basis of our language, culture, and history. But the truth of the matter is that we all "see" things differently. The same stimulus can produce very different sensory and cognitive reactions in people. Conversely, different stimuli can produce the same sensations. The route from stimulus to sensation is conditioned by education, environment, and past experience, and they vary for each one of us.

Joseph Chilton Pearce points out that, as children, we respond to outer reality by making our explorations verbal; we "talk it out" to ourselves. Later, as pressure mounts to conform to the language of society, this "talking out" of the world gets internalized. As Pearce says, "Even when actual feedback from another source is coming in, roof-brain chatter goes right ahead, prestructuring, tape-looping, resenting, planning one's rebuttal, fogging inputs, and creating static."[2] With such an intense need to establish stability and individuality through inner talk, it's a wonder we can communicate at all. Under these circumstances, much of our so-called waking "communication" is not a dialogue; it's actually a series of monologues.

Many dreams are the reflection of roof-brain chatter. Free from the constructs of waking life, a different language prevails, however. Images formed from thought, feeling, attitude, and emotion predominate. When we consider sleep to be our own sensory isolation booth, the night form of internal talk can get quite bizarre, indeed.

If we are in the habit of engaging in roof-brain chatter in the waking state, then we shouldn't consider it unusual that our dreams also reflect this mode of noncommunication. Caught up in the drone of our own internal monologues, about the only thing that will usually catch our attention is an emotive message. Given this fact, it's not at all surprising that most telepathic and mutual dream anecdotes are those that signal danger.

True mutual dreams require a mutual effort to pay attention to the dream partner; to shift focus from internal talk and really observe and listen to the other person. How many of us can truly say we do this in the waking state?

Finally, if correspondence between dreamers is not found to be the result of a common waking stimulus, then we must factor in the psychic components. Dreamers vary in their ESP abilities. Those who are psychic may not know when their abilities are active and when not. The degree of accurate perception and information retrieval can differ from one dream to another.

Cayce and Psi

The holistic worldview is best applied to mutual dream research through suggestions and philosophical theory that come from the channeled material of Jane Roberts' Seth and Edgar Cayce.

Edgar Cayce believed that psychic phenomena would not be understood if the orientation was to "prove" their existence, because the very act of trying to examine mental contents singled out and separated them from the people involved. Rather, he suggested, a better approach to understand psi would be to bring people together in such a way that they would have a desire to help one another but have no other way of doing it except by telepathic means. That way, they would focus on serving others *through* telepathy.

Most research into dream telepathy follows the scientific model: experimentation in a laboratory setting under restricted conditions involving such elements as random selection procedures and double-blind judgments. The intent is to keep the experimenter in an outsider or objective stance, to preserve the observer/subject relationship.

This approach is appropriate to those fields whose primary modus operandi is logic or reason. Dream research benefits from intellectual analysis and cognition, but stretches far beyond it into the intuitive, emotional, and creative realm of perception. In this realm the logical boundaries between self and other begin to dissipate.

Edgar Cayce's participant-oriented type of philosophy indicated that experimenter and subject should cooperate and work together for the mutual revelation of whatever it was they were trying to do. The experimenter would fully disclose the hypothesis to the subject; he wouldn't distance himself from, observe, and operate on the subject, obtain secret facts, and report them to his colleagues, leaving the subject in the dark.

John Wheeler, a leading theoretical physicist, seconds the motion. He states that the very nature of consciousness means that the observer's involvement in an experiment is a determining factor in the outcome of that experiment. The psychic researchers have already discovered this. They call it the "experimenter effect." It refers to the thesis that subjects' responses can be influenced by the experimenter's attitudes and feelings, such as expectations about high or low scores on a psychic test. The experimenter efffect has been continuously demonstrated in the laboratory.

It's been demonstrated out in the field, too. The concept is called "doctrinal compliance." In this form of ESP, a therapist's emotional interests unintentionally transfer to the patient. If there is good rapport, the therapist's concerns, ideas, and beliefs can be mirrored in the dreams of the patient. A patient with a Jungian therapist begins dreaming Jungian-oriented dreams, for instance. And the patient's dreams can pick up personal information about the therapist. Perhaps this is one reason some psychologists even use the term "participant-observer" in their work.

This is also why the participative model makes the most sense in terms of mutual dreaming. It doesn't matter if a "group" is two or twenty. All members of a group, including the experimenter, are in fact participants in the group results. All members might as well hold the conscious intent to dream together; they're going to do so anyway.

The scientific researchers agree. In order to maximize psi results, declared researcher Steven M. Rosen, "The experimenter as well as the subject must operate at a level of consciousness appropriate to psi."[3] Michael Grosso even urged consideration of the possibility of a "psi conducive community," in which group interaction could reinforce and develop individual psi ability.[4]

Henry Reed and Communal Group Dreaming

Researcher Henry Reed had this community idea in mind with a group dreaming project sponsored by the Edgar Cayce foundation, Association for Research and Enlightenment (A.R.E.). In 1976, the Dream Research Project directed dreamers to spend twenty-eight days in intensive home study using a packet of material that utilized methods of dream incubation and interpretation. As the dreams came in, it soon became obvious that some of the dreamers were quite capable of picking up information about Henry, himself. One person honed in on significant details of his personal life and psychological aspects of his involvement in dream research, including the design of the A.R.E. project. Other people sent in dreams that contained explicit references to intimacies in his life, both actual and fantasied. Thus, in these cases, Henry was a more personable target than the project itself.

When Henry began publishing the *Sundance Community Dream Journal* later in 1976, he used a format similar to the A.R.E. Project. He suggested that prospective subscribers to the *Journal* write a letter to their dreams, asking how participation might affect them and their dream lives. Henry asked that dreamers wrap the dream letter with the subscription notice and place both under their pillows for a night or two; then send the resulting dreams, along with the subscription, to the *Journal*. Responses came in over a two-year period (1976–1978).

The dreams of the *Sundance Community Dream Journal* subscribers reflect the advantage of the higher energy created by group activity. Not surprisingly, the image of dancing was featured prominently, as well as circles and other connective symbols. On the other hand, there was expressed the need for individual activity, a need for privacy, and a concern for maintaining one's identity. Through their dreams, the participants were asking, "Who am I?" and "Who are we?" Henry called this the "creative tension inherent in the very notion of community—how to reap the benefits of cooperation and at the same time encourage and provide for the vital uniqueness of the individual."[5]

Later dreams brought up the issues of control, difficulty of collaboration, and whether or not there might be safety in numbers. Anxiety was expressed about self-exposure, rejec-

tion, emotional inundation, and crowding. But certain thematic imagery remained constant: music, fertility, and
communication. There was an increase in the images of man-
made structures, indicating that the *Journal* was a technological form of connection. In all, the dreams reflected a tense-
ness between enthusiasm and trepidation; an inner conflict
between longing to be part of a larger whole and insisting
on one's own individuality.

Henry has reported that dream group participants can
achieve a sense of oneness when their dreams are reenacted
in the waking state in the form of a nonscripted psycho-
drama, but sleeping reports are more akin to the pieces of a
jigsaw puzzle. A puzzle, I would add, where often some of
the parts are missing.

A Joint Dream Helper Project

In 1978 Henry Reed and several others from the A.R.E.
cooperated in a joint Dream Helper project with people from
the Poseidia Institute, an organization that offered psychic
readings and psychological counseling. It was decided that
the next local person who came to Poseidia requesting a
reading would be offered the bonus of being involved in the
project. This meant that the individual would also receive
presession and postsession counseling with one of Poseidia's
psychologists and would meet for at least two sessions with
a Dream Helper team composed of seven members of the
combined Poseidia and A.R.E. staffs. In addition, readings
would be done on the Dream Helper process itself.

The purpose of the project was for the Dream Helpers to
intuit the person's problems without verbal assistance but
through their impressions and dreams. They also were to aid
in the healing of the problem.

A young college woman was selected, and the Dream
Helpers met with her one evening for meditation. Each team
member was asked to go home and write down any intuitive
impressions of the target individual. Five of the seven mem-

bers picked up that the problem involved a trauma or risk, and four felt that this had to do with difficulties in the pelvic area; two saw this as having to do with children or the loss of a child. Then the team slept and recorded their night dreams.

The next day the team met with the young woman and presented their intuitive impressions and dreams. Outwardly, the issue had to do with the young woman's doubts as to whether she should pursue a singing career. But by talking with her, the Dream Helpers discovered that the woman had been experiencing difficulties with her reproductive organs, for which she had been seeing a physician; she was facing a traumatic conflict of involvement with an older married man, about which her family knew nothing and would certainly not approve; and while still in high school she had experienced a traumatic abortion that very few people were aware of outside her immediate family (including the man in question). Her abortion had been a secret because of potential scandal. She was very gifted musically as an organist and soloist. Her church minister had taken her under his wing, they had had an affair, and she had become pregnant. Thus this trauma had a direct relationship to her doubts about whether she should pursue the singing career.

Sharing her problem in a supportive atmosphere where she could hear the Dream Helpers respond had a healing effect and meant a change of direction for her. The young woman went on to music college.

The team's dreams centered around several themes that included: cars with defective parts, foreign objects, earthquakes or earth splits, fires or explosions, energy in a circular motion, parental disapproval, young people or children at play, and other Dream Helper members. About the target individual, dreamers dreamt "the man has a knife and is slicing at me," and "a Buick . . . was having trouble with its pipes," but that now there was hope because the dreamer was "moving into a new house." About the team members, dreamers dreamt "I say to the [Dream Helpers] that we are dreaming. Some of them seem in doubt, or maybe doubting that we should recognize the fact," and "we as a group were all riding around a roller rink on children's tricycles, very awkwardly manipulating and colliding with each other."[6]

Interestingly, the intuitive impressions honed in on the specific inner problem of the individual, while the dreams told a much larger story. Although stimulated by the target individual's problems, their dreams included a depiction of the philosophical and emotional conflicts *among* the Dream Helper team members.

In this joint project, Henry's group came from the Edgar Cayce organization. But the people at Poseidia Institute were influenced by the Jane Roberts's Seth material.

The Contributions of Jane Roberts's Seth

When researcher Charles Tart proposed the model of the "state specific scientist," he argued that proper scientific investigations involving altered states of consciousness would require "a group of highly skilled, dedicated, and trained practitioners" who would learn to enter into precise states of consciousness such as those that can be found in dreams and mutually "agree with one another that they have attained a common state." He said that individual self-understanding would have to be central to such learning.[7]

Tart's idea sounds very like the Jane Roberts/Seth model of the "dream-art scientist." Both Cayce and Seth held the belief that dreams play a crucial role in the creation of past, present, and future reality. According to Seth, a dream-art scientist is one of several future professions waiting in the wings of historical time.

A dream-art scientist would not just study the dreams of others from the outside. She would learn how to dwell *within* the inner reality, becoming as well-grounded and secure there as in outer life. A dream-art scientist would learn how to be lucid while dreaming; how to understand the symbols in her dream and how they correlate with symbols in waking life; how to recognize the many different levels and kinds of activity in dreams; and how to begin to perceive the inner blueprints for the outer world. As a dream researcher, the dream-art scientist is the model I try to emulate.

Such principals were put into practice when Seth suggested various "practice elements" for his readers and for Jane Roberts's psychic class. These elements were used to stimulate dream recall, insight, and dream control. He asked the class to remember their dreams and report them to one another.

Seth indicated that the class members were *already* meeting in their dreams, but that they needed to become aware of the fact. He kept urging the class to pay attention to their dreams, to look for correlating elements among them. This the class did, with regular success.

Then he laid a bombshell. He told class members that not only were they meeting in their dreams, but they were engaged in a communal project. Together, they were building an "Inner City." And, because of the holographic nature of the universe, this "Inner City" would someday become fact, in the outer world.

It's one thing to hypothesize a holographic universe or believe in a holistic world. It's quite another to have the opportunity to experience it firsthand, to explore and have adventures in it. But to say that we actually participate in creating, building, and maintaining the "dreamtime" world?

Now, that takes participant-observer to the max.

A Shared Meeting Place: The Inner City

Seth's blatant suggestion that the dreamworld was a meeting place for dreamers resulted in the discovery of mutual dreams among the members of Jane's class.

Two airplanes zoom in circles over the house. Oddly shaped, like hang gliders, they are from another time and space, I think. One rams the other and threatens to crash into the house. . . . I see that the house and property are really carefully maintained museums; illusions preserved in the middle of a giant and filthy city. It occurs to me that this is a pretty tacky way to preserve history—to make a "Looking-Glass Zoo" out of us.

SUE WATKINS

A group of several people go to a field where there is a sort of tacky Stonehenge made of plywood and cardboard. People are hang gliding in the distance. We want to take some of the plywood and make hang gliders. Then in a big room—apartment?—somebody helps us make hang gliders out of a two-by-four fastened together at one end with a bolt.

GEORGE RHOADS

I was driving along the road with some class members, stopping to visit various museums to look at the artists' works.

DEREK BARTHOLOMEW[8]

"I think that spontaneity and adventure are really all you need," class member Sue Watkins wrote me about the Inner City. "Then you just get what you get. Keep records, keep your common sense, keep your sense of the Oregon Trail. Also, as I think about it, I don't think Jane's class ever set up frameworks even for its dream experiences. We'd just suggest a class dream or a City dream and then wrote down what happened. The most important thing was our sense of fun—of playful, childlike pretending, even. We threw out any other requirement."

Even with this low-key approach to dream connections, there were many reports of dream meshing among class members. Please keep in mind that the class met over a period of years. During such an extended time, they had ample opportunity to reach a sense of comfort with one another. Meeting dreams were noticed and reported among intimates: husbands and wives, and two sisters who were both members of the class.

After Watkins's books *Conversations with Seth (Vols. I & II)* were published, readers attempted to dream up the Inner City, too. Then in 1984 the Seth Dream Network, under the leadership of Lenore Jackson, collected dreams on the subject from such readers. A review of the collection revealed that the "Inner City" had undergone a metamorphosis.

The scene is rolling low hills. Small groups of people are strolling about, like Sunday in the park. The sky is overcast with cirrostratus clouds at about twenty thousand feet. People begin to point to the sky, "There's a castle, there's a church, it's a city, etc." Apparently they can really see a city in the sky. For the life of me, I look and look, and can see nothing but clouds. I wonder why I can't see it.

Then a big hole appears, perhaps half a mile across, in the clouds. Air and clouds are being sucked up higher into the sky. Wisps of cloud can be seen swishing into the hole at great velocity. This is nothing like a tornado or typhoon, which have a column going up. More like a whirlpool upside down and not whirling. No sound. It seems to be getting lower. Surface wind is picking up.

. . . I have been going to the inner city for years, seemingly after crawling out of a tunnel cut in a mountain that is on the edge of the city. I enter the tunnel from a mine up near the top of a mountain.   KEVIN D.

I am on top of a very high mountain looking down at a Shangri-la type setting, similar to that in Lost Horizons.

I walk down the hill to a very large dome-shaped building, and as I enter, it is nothing at all like one would expect a domelike structure to be.

The room is all paneled in rustic wood . . . a fireplace

at one end . . . two walls lined with books. Near the fireplace
are two comfortable chairs. In one I see my "lady in blue."
I sit in the other, and I know this will always by my Inner
City where I shall go to meet my teachers and my friends.

KENDRA T.

I am showing a friend the city in which I live. This is a
special day that draws people to the city. We are walking
beside some very tall buildings. There are no cars or traffic.
Everything is very spacious, open, and clean. One building
has an enormous dome in which is suspended a replica of the
solar system. The planets are huge globes. The earth is
covered with small bumps and is more pear-shaped than the
other planets.

MALLORY K.

In a sunny park, I'm standing near a water fountain and
walk over to a sculptural piece. It's a sundial, or planetary
sundial, or a planetary dial. It has something to do with the
planets. I walk near a big government building with about
forty steps leading up to the Doric columns. . . .

I am going to a school or library with a group of young
people. Our room is circular and we enter, climb stairs to a
walkway around the periphery of the rotunda. There are
books in the dark walnut shelves along the circular walls, and
a patterned carpet on the floor. Our instructor enters through
a paneled door, and we shoot rubber bands at him. Everybody
laughs, then he gives us assignments.

SEAN Y.

I am in a narrow, white corridor going downhill underground. The air is getting thin. After a long time we come

to a huge, lit cavern with a lake in the middle. In the lake there are several larger-than-life-size white paper boats, all made of intricate paper, folding in many different designs. They are moving slowly, but at slightly different speeds in a counterclockwise direction around the lake.

All around the lake is sort of a bowl-shaped racetrack, with many colored lights of all sizes and configurations circling around the lake, also in counterclockwise direction, and at different speeds, but much faster than the boats. As I stand watching this spectacular scene, I realize it has been worth it to come all the way down here through the thin air corridor.

LUCY C.

These reports seem to favor expansive, circular themes, including caverns inside the earth, cities in the sky, or huge domed-shaped buildings.

Later, during the shared dreaming projects, suggestions to dream up an "Inner City" met with resistance. Perhaps it was because the term "inner city" has such an unfortunate association with images of drug- and violence-filled streets. Dreaming together invoked interior scenes, but they tended to be either cozy homes or large communal meeting places like auditoriums or restaurants. Seen from the outside, the buildings seemed to reside in the middle of greenbelts: acres of foliage, not miles of concrete. Dream locations might be a park, a swimming pool, watering hole, or near the ocean. The civilized Inner City had evolved into an Inner Countryside.

When today's mutual dreamers propose meeting "places" that are earth-proper, they are usually influenced by out-of-body legend and lore. Paris at the Eiffel Tower, Runnymede at the signing of the Magna Carta are examples of such targets. However, if the selected meeting place is imaginary and especially if it is constructed either in the mind prior to the dream or within the dream itself, it's very likely that dreamers have been influenced by the Inner City concept.

Internet Dreams

These days the Sethian dreamers have gone high-tech. You'll find them on the Internet. They, and the lucid dreamers, are most likely to try out mutual dreaming projects in cyberspace. For example, in 1995, the SethWorks mailing list members (who call themselves "Moose") engaged in a couple of mutual dreaming projects they named the Tropical Moosemeet and the Moosequerade.

The folks who read the newsgroup called alt. dreams have participated in experiments like the Dream Train, the SS Dreamers (in 1992), and Cafe Dreamers (in 1993). A description of a particular place was posted to the newsgroup, and people were encouraged to go there in their dreams. A person not involved in the experiment collected the dreams via e-mail and looked for similarities among the reports.

There have been groups of dreamers who have attempted to launch meeting dreams with each other by suggesting such an event via computer on-line services like CompuServe®, Prodigy®, and The Well®.

If you were to follow the Internet highway to those messages, you would discover the dynamics of preparation and the questions raised by folks who have desired to meet in a dream. The messages ask:

When shall we meet? Sunday, Saturday, Thursday? Where shall be meet? In someone's home? In a more public place like the Golden Gate Bridge? But exactly where? In the middle? Up on the towers? In the headlands to the north?

The dream date comes and goes. Dead silence on the network. Then, a hesitant few apologies. Whoops, I didn't even remember a dream that night. Sorry, I went lucid but forgot about the project. Yes, I remembered my dreams, but none of them had anything to do with the Golden Gate. . . .

Gosh, we failed, is the consensus. Unfortunately, under these conditions, there's usually no one around to provide a reality check. Hey, folks, did you really expect a home run the first time up at bat? After all, most folks first invite good friends into their field of dreams, not a bunch of strangers.

In the realm of the Internet the issue of privacy has raised its timid head. The current wisdom from Internet gurus is: When you contact other people via a public computer network, don't use your real name. Use a first name, your initials, a pseudonym. But when you are hiding behind a pen name, do you really meet?

I'm not saying that you can't intentionally dream with strangers. I've found that you can. But I suggest that you choose folks you wouldn't mind inviting to your home in physical reality. Otherwise your dreaming psyche may close the door on your conscious effort, and with good reason.

I wish the dreamers had looked further. What happened to their dreams in and around the target date, whether they were lucid or not? Maybe there were some base hits or walks or double plays, some meshing or telepathic dreams. Maybe the connection *was* made, but with other people not in the computer group. Like friends. Like family.

Groups of people can make cross-connections when and where they least expect. Mutual dreaming actually taps into a network of events in the holistic universe. This was demonstrated even more clearly during my own shared dreaming projects.

CHAPTER 9

✦

$\mathcal{S}$HARED $\mathcal{D}$REAMING:
INTENDING TO MEET

$\mathcal{Y}$. ✦ our best chance to deliberately induce a mutual dream is shared dreaming. **Shared dreaming** occurs when partners go to sleep with the intent to *meet* in their dreams. In group dreaming projects, meshing is vague and usually consists of shared symbols and common themes. The possibility of procuring a dream in which two or more dreamers recognize or encounter one another is virtually nil. By comparison, in shared dreaming projects, the task to *meet* in a dream results in a dramatic increase in full meshing and reciprocal dreams.

And, you can get some dreams where the clues to "meeting" are much less obvious than in the classic type.

Before the lucid dream networks came into existence, Jean Campbell, Barbara Shor, and I were the first to experiment with this new model under the influence of the holographic world view.

Group Dreaming Versus Shared Dreaming

Shared dreaming projects use both shared dreaming and group dreaming types of goals. What is the difference? Group dreaming can be thought of as dreaming with all the participants surrounding an issue placed in the center of the ring. Group dreaming is basically *dreaming for*—for something or for someone.

A volunteer for a group can benefit either from the information gathered together by the group or just from the energy of being the central focus. For four days after the dreamers in the *Nexus* project did their "dreaming for Kyla," Kyla Houbolt reported that she was entirely in a state that she termed "my powerful self." In the midst of a high-pressure, busy work week, she had a feeling of "absolute trust."

However, even if a human being is placed in the middle of a group circle, this is still a one-way street. Members have dreams directed toward the center and perceive certain elements in common. But they rarely demonstrate much meshing. Even under the best of circumstances, the multiple layers of a person can be quite complex.

When dream researcher Mark Thurston of the A.R.E. used life difficulties as the target for an ESP test, he found that such targets presented a problem. A goal such as "dream to help Alex," could be verified only if Alex knew what his real problem was. Dreams don't just stick to physical symptoms, but include individual and social psychological factors as well.

Dreaming *for* a person is not the same as dreaming to *meet* a person. It's like placing a topic instead of the person in the catbird seat at the center of a dream group.

Let's take the example: "Dream to help Alex with his problem at work." The focus of the dreamers is on the topic of discussion (work) and not on the person behind the topic (Alex). In the meantime, Alex is focusing inward on himself and his problem, not outward to meet with others in the circle. And none of the people in the circle are paying much attention to one another.

The dreams reflect this fact. They "bump" into one another as if by accident. They act like chapters in an anthology—on the same basic subject, but not overly concerned about whether one opinion or perspective matches another. The result is an encyclopedia of knowledge about a person, but little focus on the actual individual involved.

In group dreaming, the major focus is on gleaning and conveying *information*—information about a topic, information about a person. With shared dreaming, the focus in on *meeting*—meeting an actual person, meeting in a dreamscape.

Jean Campbell and the Shared Meeting

As mentioned before, the Edgar Cayce organization (A.R.E.) and the Poseidia Institute of Virginia Beach co-sponsored a Dream Helper project in the late 1970s. Henry Reed went on to facilitate more of these sorts of group dreaming experiments with Robert Van de Castle. On the other hand, Jean Campbell, the executive director of the Poseidia Institute, initiated another new model for dreaming together.

Jean had her own firsthand experience of mutual dreaming, especially with staff members and clients. She was a lucid dreamer, which made her idea of mutual dreams different than that of the other researchers. And she had had a meeting dream reminiscent of the movie *Dreamscape.*

Jean had become aware in her dream that a friend was in trouble with some cataclysmic event, so she went to help. The next day Jean asked the friend, "Do you remember the dream we had last night?" The friend paled visibly and sat down. It turned out that the friend's husband had been having a nightmare involving a fire. His thrashing in bed had awakened his spouse. After describing the dream to his wife, they both returned to sleep. This time she began to experience the same dream as her husband and woke him up. But there was a difference. She recalled Jean being there in the dream. "You watch, Jean will remember this dream," she said to her husband. And of course, Jean did.

Because Jean knew it was possible to dream with people she knew, she began shared dreaming with folks close at hand. But because of the success of the cosponsored project, she was also curious to see whether people who did *not* know one another in the waking state could learn to dream together. With roots in both the Edgar Cayce and the Jane Roberts's Seth traditions, Jean Campbell created what was to become the standard for shared dreaming projects to come: Dreams to the Tenth Power. The number 10 stood for the number of invited members of each dream team.

Dreams¹⁰: The First Two Projects

The first Dreams[10] experiment took place in 1977–1978 among one team of ten people who were either staff members or people closely associated with Poseidia. The goal of the project was to determine whether people could dream on command, to explore the symbolic content of the dreams, and to investigate the ratio of lucid to nonlucid dreams involved in the process.

The format was relatively informal, with two target goals for each of the six months it ran. Some goals were shared dreaming goals. They included meeting in the dream state at a particular place everyone knew (such as the tower of the Old Cavalier Hotel in Virginia Beach). The results of these experiments, though not spectacular, were enough to indicate that on any given target date, several team members did seem to be "dreaming together," that is, they were involved in some form of dream meshing. In addition, other staff members began to dream along, showing up in the project participants' dreams or vice versa. Poseidia staff members began to use their dreams as a way of working together in the waking state, or a way of exploring the feelings for one another.

The second Dreams[10] project, in late 1982, involved two

teams of ten people each. A facilitator from the Poseidia staff
was a member of each team. Some two hundred applicants
from all over the country were screened for stability, interest
in dreaming, and for indications that they had no professional interest in either dreaming or parapsychology. The
majority of the people were Virginia residents between the
ages of twenty-five and forty who worked at a variety of
occupations from taxi driver to college professor. They were
given seven targets spread over a period of four months.

The results contained examples of successful incubation
to the target goal, meshing dreams, and dreams of other
team members. The goals included dining at a restaurant,
partying together, and meeting at the same location.

The second assignment was to meet and describe other
team members. Seventeen of the participants wrote that
they'd dreaming of being among a group of strangers. One
dreamt of a man, woke up, and wrote down a description of
the person he'd seen. Then he went back to bed, where he
dreamt about the same man again. The man told him, "You
put down my weight at one-sixty-five; it's two-hundred-
something."

When members were asked to visit Poseidia in their
sleep, ten of them dreamed of a building similar to the Institute. Several dreamt of having conversations with women
resembling Jean Campbell and other staff.

Members knew the target dates, but not the goals, until
just beforehand. About midway through the project, the researchers had planned to ask both groups to go to the beach
in their dreams. But just before the tasks were mailed out,
one participant wrote to say that she was getting married on
the target date, and couldn't the members of her team come
to her wedding as their dream goal? The facilitators agreed
and changed the target for the team only, leaving the second
team's goal as the beach. Each team was unaware of the other's goal.

On the target night, two members of the newlywed's
team dreamt that they traveled to a wedding. Four members
described aspects of a wedding. One talked to an old girl-

friend. Two didn't recall dreams. The new bride, however, wrote to say that she guessed that she'd just had too much excitement to be able to dream about her wedding. Instead, she'd dreamed that she was with a group of people—at the beach!

As the project progressed, more and more of the participants became reluctant to respond. Some grew anxious about the potential intimacy with other people; one person per team never really participated by sharing dreams. Others reported that they had learned a lot about themselves in the process, liked the unique opportunity that the project provided, and wanted to do more.

The Third Dreams[10] Project: With Dreamworkers

The third Dreams[10] project was held for six months in 1984. It also consisted of two teams of ten members each. This time it was decided to involve other dream researchers, therapists, and community dreamworkers in the experiment—people who regularly worked with their own and other people's dreams. Invitations went out to dreamworkers in the United States, Canada, France, and England. Like the others who had participated in Dreams[10], their dream responses ranged from delight and intrigue to anxiety and conflict. As Jean Campbell noted, "Although the concept of dreaming together is intellectually amusing and stimulating, the fact of group dreaming contradicts most of society's assumptions about the role of dreams and the possible limits of consciousness."[1]

Overall, the community dreamworkers seemed to fare better than the therapeutic professionals. This probably reflects the high value they tended to place on dreaming for problem solving or for promoting closer, more effective relationships in groups. It certainly reflects greater experience in participant-observer group work, whereby a dreamworker would have the opportunity to take on a peer role in the group circle and not just relate as the leader/lecturer to the rest of the membership.

Being a published author did not assure the ability to dream together; being a renowned researcher in lucidity didn't guarantee successful lucid dreams. Those who were most successful in dreaming on demand were often those least likely to perceive dreaming as a challenge to the status of their waking egos. The facilitators, who were highly motivated to keep an eye on their teammates, also did well.

Dreamers were supposed to turn in their goal sheets whether they remembered dreams or not. Comment on the waking life was very helpful: it provided evidence of synchronicity or telepathic influence on their team members' dreams. On the other hand, one individual's long dream-work commentary about his personal dream issues was distracting to the group intent, and doing dreamwork on *another* person's dream was downright disruptive. Either would turn focus onto the separate individuals and away from the group tasks.

Facilitator Patricia L. of Team 2 was the first to comment on what she called the "third night phenomenon." This syndrome has also been observed by sharing dreaming facilitators since Dreams[10]. Pat reported that, in the former Dreams[10] project, some of the people who had previously been good writers and dreamers just didn't respond to the third night goal. Others had trouble remembering their dreams or became so "busy" that they didn't report at all.

One member of Team 2 mentioned "boredom" in one of her dreams, which underlines a prime factor in the psychic connections of the dream state: emotional reaction. If the emotional bond isn't there, if the interest isn't being motivated, there is seldom connection via dreams.

Another member of Team 1 talked about the "flat response" that her team members were showing one another. Sometimes dreamers would be so caught up in their own "stuff" that they were not be able to effectively reach out to others, either through their dreams or in waking comments, and some never even tried. This is probably a function of personality and culture, perhaps even sex. Overall, the men were much more "standoffish" than the wormen; but then more women were community dreamworkers.

I have also observed that the "third night phenomenon" can be attributable to the fact that some people join a shared dreaming group with expectations of instant psychic achievement. When this unreasonable assumption is not met, their interest and their dreams wane. Those who survive the ebb and flow of dreaming understand that shared dreaming is not a one-shot effort but an ability that improves with practice, just like any other skill of relationship.

Renowned psychic researcher J. B. Rhine noted that the enthusiasm of subjects often produced good initial results in his ESP experiments, but the curve of success dipped downward as soon as his subjects got used to the experiment. During the Maimonides dream telepathy experiments, the agents who were "sending" the picture targets to dreamers reported being bored by having to concentrate on the same target for four nights. The best correspondences came on the first or second nights.

These findings suggest that the novelty of the stimulus is more important than any possible "build-up" effect. This means that if dreamers are trying to be "one-shot wonders," they'd better do it quickly! It also means that a new goal or game for every target date would be advisable.

In shared dreaming projects, dreamers may experience "beginner's luck" during the first couple of target dates, dreaming of and with other team members. Then it may seem that their achievement rate begins to falter. An important finding is that the "third night phenomenon" doesn't have to be the end of the story, if participants' enthusiasm is kept high enough.

Dreamers can be helped through slumps by increased telephone contact. I encourage members to keep trying, since the lull they are experiencing is temporary. They are actually shifting through neutral into another dreaming gear.

Cross-Dreaming During Dreams[10]

The dreams of Team 1 members seemed much more scattered than their compatriots in Team 2. However, when the dreams of both teams were observed together, it became obvious that the members of Team 1 were practicing the art of **cross-dreaming,** just as the bride had done in the second project. That is, during each of the six goals, they were reaching out to dream with and about the themes of the other team. Without other encouragement from the facilitator, members of Team 1 were directing their energies toward the literal goals instead of toward one another. But their curious psychic radars were scanning the goings-on of Team 2 and, unbeknownst to either team, were choosing to play along as silent, invisible partners, hanging over their shoulders, so to speak.

Both teams had the same preset goals, but did not see each other's dreams. The psychic cross-connections occurred when dreams were not initiated by responding to the literal target goal, but to the symbols and issues suggested by the dreams of the opposite team. The ability of Team 1 to cross-dream may have been assisted by advanced dreaming skills. For example, when the goal was to "explore dream lucidity," six members of Team 1 reported dreams involving that theme or skill; but only one member of Team 2 was able to become lucid on the target date.

However, two members of Team 2, the facilitator and one other, had been sharing dreams about bikes *prior* to the start of the experiment. Not too surprisingly, they managed to incubate corresponding bicycle dreams on the first target night.

PAT: *He invites me to a party. . . . [He], I, and an old friend [are] riding bicycles. . . . We ride to two very steep roads, where I walk my bike down while they ride down. We turn to the left at the bottom.*

KONRAD: *Traveling by foot, up a hill . . . on my way to a party. I have my bike, though sometimes I'm riding, sometimes I'm walking. . . . I get to a corner, and there are some people behind me going to the same place . . . the administrator in my office is with them. I stop to fix my bike. . . . Then I remember I'm dreaming, and I say, "Oh, let it go, it's just a dream."*

But this bicycle ride for two members of Team 2 fused a nucleus of psychological "energy" that attracted the interest of a member of the opposite team. That dreamer was also lucid.

WENDY: *As we again turn toward the right to enter a room, I think momentarily that there should be no room in that direction. Just as quickly, I reaffirm that this is a dream and decide to go along with it.*

The room looks like an old government office. . . . The man indicates I should take a seat [that] looks like a combination bicycle seat and secretary's chair. I do so, though the seat has a rip in its cover.

On the second target date, the goal for Dreams[10] was to "build a dream platform or choose a meeting place." Pat, as facilitator for Team 2, added her own energy by incubating a specific location.

"As I was going to sleep I thought about the kind of place I'd like to meet with all of you. What really seemed nice to me was a meadow with trees and a clear, sparkling creek nearby—on a comfortable, sunny day. I was picturing the countryside I saw in a Woody Allen movie, when he had a two-story Victorian-style house. I think the title was *A Midsummer Night's Dream*." Sure enough, this reverie did spark a dream response from one of her Team 2 members.

CHARLENE: *A somewhat distant, hazy view of a large two- or three-story white frame structure, with touches of Victorian carpenter Gothic on the eaves, balustrades on the verandah that run around the first floor, and steps down to the lawn. It is set in an expanse of acres of rolling emerald green lawn. It feels totally out of time and space.*

But then Team 1 used the same impetus to begin a chain-like description of the meeting place.

GLORIA: *I'm sitting reading . . . on the long, open verandah of a building which is like a hotel or country boarding-house.*

MALLORY: *A long building of unpainted wood, very old and shabby. I turn a corner and go down some wide blue-carpeted steps. I pass through many different rooms and realize that they are infinite and that I am creating them. Off to the side a wall opens, revealing a vast green carpet sloping to the center.*

WHITNEY: *I complete circling the house—same shape course as a curved parallelogram. The interior is blue.*

WENDY: *[It's] like a tour of elegant blue Victorian homes.*

Then after the goal date, one of the members of Team 2 wrote the facilitator, "I live in an old, Victorian three-story house with Gothic trim on the front porch." So there was a literal as well as fantasy target available for a dream response.

Dreams[10] was the first project to display the "half full/ half empty" syndrome. Jean Campbell had sent out the same invitation to all participants. It said, in effect, "We are having an experiment; would you like to play?" One group (from both teams) honed in on the serious specter of a scientific experiment; the other group reverberated with the image of play.

On the first goal, dreams from both teams painted a picture of tension between two "games." The first was a conflict/therapy game that was reflected in the grave tenor of administrative and psychiatric references by six of the dreamers. Four more dreamers would dream about military encampments or war-related endeavors.

Pat had stated that her team's "original idea had been to work out problems and conflict through the dream state." Pat then set the stage for this effort by having a hospital dream on the first goal date. By the third goal, members from both teams were cross-dreaming about operations and white clothing.

Pat had actually provided an "out" from this dilemma with her first goal dream. She boldly flashed the therapeutic facade. She invited members of both teams to openly reveal what was behind their long, white, safe robes. So what was beyond the coverings? Teammate Kelly perceived "bathing suits under their clothes."

Some participants bounced back and forth between the two types of game playing. Others concentrated on the second type almost exclusively. Unlike the clinical and military atmosphere of the first game, the second game arena could be likened to a summer camp.

WHITNEY(1): *A game of life is being played. . . . We are all wearing gees [martial arts uniforms] with white belts.*

KELLY(2): *[On a karate/canoe trip], but I am not interested in the karate part . . . I would hate to miss the swimming.*

HAROLD(2): *A shiatsu type of person [is] at the end of a sandpit [where] a person runs and jumps on a diving board.*

CROSS-DREAMING BETWEEN TEAMS

Team 2

4/21/84

    I am taking my mother to the hospital. I am in a cafeteria with a laboratory next to it. There is a man there in his thirties, a nurse, and a lab technician. I tell the young man about my mother. A psychiatrist comes in and sits at at table. He isn't taking this seriously, and I go around in front of him and am going to tell him off. I realize that I don't have any clothes on and am carrying my white winter coat. I am trying to be real cool and wrap the coat around me. The other people in the room are amused by my discomfort. I walk over to the therapist and tell him angrily, "Don't you go to a therapist?" He is backing his chair into a corner and says, "Yes."

    I say, "Well, you should. People who are giving therapy ought to take therapy." I flip the coat open and say, "Check this!"

PL

6/16/84

    I feel a lump in [my mother's] chest . . . I'm concerned—she should see a doctor . . . she says it dissolves now and then.

TT

    I'm going to see Doctor T. . . . I see someone lying on an operation table or bed with Doctor T. . . . I come back into the office and he comes out to me, and I was dressed in white, which he says is quite different from what I had on the other time. I show him my warts . . . he just cuts them off with a knife . . . and I think Yuk!

HC

Team 1

6/16/84

    I am being operated on by a group of white gorillas. One remarks on how ugly I am. They then see that I am wearing a gorilla suit and so are they.

TM

WENDY(1): *By an outdoor swimming pool [next to] a smiling man with short dark hair.*

The "half full/half empty syndrome" became a choice that dreamers were challenged to make. Should one dream about clinical applications or traveling by the sea? Should one dream of war games or ball games? Should one indulge in fear or seek an optimistic perspective?

Some dreamers showed a predilection for one or the other viewpoint. But those who most consistently experienced mutual dreams were those who, at least some of the time, journeyed into the land of the summer sun.

In the end, the people at Poseidia had fostered a format that included six or more target dates for dreaming and required facilitators to coordinate the paperwork and write commentaries on the dreams. Most projects included specific target goals. Because it was not necessary that team members know one another, the projects could be carried on by mail with photographs exchanged before or after the project began to help incubate the dreams.

Most importantly, because information was funneled through the facilitators, the projects enabled them to see the raw dream reports *before* the dreamers had the opportunity to talk with one another. This criterion is necessary because comparing notes and ideas might modify the results.

On the other hand, the facilitators could not edit the dream content themselves before they passed on copies of all dreams to the rest of the team members without the change being noticed by the original dreamer. Thus, there was a built-in system of checks and balances.

On the last project night, the goal had been to have a going-away party. Pat had sent each of her Team 2 members a photocopy of a photo of her house and invited the team there for the party. She also said that since it was autumn, there'd be a big pile of leaves in the backyard to jump in. Although her team members dreamed of the party, no one remembered to play in the leaves . . . until two years later.

The Shared Dreaming Projects of Barbara Shor

One of the members of Team 2 went on to use the Poseidia model in her own shared dreaming projects. Barbara
Shor's first experiment was with the 1986 Living Systems
Approach to Creativity group, who were participants in a
seminar give by Dr. Mary Schmitt in New York City. There
were sixteen members of the group—artists, educators, therapists, and physicians—many of whom had known one another beforehand. The project had five target dates with no
specific goals, although members of the group were reading
the Willis Harman and Howard Rheingold book, *Higher Creativity.* Some of their dreams followed themes encountered
in discussions of the book.

Again, the group encountered issues common to the first
stages of shared dreaming: fear of loneliness or losing
uniqueness; loss of personal control; a sense of danger; ques-
tioning one's ability to trust; and a lack of relatedness between men and women. Large windows with or without
curtains that the dreamer could close became the symbol
for control over privacy. Baffles—screens, barriers, and
fences—signaled barriers and resistance to both change and
communication. Water—from tidal waves to laundry wash—
symbolized emotional responses to the awareness of dreaming in a group.

After the group met at a restaurant for dinner, there was
some mention in dreams of dining in restaurants, but
the best incubation of a meeting place harkened back to
Dreams[10].

At their third session, Dr. Schmitt led the group through
a waking visualization in which they all met at a big pile of
leaves in the woods! That night three dreamers dreamt of
jumping into the leaves and watching others bounce off and
fly around the pile. For the remainder of the experiment,
some dreamers continued to meet at the pile of leaves, to
work out new ways of relating to one another.

In February of 1989, Barbara Shor gathered a group of

seven dreamworker friends from the New York Dream Community and began seven months of shared dreaming. The target dates were the three-night period just before, during, and after the full moon. The meeting place selected was the grand staircase in the lobby of the Metropolitan Museum of Art, and the dreamers physically met there before the project began. Then they proceeded to have dreams about museums, but none except the facilitator actually dreamt of that specific museum.

In the same year, beginning in April, 1989, Barbara also gathered seven dreamers from six different states. These dreamers had never met before, although they exchanged photos at the beginning of the project. This group attempted to meet in dream in the crown room of the Statue of Liberty. The project lasted until November of that year.

On two of the May target nights, windows and darkened lights figured prominently in the dreams of the Statue of Liberty dreamers.

On 5/20, Barbara H. dreams of a commanding female dream figure: "She walks me over to the window and tells me to look into the night sky. [She says] this large place is connected to my 'dream house,' and that all the windows and doors will be wired to my personal home."

On 5/27 Dale dreams he's hiding from a school bully: "I was next to a window and could see him looking in, but he couldn't see me."

On 5/27 not only do I dream of the harbor and the statue being totally dark, but Norma dreams that she's been instructed by an elderly lady she's caring for to switch off the lights.[2]

Shared Dreaming: A Joint Project

Barbara Shor had honed her shared dreaming skills as a member of the second team of the third Dreams[10] project; I was a member of the same project, but on Team 1. However, the two of us were not to meet in the flesh until the day of the San Francisco Dream Festival, in October of 1987. We agreed to collaborate as the facilitators of the Shared Dreaming project and, thereafter, as coauthors of a chapter on shared dreaming in a dreamwork anthology.

Shared Dreaming was set up with monthly target dates and ran from November 1987 through the entire year of 1988. Each of the ten members were community dreamworkers. That is, each had experience in leading dream-sharing groups or giving presentations and workshops to the public on his or her particular dreaming expertise. All had a sophisticated understanding of their own dreams through journaling and dream interpretation, incubation and visualization techniques. Most had been involved in some form of advanced dream study and had experience with lucid and psychic dreaming. And, most importantly, all had experience in partnering with other dreamworkers, through dream and waking projects and associations. Six were members of the Bay Area Dreamworkers Group; three others from the East Coast and Canada were members of their own respective local dream communities. Everyone knew at least one other dreamer, and all were destined to meet in person at the annual conference of the Association for the Study of Dreams (ASD), which was to be held in Santa Cruz, California, in the summer of 1988. Because of their breadth of experience, it was decided that each member would take turns analyzing the dreams of the group and writing the monthly commentary.

Before the project began, participants exchanged ideas, written or verbal, on where to meet in the dream state. Several had similar inner pictures of a private space, so it was decided to put those images together to form the targeted space: a sunny green meadow with woods and mountains to the north and east, and to the west a high cliff overlooking the sea. The first night found several members dreaming of the meadow, either cooking or building structures there with groups of people.

Over time, the buildings resolved themselves into warehouses, restaurants, and auditoriums—all structures that would prove true for the University of Santa Cruz campus, where the Shared Dreaming members would eventually meet in the waking state.

Another common symbol, the helicopter, would resonate with the waking experience of two of the Shared Dreaming participants, who would go to a workshop of a third member of the group. There were plenty of vehicles, from bicycles to buses, skateboards to station wagons.

Shared Dreaming experimented liberally: with preset meeting places and goals; no goals and meeting places that appeared spontaneously; precognition, clairvoyance, telepathy, and lucidity. Shared Dreaming was the first to experiment with "x-ray vision," or learning to recognize one another by vibes alone, even when team members didn't resemble their waking selves. The same discovery was acknowledged as applying to the meeting space. The details for the dreamscape did not have to match perfectly in order for dreamers to assume that they had been hanging around in the virtually the same "place." Dream images and events were found to be flavored by individual perspective much more that they might appear to be in the waking state.

During one Shared Dreaming date in the spring of 1988, two members of the project had different versions of a dream meeting. While dreaming, Charlene was able to overhear a conversation going on between two people, although she was unable to identify them. Charlene had an audio dream. An audio dream consists of voices without any visual images at all. It is as if the dreamer is dreaming "in the dark." Here's what she heard two voices say to one another.

"Moving through different dimensions . . . ," said one voice.

"You didn't have to elevator here?" asked the other.

"Yeah, I did."

"Now she has to find her own way back."

On the other hand, her teammate Nora had the more usual visual dream. This is Nora's version of the event.

As I am waiting at the elevator, I hear, then sense Linda. We talk together about Charlene. We are trying to point out that we realize she is traveling through dimensions . . . spot checking in. But we also know that this is her choice of traveling and she may not realize that we can not help her get back at this particular time. Besides, why doesn't she use the elevator and el . . . levitate like we do?

Nora's dream revealed the identity of Charlene's conversationalists. Nora and Charlene's dreams seemed to indicate that they were meeting not only with one another, but with me as well. Unfortunately, I remembered nothing of this dream meeting.

Part Three

◆

How to
Dream
Together

CHAPTER 10

✦

THE PARTNERSHIP PARADIGM

T hose who attempt to dream together are the new
heroes of dreaming.

When I say "new heroes" I mean in the Joseph Campbell
sense: The hero's journey is the metaphoric voyage of our
lives. This new notion of the hero's journey is being suggested in the midst of a Western civilization whose most
popular physiological and psychological explanations hold
the dream to be private space. As such, the new heroes have
very little cultural support for their voyage, even *within* the
professional dream field.

Unlike the "Lone Stranger" of Campbell's model, however, this new hero travels, at least part of the time, with
other human companions. But there's a difference between
this new shared journey and what has gone before.

In the former view of mutual dreaming there were basically two models. In one, you could be part of a group consciousness in which the boundaries between self and other
were not as well distinguished as today, where your original

identification was as a member of the clan or the tribe.
Whether asleep or awake, you would participate in a one-
mind "dreamtime."

The other option has been around for quite a long time,
too. It's the one in which you get to travel into the land of
dreams by playing follow the leader: your local shaman,
guru, ascended master, or sorcerer. This seems to be a later
evolutionary development. Previously, the shaman's journey
had emphasized contact with gods, animals, and spirits, not
fellow humans. Today's tour guides might well be psychics,
healers, therapists, or researchers.

When I began to reach out beyond my intimate circle, I
ran headlong into the effects on dreams of different beliefs
systems, morals, and ethics. Fortunately, I emerged from the
family cocoon just in time to catch the growing wave of the
partnership paradigm. This new paradigm does not sup-
plant the other two views of mutual dreaming—it coexists
alongside them. With this shift in emphasis toward separate
and distinct partners, meeting takes on increased emphasis,
and the idea of meshing changes. The image of a group mind
dancing to a uniform beat gives way to the idea of an individual stepping forth to the empathic tune, looking out the
other person's eyes and feeling and seeing things from his
or her perspective, then stepping back to improvise an individual counterpoint to the original melody.

Multicultural Dreaming

In the broad scope of history, group dreaming has been
the norm, rather than the exception. Many cultures valued
dream sharing, because of the belief that the soul leaves the
body during sleep and returns with useful information. The
songs, dances, or visions gleaned from dreams were expected to be shared for the enrichment of the entire community. The dreams were related so that physical and mental
healing could take place, spirits could be rejuvenated, and
cultural identity reaffirmed. For example, the Iroquois Hu-

rons regularly held dream festivals to act out hostility toward members of other tribes. By pooling their dreams, they sought common themes and patterns to create tribal policy.

Traditional clans and tribes found dreams useful for future planning because of their propensity to reach forward in time. Robert D. Bruce reports how the Lacandon Mayas of Mexico interpret dreams to foretell future events. One case shows how such practice resulted in corresponding dreams.

On May 31, 1970, Robert arrived at Lake Mensäbäk to study the Lacandon Mayas. The same day, in the town of Najá, his future host, Chan K'in, Sr., dreamt of seeing a puma near Lake Mensäbäk. When Chan K'in tried to shoot the puma, his gun didn't function. Chan K'in interpreted the puma to mean an upcoming encounter with *ts'ul* (Americans or Europeans).

Then on June 6, the night before Robert's arrival at Najá, one of Chan K'in's wives had her own dreamed version of the coming meeting with Robert. She dreamt of a puma entering the house. Her cries of *"Ts'aneh!"* or "Shoot it!" woke the household.

Some cultures hold a belief in an objective dreamscape. After entering the dream, believers might expect meetings with demons or spirit guides or have other events occur at specific "places" in dreamland. Several people with similar expectations can have mutual dreams. They will also assume they can visit one another in their dreams.

Like others of the mystical genre, the Sufi believed that a human helper could enter into another's dream. In one tale from the mid 1500s, a Sufi master visits the sultan, Suleiman the Magnificent, in a dream.

It is claimed that in some of the Eastern traditions, any two people sharing a close bond can visit each other at will in dreams. Both will be aware the following morning that the visit has taken place and will agree on what has been said. Tibetan Llamas trained in Highest Yoga Tantra assured researcher David Fontana that they had experienced such intentional dream visits.

Historical Incubation

Dreamers have tried a variety of methods of incubation based on practices drawn from many sources. The ancient cultures of the Greeks, Hebrews, Egyptians, Babylonians, Phoenicians, and Muslims all practiced incubation. In addition, it was a common practice among Chinese, Japanese, and Tibetans.

Strictly speaking, "incubation" refers to the practice of going to a sacred or magical site, such as a temple or natural landmark associated with a divine power, and there asking for a dream or visit from a god or saint.

At first, the practice was akin to consulting an oracle: dreamers sought prophesy or spiritual insight. In Egypt and Greece, the practice involved requests for healing and well-being. One might dream to obtain a remedy for sterility, to receive divine instructions to construct a building, or even to write a book.

A dreamer would trek long distances to spend a night in a Greek dream temple to incubate a special dream for healing or problem solving. In the latter days of the Greek dream temples, the priest or priestess would not only interpret the dreams, he or she would take on the task of dreaming by him or herself. Egyptians had the practice of sending delegates to holy places in order to dream on behalf of a third party.

Petitioners might prepare for their dreams by abstaining from sex or from eating meat and by only drinking water for forty-eight hours prior to making the request. They could bring along a gift or offer a service as payment for the anticipated dream. They would visit the site where they might join in some ritual, including prayer and meditation. Then they would sleep in or near the site, often near a source of flowing water.

Sometimes the dream answer would come the first night, but there was no guarantee. In medieval times, Christian pilgrims would stay so long by the grave or holy relic of a saint that special cells had to be built to house them.

Induction is the term that has been given to dream requests that don't involve sleeping in a special place. Indians of the Americas induced dreams for specific purposes, such as to choose a vocation or to accompany rites of puberty or initiation. Dreams were also induced when the community was to make a decision and to prepare for hunting or war. Shamanic leaders induced dreams and visions though the liberal use of drugs and chanted suggestions to define the shared journey into an altered state of consciousness. Other rituals included communal prayer and dancing. Medieval alchemists used special symbols and induction devices as signposts in their journey.

"Induction" has also been used to describe those procedures used to obtain a certain type of dream or to program the events that will occur in the dream ahead of time. Thus, to request a lucid dream would be a form of induction. So would be the intent to dream of swimming in Hawaii.

However, today it is most common for dreamers and dreamworkers to use the term **incubation** to refer to any practice of requesting or programming dreams. This is how the term is used in this book.

Incubation is one way to provide organization and purpose to the seemingly random patterning of the usual dreaming process. Incubating a dream means being able to set up the circumstances to become more aware of the dreaming process and content.

Now let's look at this idea in practice. Remember the prophet Daniel's petition for a dream? What impresses me about this Biblical story is that, by not telling Daniel his dream, King Nebuchadnezzar would be able to determine the difference between an actual psychic experience and flim-flam. Daniel then successfully produced a mutual dream through the means of prayer. But it came about only after he had been put into a position where he feared for his safety.

Being threatened with dire consequences seems to be a great generator of mutual dreams. Nebuchadnezzar probably learned that lesson from his wise men. Xerxes learned it even better.

The Mutual Dream Story of Xerxes and Artabanus

A hundred years or so later, the Persian King Xerxes was at the point of deciding whether or not to invade Greece. Two nights in a row, he told his advisors that he had dreamt of a tall man of noble aspect who stood by his bed and spoke to him. The phantom warned the king that if he did not undertake the war against the Greeks, Xerxes would be brought low just as quickly as he had risen to greatness and power.

There was only one person to openly oppose the war. Twice Xerxes tried to convince Artabanus that his dreams were a directive from his god. Finally he told his senior advisor that, if the dreams were true, the same vision would appear to Artabanus and the phantom would give the same command that had been given to the king.

Xerxes convinced Artabanus that this was most likely to happen if he were to put on the king's clothes, take a seat on the king's throne, and then go to sleep in the king's bed. Hoping to prove Xerxes was mistaken, Artabanus reluctantly agreed to the king's entire request.

After falling asleep in the king's bed, Artabanus dreamt that the very same phantom stood over him. The phantom was incensed that Artabanus had tried to dissuade the king from making war on Greece. He uttered threats of punishment against the advisor and was on the point of burning out Artabanus's eyes with hot irons when Artabanus awoke with a shriek, leapt from the bed, and ran to Xerxes.

After that, there was no more opposition to the king.

Leader-Directed Dreaming

The shock treatment works. A rather large number of dream masters, especially in the shamanic or sorcery genre, use it.

Sometimes this means physiological shock, a shock to your mind-body system caused by any number of methods such as fasting, ablutions, frenetic dancing, drugs, or drumming. Physical movement, performed in unison, serves as a kinesthetic affirmation of group identity. The drugs or mind-numbing repetition put you into an altered state of consciousness. Then a song, chant, or mythic story told by the shaman programs you and other participants in the ceremony. Voilà! You all have mutual dreams.

But if your tour guide to dreamland is on a "power-over" trip, he believes he alone has the discretion to decide when he will enter into your dream. Then he will take you on a journey that is guaranteed to be full of bottomless chasms and sea monsters. That's why you need the guide: because his dream world is so dangerous.

There's also a process found in some master/student relationships that I call "piggybacking." The dream is used to obtain entry to the student's psyche, and when defenses are down, the psyche is imprinted with new information. In this process, the student relates his dream or vision. The master responds with the assurance that he has had the same dream. The shock caused by this revelation provides a perfect pathway to insert the teaching following the pronouncement. It doesn't matter to the master if his statement is factually true or not. It's the teaching that matters. The student is too awed to ask for validation. Or, if he does, he gets a roundabout answer that blurs the boundaries between waking and dreaming reality.

Then again, the mutual dream may be perfectly legitimate, but the initiator tries to confound his cohorts by strutting his psychic abilities. I've heard too many stories where people have showed off and crowed about their great psychic prowess and their power to enter into another person's dream. But I've also heard from the other side—those who were the victims of "dream invasion" and psychological manipulation.

At this point you might ask yourself, am I interested in incubating cross-connective dreams, no matter how, no matter why, no matter with whom? Not me. I don't define this sort of power trip as truly "mutual."

My own awareness of the need to dream as a partner results directly from the fact that I am, and always have been, emotionally sensitive. Because of childhood programming, I am particularly vulnerable to the chaos of relationship and highly motivated to change it. For my entire life, I have sometimes been able to soak up the emotional "vibes" of other people, especially if they are anxious or stressed. This negative energy can then be translated into my own dream imagery. In the first four decades of my life, I remembered nothing but nightmares, bizarre conflict-ridden and anxious dreams. Since then, I have been highly motivated to determine a way to be less vulnerable to negative emotional energy, whether self-generated or not.

To achieve that end, some people make use of protective defense mechanisms such as images of "light barriers" and "energy shields." Unless carefully chosen, such imagery can either have the dual result of blocking positive energy as well as the negative, or can actually attract the very energy it seeks to avoid. Instead, I hold close a belief drawn from Jane Roberts's Seth material: the dream world is a safe universe. This way, I experience all potentially troublesome dreams as being capable of resolution, in-dream or out; all fear as being due to a temporary lack of knowledge, maturity, or experience that I am willing to remedy. But the point is to discover what works for you.

I have heard many tales of intentionally troublesome dreaming partners, but wondered why I had never experienced this sort of "dream invasion" by another human being, myself. I've come to the conclusion that this is not a matter of luck; it's because of the ideal for mutual dreaming that I hold in my own mind. This means I am continually broadcasting the subliminal message that I am only interested in dreaming with those who have decent dream manners, who are willing to be in a peer relationship, to be vulnerable to one another, and, most importantly, willing to take responsibility for those daily actions and attitudes that impact their dreams. I want to practice the dance of dialogue, to learn the lesson of give-and-take.

None of the mutual dreaming groups with which I've been associated contained anyone who consciously harbored a malicious intent. Antipartnership dreamers seem to weed themselves out via vehement letters or claims of self-importance; I simply don't invite them to participate. My reaction to those who might have slipped in is to quickly show them the door, no apologies. Those that pass scrutiny go into the project with the idea that we're going to play by certain rules. Should anybody attempt to circumvent those self-regulations, they must contend not only with the facilitator, but with the rest of the group. No one can play one-upmanship games in a partnership group without being challenged by other members. Thus, the shared dreaming model has built-in structures to help keep the members comparatively safe.

Those who deal with dreams exclusively in a teacher/student or therapist/client relationship can sometimes find it difficult to make the transition to a peer relationship. Those that do, find it worthwhile. They are certainly helped by living out like kinds of relationships in the waking state. There is a direct correlation between those who are willing to be peers in waking life and those who adopt a similar attitude through their dreams.

There are some people—some extraordinary lucid dreamers and out-of-body folks, some psychic sensitives, some vivid archetypal dreamers—with whom I wouldn't dream on a California bet. They have all the dream manners of a muddy wildebeest trampling through a crystal shop. I've run into these people several times on my quest. It's not a fun experience.

I have chosen not to engage in dreaming with the following cast of characters who do not fit the partnership dreaming model: (1) the man who was fascinated by hallucinatory monsters—in his waking state; (2) the woman who, after dreaming several times that she made love to Burt Reynolds, was ready to divorce her husband, board a plane, and fly to Hollywood to wed the real Burt; (3) the man who practiced the art of "kything," or being in spiritual presence with another, but never bothered to check to see if his perceptions were as true for the other person; (4) the man who arbitrarily interpreted my dreams, in order to try to establish his authority over me, and prior to making the suggestion that he, indeed, was capable of entering my dreams; (5) the woman who decided on her own that I would make a good target for a dreamt "psychic reading" and didn't offer herself to be read; (6) the men who were so enamored of psychic powers that they told stories of how they startled women awake in the middle of the night or "zapped" the women in their private parts; (7) the group who chose to do a dream healing on someone who didn't request it and did not appreciate it; (8) any of a number of folks from amazingly diverse kinds of cultural backgrounds who believe that, as adepts of their particular spiritual system, they have every right to try to enter and influence the dreams of those poor schmucks who are less fortunate and less evolved than them, *without asking permission.*

For me, a good dreaming partner means one who plays fair. I believe a lot of hassle can be avoided if you determine your own standards, *before* leaping into bed with potential dreaming partners. Ask questions, observe, use your common sense. And if you do find yourself trapped in a dysfunctional dream relationship? Get out of it. You have every right to leave and find partners who will better suit you. The psychological methods that are used to heal a problematical waking relationship can apply just as well to dream relationships.

Realize, as an individual dreamer, you have a choice! Decide on your criteria for a partner. Apply them. Screen out those who don't qualify.

Historical Reciprocity

Some of us in the U.S. have been experimenting via dreams with a democratic model of dreaming that begins to incorporate exchange and balance between distinct and individual dreamers. The stories from the past reflect this fact.

When America was still being settled by Europeans, a wealthy and fastidious Englishman by the name of Sir William Johnson was appointed Superintendent of Indian Affairs. He sent home to England for some richly textured and laced suits. When they arrived, he was hosting Hendrick, King of the Mohawk nation.

A few days later Hendrick visited Sir William again and told him he had had a dream. Hendrick said that he had dreamt that Sir William had given him one of the fine suits. Sir William took the hint and immediately handed over the finest of his clothing.

A few weeks later Sir William told Hendrick he'd also had a dream. He said he dreamt that Hendrick made him a present of five thousand acres of the best of the Mohawk Valley.

Hendrick gave Sir William the land. Then he told him, "Now, Sir William, I will never dream with you again. You dream too hard for me."

Then there's another tale from American folklore about a minister named "Uncle Billie."

A notorious character of the community thought he would be able to take advantage of Uncle Billie because of Uncle Billie's belief in mystical visions. So one morning he drove his wagon up to Uncle Billie's corn crib and said to him, "The Lord told me in a dream last night to come to your crib and get a load of corn."

Uncle Billie reached up over the door and took down his long rifle. "Yes," he said, "but the Lord must have changed his mind, for He told me this morning not to let you have it."

Reciprocity is the idea that relationship is a two-way street. No one is stuck in a particular role. Rather, the roles fluctuate so that the teacher becomes the taught, the leader takes a follower's position, no becomes yes and vice versa.

Partnership

In the late 1960s there were some new heroes who had finished their individual hermits' journeys and who were ready to go out and be social again. They gathered together to share dream reports and to try to dream together. By the 1990s these types of folks had made a major impact on the field of dreams. They used a new kind of terminology. They talked about things like "community," "networks," "sharing," and "reciprocity." They were describing a new model of dreaming relationship called partnership.

What **partnership** means in dreaming terms is, instead of a hierarchy with an authority figure as leader, there is instead a peer relationship where authority comes down from the pedestal, joins the group, and shares his dreams along with the rest of the folks. This makes the leader as strong or as vulnerable as any other person in the group.

There were new terms for the new positions of the people who were spearheading this movement. They were called "facilitators" and "coordinators" to indicate that they were part of the partnership model. The idea of partnership emphasizes an egalitarian, peer relationship among comrades. It teaches *power with,* rather than *power over.* It provides the opportunity to practice good dream manners . . . and to get quick feedback when they are lacking.

Partnership dreams focus on a new dynamic of interpersonal relationship. They quickly point out the distinction between peer and hierarchical relationships. If one person assumes the role of student and the other plays the helper, teacher, or manipulator, the resulting dreams may be psychic, but they won't necessarily be reciprocal. The ideal of mutual dreaming is reciprocal dreaming in an egalitarian relationship.

In a partnership group, the decision-making style is participative and encourages a "bottom-up" flow of ideas aimed at generating consensus around the issues. This distributed leadership means that all people at a gathering have the opportunity to speak. Consensus means the absence of undermining or interference in any given activity. It does not mean that everyone has the same opinion, idea, or strategy. In terms of mutual dreaming, partnership allows anyone to suggest projects or dreaming goals for the group.

Partnership groups might get together simply to relate their dreams. Perhaps they might do dream interpretation work or share techniques to program a dream. But several took this group one step further. They agreed to dream about the same theme.

Gate of Horn. Guild of Asaph. Tandem Dream Group. Dream Bridge. Montreal Dream Network. Seth Dream Network. Sundance Community Dream Journal. Metro D.C. Dream Community. The Dream Community of New York.

These partnership groups dreamt together on a variety of topics that ranged from the health of a single one of their members to the welfare of the entire world.

Fred C. Olsen and I cofounded the Bay Area Dreamworkers Group (BADG) with the intent to create a home for the community/partnership paradigm. Dream sharing and group dreaming were integral to this process. Dream sharing alerted us to the underground unconscious dynamics of our conscious waking activities. Our dreams painted vivid pictures of our social-emotional process. We were on a trek through the desert seeking water. The water was pure, the water was salty, the water was frozen snow and ice. We were swimming in the sea of unconsciousness, swimming underneath the sea, bobbing on a small boat on the surface. We were surfing the tops of the waves, we were inundated by cyclonic tidal waves! The partnership paradigm allowed us to "act out" our tensions in the waking state via dreamwork techniques rather than suppress them.

The dreams described the problems of being bogged down by dreamwork. They gave early warnings of anger and frustration around the 1987 San Francisco Dream Festival and early predictions of the success of our endeavor.

Under the group dreaming model we asked questions of our dreams. Should BADG formally merge with the Dream

Training Institute or incorporate as a nonprofit corporation? (We did neither.) Where will the next Dream House be located? (Dreams helped triangulate the eventual location.)

We dreamt up holiday dreams for the Christmas tree and dreamt inspiration for the coming year. We dreamt with, for, and about one another in matters both esoteric and practical. And along the way, our dreaming skills improved. For these are not skills acquired for perpetuity. Instead, they are mind muscles to exercise, lest they atrophy.

Intentional Dreaming Leads to Improved Dreaming Skills

Mutual dreaming is, without any doubt, the most challenging type of dreaming I know. It evokes a veritable plethora of abilities, some of which are practiced concurrently.

What skills are necessary for a successful shared dreamer? Incubation is the prime tool for the intentional dreamer. Plus dreamwork skills like recall, recording, and interpretation. Then, social skills such as reciprocity, intimacy, sharing, the development of vulnerability in an arena of trust and openness, and the ability to call a halt to dysfunctional inappropriate relationships. Psychic skills like telepathy and precognition. Content management skills like incubation of positive themes, control of negative day residue, coupled with an overall willingness to take responsibility for the production of one's dreams. Finally, the advanced skills of lucidity and out-of-body travel, and the free exercise of fantasy, which tends to shift the experience of mutuality into a whole different gear.

Nobody I know has *all* of these skills, nor do they exercise them all the time. That's one advantage of being a member of a group: dreamers can combine abilities for a synergist effect. But those that try to interest their dreaming psyches in a sense of accomplishment, discovery, or just plain fun report intermittent successes. We're still in field training. And that means we can be surprised.

Partners Dreaming Together

In 1988 Michael Oricchio from the *San Jose Mercury-News* interviewed me on how one might use dream interpretation techniques to predict and decipher the lottery numbers. In a lighthearted manner, I spoke about association techniques. "If I dreamt I was in a convenience store, I might think of seven-eleven," I said. Then I told him about incubation. "Find some sort of stimulus. No, not dirty pictures. A positive article on the lottery will do."

The *Mercury-News* article was read by radio personalities Kelly and Klein, and I was awakened at six in the morning to do a live radio broadcast . . . while still in bed. One of these gentlemen (I forget which) challenged me to "dream up" the numbers for the next go-round.

So I called every intentional dreamer in the Bay Area Dreamworkers Group I could think of and asked if they would dream along with me. (I offered to split the multimillion-dollar winnings *only* if they got their numbers from their dreams; no waking-state attempts allowed.) And they did. Most people dreamt up only one or two numbers. There were hardly any overlaps. When gathered together, it became obvious what had happened. We had "dreamt up" the California lottery numbers, all right. Virtually every one, from one to forty-nine.

When it comes to deliberate dreaming, you have to watch what you ask for . . . you just might get it.

CHAPTER 11

✦

$\mathcal{H}$OW TO $\mathcal{H}$ATCH A $\mathcal{D}$REAM

*H*ow do you begin partnership dreaming? The most important rule is: *Get permission first.* Request entry into your partner's mental space and extend an invitation for him or her to come to you.

Believe me, you will save yourself and your dream partner a lot of trouble if you stick to this rule. Could there any exception? Maybe. Just ask yourself—would this person appreciate it if I showed up at his or her physical doorstep in waking reality at three in the morning? Would it be okay with me if he or she reciprocated? If the answer to both questions is yes, an unannounced dream visit may be just fine. Or it may not be. It's still wisest to get conscious consent.

I'm especially indebted to those members of the Bay Area Dreamworkers Group who are committed partnership dreamers. Here they share with you some ideas that tend to promote reciprocity and good dream manners.

A Plan to Initiate Partnership Dreaming

1. Find a partner willing to share on a peer basis or join
   an egalitarian dream group that believes in dreaming
   give and take. Get permission to dream with, to, and
   for one another.

   Close friends and family are the most likely candi-
   dates for successful mutual dreaming. But in order to
   be a successful social dreamer, you may have to put
   out a little effort to be social in the waking state. You
   might gather your own friends or join an ongoing
   group. Check out continuing and adult education
   courses, church workshops, or metaphysical classes.
   Find information or post your own notice in book-
   stores, coffeehouses, or the newspaper. Finally, you
   might form a long-distance relationship with an individual or group. For some contacts with the larger
   dream community, see Appendix II.

2. Begin by sharing favorite old dreams.

   This is a way to learn your partner's language: his
   or her interests, values, and the way your partner sees
   the world. You can get an early indication about
   whether this person will be the appropriate partner
   for you.

3. If your partner's dreams contain a theme or symbol
   similar to one from your past, go back in your journal
   to retrieve that dream and share it.

   · This is "priming the pump" with similar imagery.
   It's sharing what we have in common at the dreaming
   level, in order to invoke continuing similarities.

4. Share current dreams with an eye for cross-connections: dream-to-dream similarities or dreams that
   contain content about your partner's waking life.

   What life themes do you have in common? What
   synchronicities are going on in your waking lives? In
   your dreaming lives?

5. At first, honor even the smallest or vaguest possibility at any dream frequency. Your particular style of cross-connection will become more obvious as time goes on.

   Emphasize what you have in common. For the moment, ignore the dissimilarities.

6. Avoid using interpretative methods that sit in judgment of your partner's dreams. They can cause your partner to self-censor relevant material.

   Comment briefly on your own dreams if you wish, but lengthy interpretive monologues are distracting to the process. Keep it short and sweet. This advice especially applies to your partner's dreams. In general, it's better to ask questions than make statements. You are trying to find out about your partner, not tell your partner who he or she is.

7. Consider sharing everything and allowing your partner to decide what might be important.

   Assuming that something is too trivial or too embarrassing to be shared can miss a cross-connection. Humor is your greatest ally, especially when you dream something uncomfortable.

8. Experiment with different kinds of sharing to discover the most fruitful.

   For example, it may be productive to phone ahead or just after the target night. Phoning ahead might stimulate incubation or provide the energy of a strong connection that can be carried into dreaming. On the other hand, too much ritual, activity, and stimulation might overload the mind. "Fasting" from waking connection can create a tension that will be satisfied only through the dream.

9. Prompt recording and sharing of the resulting dream is important to keep the reciprocal energy moving back and forth between you and your partner.

   This waking reciprocity will model cooscillation for your dreaming minds.

10. It is crucial to take care of your own shadow work.

If you are not willing or able to take responsibility for the production of your own dreams, you will be likely to project fears, anxieties, and self-importance out onto your partner, who must deal with it as best he or she can.

11. Develop patience. Mutual dreaming take time and effort. Keep trying.

Offer encouragement and affirm strengths with your partner to aid in the growth of mutual dreaming.

12. Set a specific ending point for the sharing to review and celebrate your newfound social skills.

Don't let things drift. And remember, you can call off the game at your discretion. It's your choice. Ideally, this choice will be a mutual one.

A Formula to Hatch a Dream

To incubate means to "hatch" a dream. Let's review the general formula for hatching the mutual dream. Use whichever suggestions best suit you personally.

1. Select Your Goal

You can incubate a dream on any topic you choose, but you will have the greatest success with those goals in which you have some emotional investment. Pick a problem or question that concerns you, one that you would be willing to explore. Or choose an interesting or intriguing goal, one that excites you or with which you each can have some fun.

2. Immerse Yourself in Your Goal

The more information gleaned from day residue, the more symbolic data you will have available from which to create a dream. To increase your short-term memory, engage in activities relevant to the goal. Read books or notes on your chosen subject. Utilize photos, movies, or objects to form associations. Rehearse the situation in the waking state, using role-playing or discussion. Pray or mediate to the goal, fantasize about or visualize writing the dream in your journal. Wear objects given to you by a dream partner or place them under your pillow. In short, involve your physical body and your waking life in the formation of the dream.

3. Feather Your Nest

Creating a serene atmosphere that will most encourage the dream is the private equivalent of a journey to a dream temple. Try to choose a time when you are not fatigued, in which you have not indulged in stimulants or heavy food. Have your journal, pen, and light available for recording the dream, or use a tape recorder. Retire at a reasonable time if night-sleeping, or awaken yourself in the early morning hours to return to lighter and more controlled sleep. You might also try day-sleeping.

4. Narrow Your Focus

Writing down the issue and all of its aspects helps you get in touch with how you feel about the situation, especially all those reasons for *not* wanting to resolve or experience the goal. Give yourself permission to discover, explore, and experience negative things in a positive way. Ask for help from friendly inner or outer characters. Finally, write down the phrase that most clearly speaks to your deepest desires, using the first person. It's best to make the request an accomplished fact, such as, "Tonight we fly in our dreams." Then place the request under your pillow.

5. Open up Your Expectations

Using relaxation exercises to put yourself in the mood or emotion of the goal, you might concentrate on the energy and feeling of the topic. Slipping into hypnogogia—at the crossroads between waking and sleeping—you can visualize the theme or person or place you want to dream about as vividly as possible. Then repeat the goal phrase to yourself, trying to avoid thinking of alternatives. Depending on the topic, you might choose to adopt one of the following approaches: mantra, affirmation, prayer, or command. If your mind wanders, gently but firmly bring yourself back to the topic.

6. Sleep and Dream

Suggest to yourself that you will awaken remembering your dreams. Then take a deep breath, release the topic, stretch, and prepare for sleep. Let yourself drift into sleep, and trust the dream to respond to your request.

7. Recall Your Dreams

Try to awaken before your usual rising time, using a music alarm, a partner, or by giving yourself the suggestion prior to sleep. Remaining still, try to recall the images of your dreams. Holding on to the feeling tones can sometimes conjure up the related dream visual images. After the first fragment is captured, turn over in bed to another position to stimulate additional recall. Running over the dream story several times affixes it in memory. Noting a key word to stand for each segment can help reconstruct the whole dream.

8. Record Your Dreams

In order to capture the elusive dream, record it as soon as possible upon waking. Jot down verbatim conversations quickly, as these tend to be the first memories to go. Record the visual images, the story, and the feelings associated with your dreams. If, while recording, you have any immediate associations with waking life, note them, too.

9. Reinforce Your Dreams

It is important to record each dream, as even a fleeting fragment can often contain special signifi-

cance. On nights of little or no recall, encourage yourself to try again. Sometimes the incubated dream will
appear on a succeeding night, or it may take several
nights to complete the picture through recurrent
dreams in a series. If you are confused by a response,
you can use dreamwork to decipher the dream, or you
might request that the response be made more clear in
another dream the next night. Thank dream helpers.
Then, contact your partner to compare dreams.

Some Mutual Aims

Remember, in a partnership paradigm, goals are decided
through mutual agreement.

Meshing Goals:
1. Dream together.
2. Have the same dream.
3. Dream the same issue or theme ("Dream about our
   relationship").
4. Dream the same activity or event ("Both have a lucid
   dream").
5. Both dream to the same theme, with one incubating to
   a known goal and the other trying to discern it telepathically ("What is my secret?").
6. Create the same dream environment ("Dream about
   Oz").

Meeting Goals:
1. Have a dream in which the partner appears.
2. Meet in a dream.
3. Meet at a particular place.
4. Meet and each transmit a message or single word.
5. Meet and exchange symbolic gifts.
6. Meet and do something together.

The Low-Key Approach

Mutual dreams can respond to the easy, low-key approach to incubation. Here are some examples that achieved successful results—in the view of the dreamers, themselves.

One night while Louis and his friend Carlos were playing with a Ouija board, Louis suggested, "Let's have a dream together." They agreed to incubate dreaming together before they went to sleep. That night both had dreams about a war going on outside a houseboat. For Louis and Carlos, this was a first- and last-time occurrence.

On the other hand, the mutual dream event of Fern Le-Burkien and Gisèle Perreault shows stronger evidence of meshing. That's probably because it occurred after they had participated in two years of intentional dreaming with groups in which both were members.

Fern relates, "It was after our Monday-night dream group. As I dropped Gisèle off, she said, 'Let's be sure to remember our dreams so we can discuss them tomorrow.'"

Gisèle did remember hers.

I'm shopping with [my roommate] Peggy. When we're done we walk back to the bike. Peggy gets on and takes off without me. I start running after the bike right in the middle of all this traffic, shouting and yelling for her to stop. She doesn't hear and keeps going. I'm totally pissed off and frustrated and plan on lecturing her when I get home.

GISÈLE PERREAULT, 9/17/90

So did Fern. Here's her dream response.

I'm in a store, a natural health food store [with] a shopping cart. I leave my purse briefly, to look at some vegetables. I turn back to see a man opening the coin section of my wallet. I call out and bring this to the attention of some store employees. I go to the store telephone to call the police. I look in time to see the guy run out of the store. A friend I am shopping with and I give chase on a bicycle. By this time, I've had a look in my wallet and realize that the man has stolen a hundred dollars and some of my credit cards. I become even more determined to catch him.

FERN LeBURKIEN, 9/17/90

"The elements that dovetail with Gisèle's dream is the frustrating feeling, the store (or shopping), the chase, and bike," said Fern. "I feel good that I gave chase. I'm much more likely to be chasing than to be chased in my dreams. I also feel good that I asked for help or assistance. Having things stolen or taken is not a common theme in my dream life. Neither Gisèle nor I travel by bike or bicycle."

So far we've been talking mainly about dreaming apart, in separate homes, in separate beds. What are the effects of intentional sleeping in close proximity?

Dream of the Sufi

In the sixteenth century, at a monastery on the Island of Rhodes, there was a group of twelve Sufi and their young master who decided to have a communal dream. As a group, the men prepared themselves bodily, mentally, and spiritually. Together, they recited the same secret formula. Then they all went to sleep together in one large bed to have the same dream.

For me, this way of doing things doesn't meet the test of practicality. My bed easily sleeps but two, despite odd kids and cats who may find their way there. What works for me is having a chance to sleep late and do dream recording at my leisure. It is usually a weekend, when I don't have to be awakened by alarms or children. It means dreaming in my snug bed with someone who is home in his or her bed, at a time of mutual convenience.

Dreaming Like The Kin of Ata

When it comes to dreaming in a group, dreamers nowadays have added creative fillips to the incubation process by drawing from other cultures and creative resources. A ritual to induce mutual dreams might include singing, dancing, chanting, or speaking aloud. One such example is the 1975 dream circle for women described by Hallie Inglehart Mountainwing. The women wanted to see if they could have a collective vision of how best to use female energy to build the world they wanted to live in, to break down barriers, and to strengthen the ties among themselves. Some of the women had never met one another before the weekend dream-together.

The women were inspired to sleep in a wheel formation by Dorothy Bryant's novel, *The Kin of Ata Are Waiting for You.* Each made a crescent-moon-shaped pillow and stuffed it with mugwort and psyllium seeds, two of the many herbs that have variously been suggested to bring on strong dreams. While some made music, others drove a large pole into the ground and tied cords to it. The sleeping bags were arranged like the spokes of the wheel. Sitting on their bags, each woman tied two stands of rope behind her to make a backstrap loom and two sticks crosswise to make a square frame. Using materials brought from home and gathered in the surrounding area, the women made weavings to "catch" their dreams. During the weaving they told stories and poems, shared star signs, sang songs, and chanted their names. They also washed their hands and faces in a stream, using salt as a psychic cleanser.

Before retiring, the women did not eat or make a fire. Instead they "cast" a circle, taking turns, each making a contribution. Some sang songs, some chanted, some spoke or made wishes for the group, some danced. Then they went to sleep.

So what happened? Most of the women had dreams that, when taken together, provided this message: a whole new

order was necessary and there was no point in trying to re-
form the old order. They dreamt shared symbols: bicycles,
cities, and finding new lands. But Hallie herself remembered
no dreams.

This is a recurring problem when sleeping in a new, unfamiliar place: the toll it takes on dream recall or even sleep.
Henry Reed reports of dreaming with a group in 1976 that
managed to persuade the Egyptian Government to let them
stay overnight at a sacred site. The King's Chamber of the
Great Pyramid at Gaza had hard stone flooring and was
swept with a cold wind. Hardly anyone slept.

Even dreaming in comfortable surroundings with a
group has its disadvantages. Going to bed at an unusual
hour, the noises of tossing and turning, the squeak of the
mattresses, trips to the bathroom, and inevitable snorers can
disrupt private sleep patterns. Just as it is no longer necessary to go to a sacred shrine in order to incubate a dream, so
it can be shown that sleeping together in the same place is
not necessary to produce mutual dreams. In fact, going to
sleep with a large group might actually hinder the process.

A Date to Meet in a Dream

Sleeping together one-on-one has had better results, at
least for Nerys and Marie. Nerys knew Marie a year prior to
their programmed mutual dream, but only vaguely. Then
came a time when circumstances dictated that they spend
the night together. In May 1992, while sleeping in the same
bed, they spontaneously experienced similar dreams. This
was such a remarkable event for both that the two of them
decided to see if they could do one better: have an intentional
meeting dream.

In order to help induce a meeting dream, Nerys and
Marie decided to select a location known to both of them.
They chose a graveyard! The cemetery, near Marie's house,
consisted of beautiful foliage and statues on green grassy

grounds surrounded by woods. Nerys called it "peaceful . . .
not morbid."

The following weekend, Marie and Nerys met there in
the waking state. Taking a walk together, they came upon a
large tomb built of stone. The stone was decorated with
angels and there were steps down to a wooden door. Because it had such a "fairyland" appearnance, Marie and
Merys decided to focus their intent on the tomb as their
dream meeting place.

Both had brought along a finger ring that was precious
to each. They wrapped their rings in kerchiefs and placed
the kerchiefs inside the ivy growing above the tomb's doorway. Nerys and Marie did this with the belief that items that
contained their energy, and to which they were attached
emotionally, would help pull them to that location in their
dreams.

Marie and Nerys had also purchased crystals together.
They chose purple segilites because Nerys had read that
these types of gems were energy receptive and increased
psychic powers, healing, and awareness of the spiritual
world. Ruled by Jupiter, the gems were said to be under the
influence of the water element. This idea was attractive to
the two of them, because they were both born under the astrological sign of Pisces. Nerys put her crystal and a piece of
quartz under her pillow; Marie also placed next to her crystal
some hemalite, which she used for "grounding."

That night they talked on the telephone to arrange the
dream meeting. It was agreed that they would bring their
crystals to the dream meeting to show one another. In order
to reinforce her intent, Nerys recounted the phone conversation before she fell asleep. That night she had this dream.

*I go to the graveyard. I'm there with some man whom I
can't remember. I walk down the road that leads to the tomb
doorway. I get to the doorway, but I don't go all the way
around or down the steps. I see where the doorway is, and
I know that Marie is not here.*

The dream shifts. Because I realize I had forgotten to go to the door to find Marie and show her my crystals, I become lucid. I discover that I am either a private investigator or a police officer! I'm working on a case which involves searching out men who are killers. The man, who has been with me all along, is my friend. But I question our bond because he is a man and because I'm so aware of men as killers.

Nerys says, "I became lucid because of the memory of what I had done previously. The sensation was that it felt the same to forget in dreams as when awake. I was amazed it was the same sensation and that I had forgotten something so completely. It made an impression on me."

The next morning Nerys called Marie. Marie reported that she, too, had a dream of the graveyard. But she didn't meet Nerys there.

Marie also had another dream but didn't mention it at first because she thought that it had no relevance to their project. However, when Nerys began recounting her dream, Marie responded that she also had had a dream with the "police" theme.

Nerys and Marie were encouraged because even though they had not dreamt of meeting, they believed their connection had been confirmed by having the same dream. Further attempts to dream together were springboards to other joint activities in the waking state, but not to any more mutual dreams.

Nerys states, "I thought we had failed because we didn't meet in the graveyard, but we really succeeded in dreaming the same thing." While attempting a meeting dream, Marie and Nerys had achieved a meshing dream.

The Goal Factor

Both Nerys and Marie and Hallie's group used elaborate incubation activities. But Hallie's group didn't have as much success in producing mutual dreams as did Nerys and Marie. One might be tempted to conclude that one-on-one induces better results than group energy. Actually, that's not true. The crucial distinction is the type of incubation.

Nerys and Marie wanted to *meet* in the dream. Hallie and her friends simply wanted to dream around the same theme.

Sharing a ritual does establish a sense of security among waking selves that reassures them that it is all right to try to dream together. Those dreamers already comfortable with themselves and each other generally dispense with elaborate rituals unless essential to their particular belief system.

From Individual to Group

I've discovered that it's often an advantage to have multiple partners. If I dream with several people in rotation, or in tandem, it soon becomes obvious with which dreamers I feel comfortable and what dreams best resonate with my own. At times I use this knowledge to help me eliminate potential partners with whom I do not experience rapport.

At other times I intentionally try to dream with people for whom I do not feel an especial affinity, just to stretch myself. By allowing myself to be influenced by others, I am able to try on a different style, new symbols, new levels of consciousness, new ideas for connection. Of course, I can influence others, too.

CHAPTER 12

✦

DREAMWORK AND DECODING

✦

*N*ear the beginning of my mutual dream quest, I had what *I* thought was a meeting dream. But it appeared that my dream had no equivalent for a second dreamer. It frustrated me to realize how aware of each other we seemed to be at the level of the dream and how unaware of our connection we were at the level of waking life.

At that time it appeared I had but two choices. I could either obtain some sort of verification of the event in the other person's life, or I could pass off the dream as the product of an overactive imagination.

Tracking the mutual dream over several years' time has yielded some important observations. First, mutual dream correlations do not necessarily have to be dream-to-literal-waking-life. They're mainly dream-to-dream. Second, classic meeting and meshing dreams are what might be considered "World Series" events. These types of cross-connections are clear and evident models of excellence. But just as not all waking skills produce fully developed results, so it is in the field of dreams. Whether spontaneous or planned, mutual dreams can create descriptive correlations that range from being quite pronounced to extremely opaque. What if the connections are vague or symbolically dissimilar? Does that mean the dreams aren't mutual?

Because we're dealing with the dreams of more than one dreamer, things can quickly get confusing. First, you need to be able to recall your dreams of the night. Then, it helps to write the dreams down. Because connections can be so subtle, you may have to put on your Sherlock Holmes hat and bring out the magnifying glass to detect and decode them.

Dream Recall

Whatever incites enthusiasm and interest in dreaming will increase the likelihood that you will remember your own dreams.

As a mutual dreamer, one of the strongest reasons for you to recall your dreams is that your dreams have a place to go. They are destined to be shared with dreaming partners who will listen to your dream narrative and help you remember the dream for future reference. You can share with partners your ideas on how to remember dreams, and they can provide encouragement and reassurance when you don't. Inquiring about a friend's dream will also help stimulate your own, and the sharing may induce additional recall. Having a creative goal like meeting a friend in your dreams will stimulate recall beyond normal levels.

Recall relates directly to the degree of interest you show your dreams, and that interest is reinforced by a supportive social context. A social group that gathers for the purpose of sharing dreams not only stimulates your interest in dreams, but provides you with important feedback. The group may simply listen and appreciate the dream as an audience. Responsive members will act as a mirror to you, reflecting back elements from a new viewpoint. Or they might highlight elements you haven't noticed before.

If you can retrieve dreams several times a week, you will have more data available to compare with other dreamers. The ability to recall on a specific night is often a necessity for mutual dreaming projects.

Relating a dream to others fixes the dream in memory and sharpens language skills so that the recipients of the narrative can clearly understand and appreciate the dream. The extra involvement of mind and body in verbalization helps clear the channel for new unconscious material to emerge into consciousness.

But sharing verbally in a group can be a confusing experience, requiring sharp wits to keep separate who dreamt what, and when. Because there is a tendency for dream reports to change when influenced by the reactions and contributions of others, writing dreams down before sharing provides a record of the original report, before any shift occurs. Writing also helps convince your unconscious that dreams are important enough to you to require the action of both mind *and* muscles.

Dream Journaling

"One of the most interesting dreams I've had was many years ago when I lived with a group of six or eight fun-loving friends in upstate New York," Don Middendorf told me. "I dreamt that I was teaching them to fly around our house.

"The next morning over breakfast, a number of them related dreams in which we had been involved in flying airplanes, kites, etc. A couple said that I had been teaching them to taxi an airplane or drive a boat.

"This group had no interest in dreams when we began living together, but over the years felt comfortable relating dream experiences over Sunday brunches or breakfast, even though at first I took a lot of ribbing about writing in my dream journal."

Don knows that **journaling** is more than just recording a dream on scraps of paper—it involves commitment to capture dreams in an organized manner. Mutual dreamers soon discover that they are recording dreams not just for themselves, but for others, too. This means that partners in dreaming must be able to decipher the information. It becomes the responsibility of a dream partner to present the dream in clear, understandable form. This can be crucial when there is no local partner and the dreams are transcribed by letter or electronic media. Mutual dreaming is a shared experience, requiring excellent communication skills.

What can you do *now* to make your journaling technique more user-friendly? Tape-record your dreams? Write them down? Print rather than use cursive handwriting? Use dark ink rather than pencil? Typewrite rather than hand write? Use a word processor instead of a typewriter? Change to a more suitable font?

Remember, in mutual dreaming your dreams are a *gift* to your dream partner. Just ask yourself: If I were the recipient of this gift, how would I want it packaged?

A journal that is effective enough to track dream cross-connections can include both written narrative and sketches or diagrams. The shared report is most appreciated when it is typed; handwriting can be difficult to decipher, especially if photocopied and particularly if the original draft was in pencil. Sharing multiple copies of a dream also helps protect it from damage or loss.

Giving a title to each report will capture the subject, mood, and action of the dream. Titles make dreams easier to locate when included in an index or table of contents. Adding initials in the margin for special types of dreams (A for astral visit; P for precognitive, etc.) will help speed recovery of a particular dream long after its occurrence. This is especially helpful when your dream partner inquires whether you have ever had such-and-such type of dream.

Dates are critical; noting the time is useful when trying to discover when a dream was shared. This can indicate whether the mutual dream occurred on the same date or whether there was a shift in time. It is important to get into the habit of dating dreams in order to discover dreaming patterns. This can show that one partner sets the pace, while the other follows. There may be precognitive or retrocognitive elements to be considered. Partners sometimes have different dating systems: one using the date of the day prior to the dream (in order to set the stage for incubation) and the other using the date of the morning following the dream (when recording and interpretation occurs). The clearest solution is to use both dates, for example, July 10–11, 1996, but this must be a mutual decision.

The recording process should be kept simple. A lengthy time span between the recording of the dream and its distribution slows the process of sharing and adds to opportunities for memory distortion. To avoid delays, some dreamers exchange duplicate cassette tapes or alert their dream partners to significant dreams by phone.

Writing the dream in present tense keeps the dream alive for both you and your dream partner. Capturing verbatim conversations of dream characters can be important in establishing the existence of shared messages. Because cross-connections can come from any level of consciousness, it is also useful to record those flickering images that occur before or after sleep.

As important as it is to provide clear copy to your dream partner, it is equally important not to censor the first words that come to mind, no matter how awkward, bizarre, or embarrassing they might seem. Dream partners must give one another permission to be crude, rather than smooth. Details are included, even if they seem trivial. Your dream partner can cojudge whether or not a particular dream element is significant in terms of cross-connection. Often, very mundane elements or puns can be meshing clues. And it can take more than one review of a dream report to uncover evidence of the influence of your partner.

Dream Interpretation

Okay, you've remembered your dreams and you've recorded them. What about dream interpretation?

The art of interpreting dreams, especially other people's dreams, was well established in the ancient civilizations of Egypt and Babylon, Greece and Rome. In these civilizations, divine intervention was considered a primary cause of dreams, but the Greeks began to shift emphasis to more mundane influences. Democritus, who fathered the atomistic view of the universe, believed that thought and sensation were appearances only; thought itself was really a movement of atoms in the body. He held that the atoms that composed people and objects might be able to emanate and penetrate a sleeper's consciousness. Thus, he hypothesized a kind of materialistic dream radiation. Heraclitus taught that visions of unknown places and people could emerge through dreams without the assistance of the senses or personal memory. Because psychic, spiritual, and social dreaming were cultural norms, interpretation theories and techniques took such factors into account.

It's only been in the past one hundred years or so in Western civilization that the idea that dreams are private, secular, and decidedly nonpsychic, that the best approach to dreams is a passive one, has come to the fore. This passive, private emphasis is just a blip on the radar screen of history. But it is a very important "blip."

That part of the dreamer's journey in which you turn inward and do your hermit's work is where you learn to become an individual. It's the process of individualization—self-determination, self-worth, self-esteem, and being a person with the right to make your own decisions. It's the time when you do your shadow work and learn to take responsibility for the content of your own dreams, good and bad, rather than project it onto the gods, the community, and onto other dreamers.

But eventually, it's time for the journey to turn outward again, to include mutual factors in the interpretive mix.

Dreamwork

Dreamwork usually refers to imaginative methods in which dreams are examined and processed in the waking state. By spotlighting and transforming feeling, motivation, and behavior, these methods might be used to solve problems and resolve conflicts, provide insights, and inspire creative ideas. They are especially applied to decipher the meaning and significance of dreams.

Any dreamwork method that overlays your opinion on another person's dream is counterproductive to the purpose of mutual dreaming. Such methods produce projection. Mutual dreaming requires the development of perception: looking beyond our own "stuff" and really seeing and understanding our dreaming partner from our point of view and *his or her* point of view. And conversely, allowing our partner the opportunity to have the same experience of us.

In partnership dreaming, you can try on another's ideas and beliefs for size, but you retain the authority of the final judgment of any interpretation of a dream. Your unique viewpoint becomes an integral part of the consensus whole. The Aha! of insight, the tingle of feeling, the fulfillment of emotion, and the certainty of gut instinct help guide what's right for each of you. Inquiry and feedback help guide you to what's right for the other person.

The following dreamwork methods support mutual dreaming because they encourage sympathy, identification, understanding, and other social skills. They model and rehearse dialogue with another dream figure (like the meeting dream) or empathy with the other dreamer (like the meshing dream).

Methods to Use by Yourself

To encourage meeting:

- Dialogue with your own dream character.

    Visualize any character who has appeared in your dreams and ask questions of that character. Wait for an imaginative reply. Continue the dialogue until your questions are answered. Useful questions are, "Who

are you?" "What do you think or feel?" and "What would you like to do?"[1]
- Befriend your dream enemies.

    Based on popular accounts of the dream practices of the Senoi forest people of the Malay Peninsula, this dialogue involves confronting scary images and asking friends for gifts or calling on them when in need of help.[2]

To encourage meshing:

- Become your own dream character.

    By role-playing a character in your dream in the gestalt mode, you learn how to express alternate feelings and view new perspectives. This technique helps bring alive what you might not otherwise experience.[3]
- Rewrite the dream from the character's point of view.

    You can use your dream journal to practice placing yourself in another's shoes and recording the dream events from this new point of view.[4]

Dreamwork with Others

To encourage meeting:

- Interview your partner about his or her dream characters.

    Like the first exercise, you ask questions, but about your partner's dream characters, not yours. "Who is X?" "What is your relationship with X like?" "What can you learn from X?"[5]
- Role-play the part of a character in your partner's dream.

    Psychodrama is a favorite dream group exercise. The original dreamer can either stand back and watch the group, or play a part in the action, too.[6]

To encourage meshing:

- Interview your partner *as* one of his or her dream characters.

  Ask "What is your name or what would you like to be called?" "What is your purpose in this dream?" "How would you like to see this dream turn out?"[7]
- Experience your partner's dream character as if it were you.

  This technique can demonstrate how your personality differs from your partner's and his or her dream characters, and what opinions, beliefs, and viewpoints you share in common.[8]

Dream Decoding

Dream interpreters have long used a variety of techniques to discover the hidden meaning behind the symbols that show up in dreams. Couldn't there be an equivalent mutual decoding method so we might unlock cross-connections when they aren't at all obvious? Yes, it turns out, there is. By combining the flexibility of dream interpretation techniques with the structure of dream content analysis, you can become a meshing detective.

The following decoded examples come from several shared dreaming projects. The projects include Dreams[10] (1984); Lucidity Project (1984–87); Shared Dreaming (1987–88); Bay Area Dream Team (1988–89); and Nexus (1989).

Synchronous Symbology

People who report having the "same dream" can mean that they share only a single item: a number, a surname, or a word. Sometimes the correlation between dreams is as simple as a solitary symbol. Color can be a bright banner to signal mutuality.

GWEN: *I am looking at a description on a pink piece of paper.*
LAURA: *There are pink penises everywhere.*
TAMMY: *I discover a pair of pink satin slippers.*

By itself, the color pink is unusual for dreams. But this particular correlation is enhanced by the fact that Gwen was dreaming about shopping with Laura in a *shoe* store, which, of course, relates to Tammy's slippers.

Sometimes a single color is linked to a similar type of symbol. Here, green is the primary color: a *green* caterpillar, a *green* sea serpent, some *green* celery sticks, and *green* sprouts. Each of the symbols is something long and thin.

How about these symbols: *red* Ferrari motorcycles, a *red* convertible Corvette, a *red* English convertible sports car, and a *red* biplane. Not only are all these the same color vehicles, they are all open vehicles, as well. Perhaps the dreamers were symbolically signaling to one another that they were "open" to connection.

You can count the number of times a particular word appears in the dream reports. For example, on the second Shared Dreaming date, three people dreamed of fish and another three dreamed about windows; squares and rectangles also showed up in four dreams. Some dream events were nearly identical. Sharon dreamt of a "sudden heavy rain"; Emile of a "flooding rain."

On the first Bay Area Dream Team date, a word count revealed that the most frequently mentioned primary element was water. Karl had "the intention of stealing *water* out of an outdoor spigot" as well as "some kind of *water* hose being directed at some people." Henriette had a "long thin canal of *water* with a boat traveling up and down." Wendy said, "I go out into the *water* to avoid [a monster]," while Genevieve reported, "I jump into the *water* to escape." For the other dreamers, water was implied. Lisa was walking along a beach, and Gwen made a comment about Hawaii.

But water is a fairly common symbol. It may be more

intriguing to search out the unusual. On this same date, both Karl and I dreamt about *dinosaurs*. I had been using the symbol of a "pink dinosaur" as the example of simple symbol correspondence between dreams. In fact, I'd never encountered that particular symbol, until Karl decided to take me up on it.

But looking for the same word can be deceptive. For instance, how might you group these elements: "the feisty woman," "Mrs. Chambers," and "my Aunt Mable"? Did you know that all three are referring to the same person? A single word count wouldn't indicate that fact. The situation becomes even more complicated when symbology moves from literal to metaphorical: orange as a color *and* a fruit, for example. A pine tree seen by one dreamer with 20/20 dream vision could correspond to "that fuzzy green thing" for another dreamer with inner vision myopia.

Parallel Phraseology

Parallel phraseology means that words of similar description can form string patterns in the written dream reports.

HENRIETTE: *Each diver is setting down rows of lights . . . they look like street lights on the floor of the ocean.*
BOBBIE: *Christmas lights are loose so that a huge strand dangles in an arc shape along the wall.*

Sometimes the parallels come in the form of dialogue.

FELICIA: *He finally says, "Maybe I went too far this time."*
But I tell him, "No."
EVAN: *"I didn't sound too crazy, did I?"*
"Not too bad," she says.

Parallel phrases can describe an event involving more than one symbol. On one Shared Dreaming date, Flynn dreamed, "The *wind* comes into the apartment through the closed *windows* and blows me about," while I dreamt, "Inside a white octagonal room with large *windows* the *wind* increases. I know it's coming to lift me off the ground."

As the parallels increase, the cross-connections range beyond a single sentence. Two friends in Dreams[10] dreamt in this way:

KONRAD: *I also have a book I put together, of the fifteen or twenty or so betting situations . . . I'm having a great time crisscrossing my choices, figuring out the situation, the odds and percentages.*

KELLY: *I am teaching someone arithmetic. . . . I encourage her to . . . do the book questions because I don't want to go to the trouble of figuring out the answers to my own arithmetic questions. I am happy to realize that I do remember how to multiply and divide fractions. I am teaching her how to use graphs, with the X-axis and the Y-axis.*

Aggregate Emotional Content

It can be more subtle and sometimes more difficult to detect shared emotional content, but similar symbols and parallel phraseology provide clues. Compare, for instance, these dreams from a Shared Dreaming date:

FLYNN: *Many beautiful spiderwebs. . . . He doesn't want to get wrapped in them. . . . I feel fairly detached and able to see the absurdity of the situation.*

EMILE: *. . . trapped behind one of those retractable accordion iron gates . . . there is no big deal for me, and I appear calm all the way through.*

Both dreams reported potential conflict or entrapment, and yet each of the dreamers had an unusually similar emotional reaction, calm and cool.

Conflict can be a major emotional connection. On another date, dream themes included two men fighting, a wrestling match between two men, yelling at a man, and two men driving everybody nuts. But there was also conflict resolution. One man prevented disaster by yelling to a woman friend; another had a woman trying to calm the fighting men. One man pinned his wrestler, and another had a dream in which the two men were working to resolve the conflict together.

On yet a third date, common feeling tones were of excitement and exhilaration. Symbols included charging horses, bubbling energy, joyously bouncing spaceships, singing and dancing and happiness at everybody being in synchronicity.

Parallels are most likely to be found in full-sentence phrases. But a single symbol of emotion can be the connecting element, as it was for the Dreams[10] example of group meshing on page 177.

Common Themes

You can discover the major issues that dreams address by seeking the themes held in common. At the start of a dream project like Bay Area Dream Team, dreamers produced of crop of symbols that might herald any new beginning: a wedding, a baby, white eggs, and a clutch of new to full moons.

The Nexus dreamers were much more literal on their first dream date. Symbols like a document or pilot license, two-page form, manual, adoption sheet, and legal pad all carried the stamp of bureaucracy that characterized the preproject information gathering and resulting paperwork that the dreamers had to endure before they could dream together.

What do the following buildings have in common? On a Bay Area Dream Team date, three people talked about a

GROUP MESHING

Don and his ex-wife . . . are intensely upset with each other . . . both flushed, arguing, feeling of anger.

WN

Ron has decided on some ideal situation for the house and is forcing his standards on me. I'm angry and yelling at him.

TT

Mother's planned a big party without telling me, knowing I'll do all the shopping and cooking. I'm so angry that I start to cry.

CT

[A girl] is acting kind of crazy, but it might be because she is very angry. She is fixing food for these people and it is yucky stuff.

TL

hotel, two had a department store, and two mentioned apartments. Not only were all multi-inhabited structures, but two had elevators and one an escalator, again indicating several levels of habitation. Such multiple quarters are common indicators of dreaming with a group. So are large structures like auditoriums, warehouses, restaurants, office buildings, and schools.

So when the Lucidity Project goal was "Investigate your dream location," two members responded this way:

NEIL: *I'm in a restaurant, at a table, sitting. My waitress is having trouble understanding me, and another woman comes over to help translate.*

A good number of the people in the restaurant (maybe everyone) stand up and sing in a cheer fashion. I'm eating some special national pride, I guess. I stand up and proudly acknowledge this.

PAT: *I am with one or more people experimenting with words. In some ways it seems like I am back in high school. I experience it feeling really confident.*

Everyone likes me, and I am aware of it and really feel good. There is a flag in class, and I start singing "America the Beautiful," getting everyone to join in.

Word Games

Ann Faraday has an excellent example of how dreams use **puns** as the connecting element between them. In her book *The Dream Game*, Faraday relates an experience she shared with her husband, John.

I dreamed I was staggering over a bridge with dishes of food I had cooked for a party, feeling very resentful because no one stopped to help me. On the same night John dreamed that I had agreed to prepare food for a bridge game.

Besides attaching two different meanings to the word "bridge," both husband and wife deciphered the dream to mean that Ann had allowed herself to prepare too much "food for thought," meaning that she was feeling overburdened with people's requests for lectures, interviews, dream interpretations, and so forth. John also suggested that this victimization was a big "game" on Ann's part.

Puns are a common symbol correlation. From the Lucidity Project:

FELICIA: *There is a stack of paper cups on the table before me. I take one and pour from a large container. It appears to be a cold drink of some kind.*

EMERGY: *I let my friend have the only ginger ale left and I take the Pepsi. I talk with a woman about how it got cold later since she only had a T-shirt on. I had also gotten cold.*

Third team member Sharon dreamt of drinking "more than average servings of orange juice," probably because she reported that in the waking state "I had been feverish with a cold bug." In this case, the word *cold* had been used by the dreamers in three different ways: to define a type of drink, to illustrate the effect of temperature on the body, and to indicate a case of influenza.

Dreams of several members of a group can combine forces to play word games with symbols and phrases. The symbols can go on **word association journeys:** enemies/ Civil War tapestry/fabrics/gowns/dress shop. Or consider: fire/firecrackers/crazy woman/storm/river/jumping in the water/dog jumping in the air/airborne superheroes.

Then there are **synonym rolls.** Take, for example, this string: fair haired/fairies/ferrous oxide/Ferrari, all mentioned in dreams from the same Shared Dreaming date.

Phrases can be put together to create **chains** that form a communal story. This tale comes from the first Dreams[10] date.

> **KONRAD:** *[Some people] give me forty dollars to go buy supplies for a party. . . .*
>
> **THEA:** *[When I return] people are throwing chips into a bowl of dip under the table. . . .*
>
> **KELLY:** *The lady serving food gives me a huge mound of green vegetables—too much—so I give her some back, not to waste it. . . .*
>
> **CHARLENE:** *I refill my chip bowl from a bag at the woman's feet, then realize it's her own private supply. She smiles, says, "It's absolutely all right."*

Sometimes these phrase chains wrap back on themselves. In such a case, we have a **round robin,** such as this one from Dreams[10].

> **CRAIG:** *I'm at a gas station . . . the manager points out the gas pumps. [When a customer pulls up, I see] the woman is blond, shoulder-length hair, attractive, well dressed. [Her red] car rises about five feet in the air.*
>
> **EDWIN:** *The car is on skis and on a very slight slope.*
>
> **CELESTE:** *[Who is a woman with white, shoulder-length hair] I'm floating high, high in the air looking down.*
>
> **THEA:** *[Who is a blond woman] I'm on a piece of land floating. . . . When things settle, someone knocks over a standing gasoline tank.*

Full Story Line

After a period of practice with connecting bits and pieces of their dreams, members of a shared dreaming project can finally learn to harmonize complete dreams. This example is from Shared Dreaming and describes the stops and starts that are part of any programmed attempt to dream together.

SHARON: *I drive some small vehicle into a sandy/isolated road which also has a mud-patch—perhaps the sand is used to improve traction because it is gray sand, mining sand, not white ocean sand. My vehicle is able to get over it, although I realize that others might not, yet when I get to a certain point I realize that the road dead-ends at someone's home and I have to turn around and make my way back again. I hope that the person whose road it is doesn't mind my traveling over his/her road, making tracks, etc. I am with someone, perhaps one of my sons, but that is vague, and the passenger doesn't help with the driving or directions. It is a sort of difficult passage to maneuver and frustrating in a sense, yet I don't get stuck and keep moving to where I need to go . . . out.*

CHAD: *I remember driving with someone in a convertible. I think I'm in the backseat on the right. A man is driving and a woman is on his right. We're driving down a narrow gully that's slightly higher than the car and just barely wide enough for us to pass. The road ends at a lake, and the road itself appears to have been cut by a stream.*

We drive right into the lake and go a small distance to a little sandbar in the shallows. But he continues driving out into the lake until the car fills with water, and I'm aware that my clothes and especially my shoes are wet, and I may wonder about my wallet or other personal effects that may be damaged by the water.

I don't recall if the water is up over the top of the doors or if we stop sinking with the water below door-top level. At any rate the car does stop sinking, and he continues on as if he's quite in control, knows what he's doing and where he's going.

Part Four

✦

New
Field
Research

◆

CHAPTER 13

RECIPROCAL DREAMING

◆

When I began to deliberately mutual dream, I soon discovered that my intention produced much more than the obvious classics. As in any form of dream, there are subtle variations from the classic theme. Because mutual dreaming is a successful connection between at least two people, there are cases when connection will be attempted by one partner, but not the other. Or one will inspire response, but not actively participate in the connection.

While communicating via dreams with a partner, the question arises as to what stance you might take in the relationship. Reciprocal dreaming requires that you look at the responsibility to yourself and each other and how that impacts the production of your mutual dreams.

Reciprocal Games

When I dream a symbol and later you dream the same, when I dream a theme and then you copycat me, when I dream a stimulus and you dream a response, we are playing the game of "follow the leader." Except, in reciprocal dreaming our roles can change at any time—you can become leaders and my dreams will react to yours.

On the other hand, if I dream a dream in which I have a particular perspective and you dream an alternate viewpoint, then we play the game of "agree to disagree." Your dream is positive, mine is negative; yours says yes, mine says no; in your dream you fly, in my dream I walk. I see the distant landscape, you look at the ground. You dream in black and white, I dream in color. My dream says we're in an auditorium; your dream says, nope, it feels like a shopping mall.

Once a wife and husband had dreams about a Transcendental Meditation teacher who was showing them a colorful movie. The woman remembered that the instructor spoke in Spanish; the man didn't. The woman thought that the teacher was handsome. The man thought he was ugly.

If we can argue, dispute, and dissent in waking life, we certainly can via our dreams. Independent individualism is a common trait among partnership dreamers. This is particularly obvious around the issue of the timing of our mutual dreams. We often have the "same dream" but not at the "same time."

Missed Meetings and Group Meetings

The traditional meshing dream contains similar activities to indicate empathic merging of identity. But without such parameters, a meshing dream might instead be a case of "inhabiting" the same dreamscape or "attending" the same event.

In a **group meeting**, dreaming partners have the sense of being part of a communal event, but don't specifically identify anyone in the group. Here is such a friendly get-together during the *Lucidity Project*.

HOWELL: *A party—lots of people there carving turkey and making sandwiches. There is a gal at the party I meet with a familiar sense, likely a dream friend.*

MEGAN: *I'm with my parents and sisters at a big party. The overall feeling-tone is one of closeness and deep enjoyment. I feel very connected to everyone.*

As another example, Linda Reneau and her husband, Ben, once dreamt about moving back to their old home in the Alaskan wilderness. Both saw the place as unfinished and run-down, but filled with many people. Neither identified the other. Their group event was also a missed meeting.

A **missed meeting** involves two or more dreamers who describe a similar event when dreamers do not see one another. Instead, there is some clue that they are in essentially the same dream "place," partaking in their own cell of a rolling filmstrip of events. It might be a shared symbol, like boxes.

The dreams of good friends Tom and Laura wove in and out of one another during the last night of 1987. Laura set the scene by dreaming of looking for a box on the top of a stairs. She also "dream thought" about Tom and his "stuff."

(2:30 a.m.)

A large Mexican woman is telling someone about the box she found on the sidewalk. I say please can I have it back, it has all my stuff in it. She says sure; I just put [the box] at the top of the stairs. I am very anxious about this; even though there wasn't much in it, it was all I had. There's some hint of Tom's stuff, too, but I decide I can't worry about that now.

She shows me where the stairs are, but there is no box. The stairs lead into a warehouse basement, where someone named Ralph works. I descend, calling "Hello," but no one is answering. The stairs are in brief courses with very low ceilings, and after a few moments I begin to get claustrophobic. The Mexican woman is still with me, and she laughs and says not to worry about the ceiling. I go down a few more steps, and she is gone. I give up, start to ascend, get panicky, wake up.

                                                            LAURA

For his part, Tom went lucid and flew around a palace. Then he came across a stairway stacked with boxes "guarded" by Nazi insignia. After exploring for a bit, he decided to return to his "own adventure."

(3:00 a.m.)

My recognition that I am dreaming and my successes inspire me to fly through the air, in and out of the balustrades and over the staircases and around the vaults in the ceiling, wheeling and turning within the palace.

At one point during my exploring I come across a tiny access way, like the kind you find behind storm doors in a school building, a little two-flight stairway stacked with stored boxes marked with Nazi insignia, a shabby little space with Nazi graffiti and pictures of Hitler. I moved down the concrete stairs towards the doors at the bottom. I was aware that it went to another place, that a connection could be made by opening the door. I decided to return to my own adventure.

                                                            TOM

In her last dream of the night, Laura finally discovered Tom's "palace" (although she called it a "temple"). She still seemed to find more boxy objects. Although she didn't find Tom, she did run into some "uniformed guards."

(9:00 a.m.)

I am crashing a sacred ceremony. I have done this before, or read about it. Someone is with me. Ceremony is in a large temple with courtyards and levels and terraces and windows and archways. I avoid walking through an arrangement of objects sitting on the floor at the feet of a row of celebrants or priests. I remember that this was done before, or my companion does it, or something. Then I climb into a window over a large central courtyard or amphitheater and the next step is to leap down, but I am discovered. I am not concerned, but the uniformed guards who "catch me in the act" are perturbed.

LAURA

The reality of multiple dreams is that they are seldom "real time" events. When compared with one another, they most likely engage in some degree of *time shift*.

Symbol Swiping

Neither meshing nor meeting dreams have to occur on the same evening. There can be a delay factor of days, weeks, or months between every sort of cross-connective dream. If you didn't know about the previous dream of your partner and you experience a dream after he or she does, chances are that you're probably having some sort of delayed psychic resonance. But even if you do know, and your dreams wait to respond until after a period of time elapses, this is still a form of mutual dreaming. Mutual dreams can be psychic or nonpsychic, as long as they are *social*.

As dreams multiply, group members start to play the game of "symbol swiping." This means that a current dream will contain the same symbols as those in the dream that another dreamer had previously shared with the group.

Thus, current dreams have been incubated by reading or hearing the dreams of others.

This type of dreaming is an important sign of group solidarity. It shows that our dreaming psyches find one another's dream elements intriguing enough to copy. Spontaneous psychic mutual dreaming will become more likely after one dreamer practices trying on the symbolic language of another.

During the *Lucidity Project*, Raymond shared a dream he'd once had about a crescent, because he thought it reflected very well the idea of dreaming to a target goal. He described his dream in this way.

> **RAYMOND:** *Dreamt of a machine from another place or time that looks like a gold crescent on a pedestal, with a circle or sphere now frozen in position at the top end. The sphere will, at the "right" time, fall free and come to rest at a certain position along the crescent, indicating the vibration of the target material.*

Several members of the *Lucidity Project* resonated with the symbol and responded by sharing past dreams of a gold crescent. But Neil did them one better. His dreaming mind responded to the dream of Raymond with one of his own.

> **NEIL:** *I drive to a combination bookstore and library in my hometown. I go to the occult section. At the top shelf is a sign with the word B-A-B-Y and a crescent moon shape underneath the B.*

Neil's dream psyche was saying, in effect, "I like this symbol!" But the symbol was put to use for his own creative purposes.

Symbol swiping is an assertive attempt to learn one another's dreaming language. If imitation is the most sincere form of flattery, then it is also a way to learn to appreciate one another. As Neil's dream suggested, he was taking a first "baby" step toward dream harmony.

Dreamers aid the process of creating common language by suggesting symbols such as a meeting place or objects to be dreamt ahead of time.

Echo Dreams

When the harmony is most complete, an echo dream is produced. The dreaming self can spontaneously respond to the waking report of another dreamer by creating an "echo" of the first dream. The echo dream serves as a personal variation and parallel to the previous dream. Dreamers copycat one another as a way to learn each other's dreaming language.

In an echo dream, you create your variation of complete dream sequences that you have already seen or read. The echo dream might be the result of cryptamnesia—the unconscious recording of a scene, a landscape, or a piece of information or knowledge that is completely forgotten by waking memory. But your dreaming psyche will remember the dream, and, as Raymond's dream suggested, at a time of its own convenience, the dream will resurface as a new variation. Journal keeping will provide you and your partner with evidence of the original dream. I have seen dream echoes that lag in time as long as a year.

This original dream was dreamt in November of 1988 by one of the members of the *Bay Area Dream Team*.

HENRIETTE: *It's my job to take care of the animals and plants. The compound is a huge place. There's a high wooden fence around the animals and no door to get in. I jump over the fence and proceed with my duties. I am quite content doing this.*

Two weeks later, after her teammate Laura read Henriette's dream, she dreamt an echo of the "caring for animals" theme.

LAURA: *I am at the edge of a fenced field, tall brown grass, wooden fence. In the field are kept animals—cows and dogs. A sense that this is an area of convalescence; the animals are recovering. I interact specifically with one animal, a dog. Lots of love.*

A Case of Intensive Dream Sharing

Early in my quest I was fortunate to link up with another highly motivated dreamer. Melonie was interested enough in mutual dreaming to agree to dream with me on a consistent basis, just to see what might happen.

Melonie and I began by sharing letters. Then "coincidentally" we both joined the same group dreaming project. There, we had the chance to sample the "flavor" of each other's dreams in an arena where our focus was not directed primarily at one another. We simply observed from afar. At the end of the project, we both felt discouraged at the lack of enthusiasm most members seemed to have shown. Conversely, there had been a couple of times when several of our own dreams had sharp correspondences. So we decided to take things one step further. We would engage in intensive dream sharing together, just the two of us.

For thirty-seven days in late 1984, we recorded every dream we could remember. Then, at the end of each week, we'd send each other all the dreams of that time period. Mail between us took about three days' travel time. To help spur mutuality, we selected once-a-week goals for special incubation on the weekend. We also exchanged color photos for the duration of our dream sharing. We talked on the phone perhaps twice (before and after this period) and never met in the waking state.

We didn't make our experience a chore; it was an experiment, a game we were playing. We were not attached to any model of a "successful mutual dream." During our megamonth, between the two of us, we recorded 3 cases of precognition, 1 false awakening, 4 OBEs, and only 1 nightmare apiece.

We each averaged slightly less than 3 recorded dreams a night. By comparing data, we were able to find 43 total correlations, on 18 out of the 37 days. Nine of them occurred on exactly the same date, as these did:

10/10/84:

MELONIE: *I am sleeping in someone else's house (an older woman?)*

LINDA: *An old woman's house is being used for a party.*

10/11/84:

MELONIE: *An outdoor party, people selling balloons and toys.*

LINDA: *I am within a circle or balloon hanging from the ceiling.*

10/12/84:

MELONIE: *Susie and Roy have found a way to make a lot of money playing bridge. [Roy is dark-haired; Susie is his married sister].*

LINDA: *I am at a food counter with a dark young man. His older married sister has just purchased $206 worth of food and taken it home, leaving it to him to pay out of his "winnings."*

There were lots of time shifts: 24 correlations where Melonie's dream preceded mine and 10 correlations where mine preceded hers (by 0 to 7 days . . . before we got notice of each other's dreams). We figured out cause and effect by having a good knowledge of our own dream vocabulary and waking-state events.

During our intensive month, I discovered that correspondence could come from audio as well as visual dreams.

10/13/84:

MELONIE: *(Visual): I see the doctor and try to turn off the lights. I can't find all the switches.*

LINDA: *(A voice only): "In the model that I'm talking about, you remain in the same place. It's as though someone turned on a light switch."*

The clues that had alerted me to our potential compatibility were a couple of dreams during our group project. In one case, Melonie dreamt "A family where the mother is a man and the father is a woman." A couple of days later I had dreamt that a man objected about a home for unwed mothers. "What about a home for unwed fathers?" he had asked. "Sure," I had quipped, "When men can get pregnant!"

Of all the possible symbolic contributions that can occur in dreams, a female man has got to be a statistical improbability of a high order. In addition to that anomaly, what intrigued me was that my dream also stated blatantly who the corresponding dreamer would be. For in the same dream, I had dreamt of Melonie by name. Then, during our intensive dreaming, I dreamt of Melonie by name six times; she dreamt of me by name twice. Four of those occasions were correlating dreams (2 each).

The other dream pair from the project was a "missed meeting." Again, I dreamt of Melonie by name. But this time I was lucid and did it on purpose. I associated her with a picture I was viewing. When I awoke, I noted the time was 8:00 A.M.

LINDA: *"Melonie?" I ask. The dark shadow moves back, revealing an oil painting of a shoreline water area that wild-*

fowl might inhabit, overhung by trees. The colors are brown and green, the picture frame ornate.

MELONIE: *A male crocodile is pursuing a female crocodile . . . he meets her in several different canals.*

After seeing my dream, Melonie reported to the project, "My crocodile dream was the result of forcing myself to return to sleep and so occurred at approximately the same time (8:00) as Linda's. In her dream 'shoreline water area,' 'overhung by trees,' and 'brown and green' all apply. 'That wildfowl might inhabit' makes me think of all the shorebirds I have photographed this summer. And the 'ornate' which she used to describe the frame could very well apply to me."

So we had a "missed meeting," even though we were dreaming at the same time!

Later, during our intensive dream sharing, we experienced some "group meetings."

MELONIE: *High school. Walking through the halls. Mothers volunteering to work on some project.*

LINDA: *In an extended classroom there is going to be a children's play. But first their teacher will address the parents. Halfway back a group of mothers are talking animatedly to each other, not paying attention to the teacher's speech. I walk out the door.*

So there were indications that we were dreaming about the same place. But although there might be other people around, none seemed to look like the photos we had sent each other. Where were we hiding?

Sometimes the goals we chose worked, sometimes not. The one that worked the best echoed our first case of meshing. It was "Find the relationships between our inner and outer selves."

11/3/84:

MELONIE: *I am in a bed in the corner of the room. I seem to be a man. When everyone leaves, I leave too.*
LINDA: *I feel myself to be one of four men who have been planning a rendezvous or vacation for two weeks. We will not tell anyone—spouses or employers—just leave.*

Retrospectively, I realized that we had been dreaming about one another not just as our literal waking selves, but as alternate aspects of the opposite gender. For example, on the 4th of October, Melonie dreamt:

I am staying somewhere separated from the land next door by dense brush. There is a man who is there. He and I think there is no way to get from one property to the other. But I find a path, very steep and through the brush.

I wrap a light green wood muffler around my head and push my way through. The man is talking to a Japanese man (gardener) who is facing me. When the man turns around he is very surprised to see me and wants me to show him the path.

Besides talking to me (in my male aspect) and the symbolic difficulties we were having trying to "find the path" between one another, this dream was precognitive of the hike Melonie took the next day. The hike was in the mountains. The starting point was the site of a now-destroyed inn with rocks outlining the original floor plan. The trail began over a swampy area on wooden planks. It ended in a rocky area in front of some ice caves.

Melonie walked on to the right of the caves around a large knoll covered with trees and dense brush. She thought that if she could just go all the way around the knoll, she could get back to the trail without backtracking. She didn't want to backtrack because it was so difficult, so she tried following some little creek beds without luck. Then she noticed it was past time to meet the rest of her hiking group. Just as in her dream, Melonie forced her way through the very dense brush and eventually found her way out. She remembered her dream while doing this, hoping that it meant that she could get through. It did!

I had the corresponding dream the day before Melonie's, on the 3rd of October:

I am climbing a mountain with some friends, including a male companion. The path is very narrow here by the cliff, but over on the right is a one-laned dirt road, wide enough for a single car to drive on . . . (I become lucid and find myself walking with two male companions. I'm amused that one of them has an Oriental appearance. I begin talking about the waking state.)

The three of us are now on foot, walking down a narrow path. I continue talking. "You know in that existence they can't even put their hands into the ground!" I bend down and push my hand partway into the dirt. I can feel the irregular layers—as though there are pebbles inside. . . .

I am walking up a wooden plank walkway which seems suspended about the ground, or over the water. There is a rectangular pool to the right around the perimeter of which I now seem to be walking. . . .

So far, so good. A hike in the mountains with male companions, circumventing the perimeter of a rectangle, a path over a suspended wooden plank walkway. These were consistent with Melonie's dreams and waking events. But then my dream took off on a wild ride of its own:

Out of the pool arises a huge dragon. I walk back to the end of the pool and out onto a platform and onto a diving board.

It seems as if this is a ritual. I will grab on to the dragon's two bottom "eye" teeth and he will raise his head up so I will be carried into the air, hanging by my hands from the teeth of his lower jaw. It seems I'm the only one who can appease him.

His huge face comes close to me—I feel proud that I'm only slightly anxious. (This is a lucid dream, after all.) I reach out and grab his teeth (stage one). He breathes/snorts through the holes in this nose. (Vague appearance but seems like a human face with reptilian nose-holes.) I turn my head to the left to avoid his bad breath (stage two).

He opens his jaw. On each side of his mouth are "eye" teeth grouped in twos. On his right/my left the tooth toward the inside is decayed. "Oh, poor dragon!" I exclaim.

I'll have to hang on only from the other tooth (stage three). It's becoming old and decayed too.

Part of my dream was day residue. The previous day I had lunched with lucid dream researcher Stephen LaBerge (he told me that *berge* is "cliff" in French). Talking about lucid dreams probably prompted lucidity that night. Then I went home and read of Henry Reed's use of dream ritual, and that information found its way into my dream, too.

This last part was precognitive, too, but of *my* life. The next morning I had my left lower bicuspid crowned. The dentist remarked about how the tooth was out of alignment with the rest. I grabbed a mirror to look. The tooth was in the exact same location "toward the inside" as in my dream. And my dentist? Just as Melonie's dream that night would describe: The "gardener" of my mouth is Japanese.

Finally, on October 15th, after seeing my dream and sharing her experiences, Melonie had the dream that echoed the latter part of mine:

My newphew Jason and I are together. One of his teeth has an ugly brown spot. It had been capped by a dentist and a hole has worn through. The dentist told Jason he had been brushing too hard.

Talk about "dense brush"!

Reciprocal dreaming made our dream contributions even-Steven once again. Our intensive dream sharing had painted a bigger picture of mutual dreaming than I'd first imagined. This wasn't just a case of paired dreams. Meshing dreams, missed meetings, group meetings, meeting and meshing events combined with alternate aspects to form a whole network of inner and outer events. Hmm, I thought. Things in dreamland must be a bit more complex than the simple model of waking sociability. Maybe the world of dreams was magical in ways unsuspected.

CHAPTER 14

◆

$\mathcal{T}$HE $\mathcal{E}$XPANSIVE $\mathcal{F}$IELD
OF $\mathcal{D}$REAMS

$\mathcal{I}$ ◆ f there's one thing a shared dreaming project can
do, it's to allow us to peek into the field of mutual
dreaming and come away with the understanding of just
how large and complex a social phenomenon it really is. You
just can't get that appreciation of social dynamics from reading one-shot cases or experiencing a mutual dream a couple
of times during your life. In reality, mutual dreams are not
stable: they shift, to other places, other times, other people
than the date, place, and person to whom they might have
originally been intended.

Shift in Space

Remember when we were trying to decide if mutual
dreams are psychic or not? It can be hard to tell, if you know
someone, and especially if you interact with him or her on a
daily basis. But the telepathic hypothesis is especially com-

pelling for connections between people who have never met in the waking state. Because dreams are not limited by waking space and time restrictions, connections can occur between people thousands of miles apart.

Here are two "coincidental" dreams from the same date by two dreamers who were participating in the same shared dreaming project facilitated by me. I happen to own a house with Mexican artifacts in the living room.

I enter a room. It is like a showcase or an exhibit room you would see at an anthropological museum. It looks like a desert scene with maybe some cactus, a smoke tree, and sand. Four people dressed in Mexican caballero clothes (big floppy sombreros, striped red trousers cut Western-style, and similar shirts of the stereotype bandito). They appear to be dark-skinned Mexicans and have a sleazy and unclean feeling. I take a great dislike to them immediately. After seeing them, I turn my back away so I won't see them.

I move away into the room I am in and meet more people. I am very aware of the four, however, and realize they are important for me. Yet, they are not part of the circus-group here.   ROBERT WARWICK, 10/20/85

Robert Warwick commented, "Waking up I realized that the four 'banditos' were a part of me. An instant grab for the title (as I type this) comes up with 'A Midnight Visit.' At the time the dream finished, I wanted to call it 'The Circus.'"

I'm somehow in this place with a number of "spiritual" people. It looks like we're on a knoll that's dry, dusty as a desert—reminds me of New Mexico. I look over at the people, and it's a pretty weird group! One woman is wearing headphones; possibly, these put her in touch with God? And one bearded guy is rhythmically pounding something in his hand that he calls a "don-ton" (rhymes with wonton). Most everyone is dressed in sixties garb, and I know that everyone is on a spiritual journey of sorts—but it seems to be manifesting itself differently than mine! I wonder about my being here, my connection.   ROBERT WAGGONER, 10/20/85

Robert Waggoner had this to say: "My dream helps to dramatize my sub- and conscious thoughts about the Lucidity Project. In that way that dreams sometime exaggerate things to make a point, I obviously think that I'm somehow in a pretty far-out group of wide and crazy spiritual people who are trying to get in touch with god in some odd ways. So this dream made me think. I decided that everyone is going to have their own views, their own methods, their own ways of expressing themselves, and I don't necessarily have to agree with them, nor they with me. But as an individual, I applaud their individuality as well as my own, and wish them the best. Also, as a member of the group, I have to recognize that there are basic beliefs that we share in common, and so in many ways we are similar."

Robert Waggoner lives in central Iowa. Robert Warwick was teaching in Tokyo, Japan. With the suggestion to dream a "True Dream" as their only common stimulus, what do you suppose is the probability of mutual dreams with Southwestern themes on the same night, by two men with the same first name and last initial, who lived halfway round the planet from one another?

The Lucidity Project

As an alumna of Team 1 of the third Dreams[10] project, I'd had a slightly different experience of shared dreaming than did the members of Team 2. My team had less overall coherence with one another, but did have some members who would occasionally evoke advanced dreaming skills. There were lucid dreamers and astral travelers, those who could dream precognitively and telepathically of a team member's waking life, and those who made use of fairly liberal creative symbols such as artwork and balloons, in addition to the recreational and sports-minded themes. Whereas both teams had shared issues of privacy, individuality, and balance, Team 2 was more susceptible to themes of anger and pain; my team's symbols were, on average, far more positive. Finally, I noticed that the most successful shared dreamers from our team had one thing in common: they were all readers of Jane Roberts's Seth material.

These factors led me to seek new dream partnerships with members of the Seth Dream Network, an informal group sponsored by the Austin Seth Center, in Austin, Texas. The executive director, Maude Cardwell, and the Seth Dream Network coordinator, Lenore Jackson, agreed to have me facilitate a project involving those members who'd had the experience of lucid dreaming.

The Lucidity Project of the Seth Dream Network ran for three years, from 1984 to 1987. There were thirty target goals in all, for as many months, to serve as the focus for dreaming. Each goal was suggested by team members and ran a gamut of subjects. Some were set up to encourage lucidity; some to elicit examples of precognition or telepathy; still others had an interpretive or symbolic nature. About eight of the goals involved meeting locations or intentions. The Lucidity Project was a drop-in, drop-out group with a core of approximately six to eight consistent contributors.

They all reported excellent health. Almost all had had college, some with post graduate work. They had been lucid dreamers since childhood or for any period up to two to three years prior to the starting of the project. The frequency of lucid dreaming ranged from "seldom" to up to "twice a week." They reported that the percentage of lucidity in their remembered dreams ran from 10% to 85%.

The value placed on social dreaming was very high! The most meaningful lucid dreams were personal encounters with dream characters or traveling to other places and planes. There was little reluctance to share dreams, with the exception of sexual themes. The dream type labeled "most fun" was flying. Out-of-body experiences and contacts with other people were also mentioned.

During the course of the Lucidity Project, five members experimented with visitations: some nonlucid, some lucid. When lucid, they would attempt to call one another or visit each other, perhaps by going to one another's houses. Sometimes they would get corroboration of clairvoyant or telepathic information from the resident.

The Lucidity Project also provided strong written evidence of lucid meshing. Although members might not see one another, while lucid they could have dreams with strikingly similar symbols or events.

The participants, all readers of *Reality Change,* a magazine of the Austin Seth Center, were both men and women, with ages from early twenties to almost seventy. They lived across North America and in physical locations as far removed as Japan and Botswana, southern Africa.

Shifts: Space, Time, and People

The June 1985 goal for the Lucidity Project was "Determine how to have a shared dream." Two members complied, but on different dates. They dreamt about having too many clothes to pack and about the view from a high tower.

Kate Belco lives with her family in Botswana. She was a full-fledged member of the project.

Packing to go home from University. Too many clothes. Wander round very beautiful shops, lovely clothes, but decide not to buy as I have too many. A sort of saga of people and events, and I eventually find myself on a high parapet looking down on an incredibly beautiful landscape.

KATE BELCO, 7/6/85

Karen Dole lives with her husband, Kevin, in the state of Washington. Kevin was a project member. He only included his wife's dreams if they seemed interesting.

I am in a dark house which is built like a tower with the stairway on the outside. . . . I decide to pack and quietly leave. For some reason I have brought boxes and boxes of my belongings with me. I can take only a few things, to leave hastily and unobserved. . . . I can see for a great distance from my position, out over a vast dark wooded land-scape.   KAREN DOLE, 6/15/85

So Kate was influenced, not by a member of the Lucidity Project, but by the *spouse* of a member. Spouses and friends and family members play along with shared dreaming projects, too. I've lost track of the number of times my husband, Manny, has had a dream on the same theme as a project goal, whether or not I tell him what it is.

Even more common than "spousal participation in the group event" is the "shift to the intimate partner" phenomenon, which, again, I first noticed in the Lucidity Project. The members of a group will consciously target strangers with their dreams. This intent flies out into the night, makes a sharp right turn, and winds up landing smack in the dreams of the comfortable and familiar. Thus, the dreamers report, "Oh, by the way, last night I had a mutual dream with my son, (or husband, or bed partner.)"

My wife and I are sitting across a table from each other engaged in discussion. I look down between my hands on the table and into a mirror. There are three standing figures in the mirror. It appears in my mind that these three figures, all dressed in white, are my spirit guides.

They reach out a hand, each one of the three, and bring forth a light into one merged beam—which leaves the mirror and strikes me directly in the forehead. I become lucid momentarily as I feel my head recoil from the impact. As I awake, I realize the light beam contained a message to me: "Psychic Power."

"Whether the light beam was a symbolic gift, or an awakening of my own abilities, or both, I didn't know," said Nigel. "I appreciated only the gift, regardless of the source, but the mirror made me think it came from me.

"Incidentally, my wife dreamed that night of our meeting at the same location."

The classic meeting dreams were taking place outside the intended circle of strangers—with friends and family. So when we dreamers in the shared dreaming project planned to dream with stranger-colleagues, we might be having missed meetings or audio meetings or other nonclassic meeting dreams instead.

Bay Area Dream Team

Both Dreams[10] and the Lucidity Project demonstrated that day residue and shared symbols deriving from long-term relationships could not explain the correspondences between dreamers who had never met. Since I knew that the degree of dream similarity tended to relate positively to personal familiarity and interest, I determined that my next experiment would be with a like-minded group that did meet with one another in the waking state.

Fern LeBurkien, a fellow dream enthusiast and Sethian, instigated the formation of the group. She asked three other Sethians to join us, including Kyla Houbolt, who offered her apartment for the group's meetings in the waking state. Three more people joined for a total of eight: seven women and one man, all from the San Francisco Bay area. Lucid dreaming was not a prerequisite for membership. And that turned out to be a hardship to achieving a classic meeting dream.

Bay Area Dream Team project ran from October 1988 through January 1989. The primary meeting took place with seven members present. We discussed the project's parameters and, as a group, selected the six goals. I had learned that shared dreamers utilized a variety of incubation techniques, including waking rehearsal, sharing of photos, telepathic induction, and commonly agreed target goals. Therefore, a chief component of the project was experimenting with different types of incubation: dreaming to a telepathic target; dreaming for a team member; waking-state rituals; and dream-state meeting intentions.

Because of past experience, I suggested the first two goals in order to lead us gently through group dreaming into a mutual experience. I reasoned that a focus on an objective telepathic target (or me) would be less threatening than feeling as if all dream "eyes" were directed at the dreamer, at least in the beginning. So a dream telepathy experiment became our first goal. Past targets had been mainly pictures or photos, so I decided to experiment with a three-dimensional object, to bring as many sensory elements into play as possible. The result was the dreaming of objects, but not of one another.

Before the third target date of Bay Area Dream Team, we all met at Kyla Houbolt's apartment. Each person brought small, inexpensive, personal objects to share with teammates so that we could take home some gift of one another. The goal would be to meet in the dream state to reenact the ceremony that we would perform in the waking state. This "ritual" was quite informal, consisting of standing in a circle with hands clasped and participating in silent meditation, during which I suggested that we visualize "sharing energies" with one another. Afterward, there was hugging and talk about dreams. We also shared food, so food preparation or serving occurred in the dreams of five of us, although the locations and form of libation didn't parallel our waking experience. The connective element was color.

KYLA: *I am with S. in a restaurant. . . . There are children in a group like a class, being led through the restaurant to greet everyone. These children appear to be mentally handicapped. . . . They are all dressed in shades of red and orange, like Rajneesh sanyasins. . . . We are all saying "Hi" at once and playing with it so it becomes a little song or chant.*

WENDY: *I come into a cottage room filled with men. From their awkward behavior and slurred speech, I know that they are mentally retarded or crazy. . . . As I gaze at one man, I notice that he and all the others are dressed in identical bright orange outfits, like a martial arts costume. . . .*

We begin singing some song with a religious flavor. . . . I know that I am sane and . . . I realize with surprise that I can sing right on key, so I adjust my voice to mouth the words of the song, only singing a clear word every so often.

LISA: *I go into a room where people are preparing food and other things . . . a dark-haired woman is singing one of the songs from a new tape I have . . . she has no soul with this song. The feeling tone is flat and unappealing. . . .*

[Then] I lose some of my self-consciousness and begin to sway and sing the song myself. . . . It feels like this action and the feeling that it evokes is about who I really am.

In addition to these dreams, Gisèle dreamt of dancing and a band playing music; Karl had a carnival with "many musical groups playing music here and there, people milling about in thick crowds, dancing." The energy-sharing ritual had evoked symbols of musical harmony.

Bay Area Dream Team reacted to all the sensory influences with more tactile dreams than other projects. For example, Karl had this regular dream:

I struggle through some kind of harsh circumstances and problems. Then I'm tickled under the right armpit by a man who likes to act like some kind of clown or jokester. My first reaction is one of annoyance, but I realize he is doing it on purpose to try to get me to "lighten up" and not take things so seriously.

It was quite similar to my false awakening:

After a night of trying hard to sleep, with little success, I am lying on my stomach with my right arm down, palm extended upwards. I feel someone gently touch my palm, caressing it in several spots. I assume it is my husband and think how nice he is to do this, until it starts to tickle. Then I jerk and wake up, realizing immediately that this actually had been a false awakening.

By the end of the project, the group gathered for an in-dream party, where dancing and music featured prominently. Selected phrases from the dreams linked in a group meshing chain.

Nexus

Both Shared Dreaming and the Bay Area Dream Team ran during more or less the same period of time. I began to notice examples of cross-dreaming between the groups. So it was natural, when both projects came to an end, to suggest a "nexus" of the groups. The *Nexus* project included alumni from both groups as well as from the Lucidity Project. It was held from February through June of 1989.

True to its name, the Nexus project did show evidence of

CHAIN

There are some others gathering . . .
LT

. . . [at] a booth in a crowded restaurant.
TN

A whole bunch of boisterous students arrive.
GC

They're so busy talking and laughing among themselves . . .
KF

. . . with their colorful costumes and merry attitude . . .
WL

. . . [that] I envy their good spirits and sociability.
KF

An amorphous couple is dancing, swirling around the floor . . .
WL

dressed in something like a show dancer's outfit . . .
LI

. . . outrageously twirling and stomping and laughing.
HO

It is going really well in a joyful and effervescent kind of way.
GC

"cross-dreaming." But this time, the connection was *back-ward*, to a previous project. Three month before Nexus began, while they were still contributing to Shared Dreaming, Bob Trowbridge and Jill Gregory had a couple of dreams about "heads and horns."

I am in Bob Trowbridge's apartment looking around his living room. I notice many heads of stags laying about. They have magnificent sets of antlers. They have brown fur, some of them being mounted on wood like trophies. Bob doesn't seem to quite know what to do with all of them. However, he accepts them as belonging to his home.

I go lucid and recall my incubation of our mutual dream group and topic. These heads and horns must be the topic: Bob reads my mind. Looking at me while standing next to me on my left side he says with a smile: "These things seem to be popping up all over."   JILL GREGORY, 11/11/88

I'm at Y's house. We see some animals, about three or four of them, which go through some rather rapid metamorphoses, so that I'm not sure of the sequence. The first thing that happens is the sprouting of a small unicorn horn sticking up in the middle of their backs. Then the horn moves to their foreheads. The final transformation is into horses with a small stylized unicorn horn on their foreheads.

In the next scene, I'm sitting at a rectangular table, with a little girl. I'm telling her about the unicorns. Actually it feels like the two dream happenings are parallel or simultaneous. I am telling the little girl about the animals at the same time I'm having the experience.   BOB TROWBRIDGE, 11/13/88

On January 29, 1989, these two alumni of Shared Dreaming went to the first meeting of Nexus. Again, it was held at the site of the Bay Area Dream Team ritual—at Kyla Houbolt's apartment. Bob found himself sitting underneath a pair of deer antlers hanging on the wall of the apartment. He took the antlers off the wall and playfully placed them behind and then in front of his head. Since Jill had her camera with her, she took a photo of Bob. The picture looks as though Bob has antlers growing out of his head. Neither of the dreamers had remembered their previous dream content until I brought it to their attention once again.

Other Projects

The Women of Power project involved four individuals and was held from October 1990 through January 1991. It featured dreams about our alternate personas. The most important new contribution was the first shared dreaming project example of contiguous dreams, in which there's a sharp sense that your dream borders the dream of another.

Firebird Rising was held from July through December of 1992. It included only lucid dreamers, but was again a drop-in, drop-out group. As a result, despite liberal use of "meeting" goals, there was a lesser amount of dream meshing than some previous projects. But there were often examples of advanced skills: lucid remote viewing and visitations; lucid telepathy, clairvoyance and precognition; x-ray vision and contiguous dreams.

Throughout all the shared dreaming projects there were two approaches that produced the best meshing and non-classic meeting connections: actual meetings in the waking state and shared dreaming types of goals. The waking-state contacts were enhanced if the dreamers actually did something together when we met. It helped to participate in a group task of some kind, especially if it involved more than talking; if it involved gesture *and* physical contact.

The most successful goals were variations on these themes:

- Get acquainted with team members; say hello.
- Meet at an imaginary place (especially water locations).
- Have a party.

The Effect of Positive Intent and Lucidity on a Group Dreaming Goal

During the Bay Area Dream Team, the members decided to use a group dreaming goal. They wanted to try out a Dream Helper experience with energy directed to a target person. Gisèle Perreault volunteered and handed us a major challenge: she was planning to travel to Canada in order to be at the bedside of a friend who was dying of AIDS. She asked us for help through our dreams.

That suggestion set the stage for some heavy symbolism and did result in the expected thematic meshing dreams for most of the participants. But the Bay Area Dream Team had a trickster among the group.

Just before going to sleep on the target night, Kyla Houbolt wrote in her journal for Gisèle, "Let us send her a death of wild wing feathers and ringing bones, a death as solemn as the jokes of stones. . . . Is death an ending, a closing of doors, a shutting down of powers, a final good-bye? No nay nix and nonsense. Never say die say I. Close one eye open another. . . . No one goes away for good. It's just our bones change costume for the next act."

Thus, although all the dreams shared a similar disjointed quality, about half of them incorporated positive, resolving elements as well. For example, Fern dreamt that while she was auditioning for a play, she asked the casting director if there was a part for a sacred clown. "She says no, but I can play the part of an air tank with skeleton attached," was the response. Gisèle noted, "The oxygen masks were attached to tanks . . . my friend Dan was on oxygen from November 9th to 15th, when he died."

Gisèle actually incorporated the feathers and bones of Kyla's incubation into her own dream of the night. Then, that weekend, she went to see something called the "Canticle of the Sun."

GISÈLE: *Something about immortality. I have the sensation of sinking down into deep and deeper layers of understanding.*

I want to talk to the attendant, who is known to be a guide in quick and easy deaths. I see him walking along the opposite side of an indoor pool. No one else is present. I try to get his attention.

The scene switches, and I'm in a fairly dark room lit by candles. The walls are a speckled blue and white color. The door is open and a procession of people enter. All are shrouded in black cloth and are wearing red feathered face or eye masks. I welcome the visitors. There are two oxygen masks laying on the floor, to the side of the room. There is a sense of decay, and I wonder if there are skeletons somewhere.

Early morning on the same date, I had a lucid dream in which I took advantage of my awareness to call for Gisèle.

LINDA: *I go back to the corridor, take a deep breath, and bellow out, "Gisèle Perreault!" The woman who comes toward me seems quite like her. As she swings around me, I recall or change her facial features so the end result is a pretty close approximation of how I remember Gisèle.*

"Do you know me? I'm Linda Magallón." She squints her eyes and turns her head to the right as if trying to think. . . . "Are you asleep?" I ask because I know that it's late in the morning, and she might already be awake.

"What are you doing now? Close your eyes and see." I close mine, too, but get overlapping images swirling around. There are too many to distinguish, except one which I know to be the sun.

When I open my eyes again, Gisèle isn't there. I go into a bizarre scenario where I walk alone from the edge of one blue indoor swimming pool with blue walls to another and back again. The first is lit from a source high up on the wall, but what it is I cannot see because there is a fluttering squarish shape in front of it. Symbols like boxes float on the surface of the pools.

I picked up the image of the sun: that was the telepathic element from Gisèle's daytime event. Both Gisèle and I were trying to get someone's attention: that was the strongest meshing element. We also used parallel phraseology of a missed meeting: "oxygen masks laying on the floor" and "symbols like boxes floating in the water." But we also seemed to be hanging around in the same dream "space": by a blue indoor swimming pool.

The influence of a special incubation shifted my direction away from a literal negative picture to symbolic positive imagery. The presence of lucidity allowed me to try to "see" what Gisèle was dreaming. Incubation plus the presence of lucidity meant that I finally got my half of a meeting dream. I just wish Gisèle had recognized me, too. Was it because she wasn't lucid, and I was?

CHAPTER 15

✦

SHADOW WORK

✦

When we dreamers do make successful connections via a shared dreaming project, our dream reports reflect personal relationships as varied and complex as those in the waking state. They parallel the developmental dynamics of small groups as described by social psychology, educational psychology, and business management theory. Besides sociometric patterns based on these principles, models unique to the dream state are formed.

Social psychology proposes that groups go through stages that reflect the group's ability to resolve its interrelationship problems, complete its specified tasks, or discuss the topics on its agenda. But these stages do not flow from one phase to the next with any consistency or clear-cut divisions. Instead the organic nature of the group dictates a process that is more akin to a complicated dance with steps going to and fro, back and forth, rather than always in one direction.

Nor are the individuals in the group always moving in

sync with one another. Not everyone is at the same stage of experience and maturity in the social matrix. It's quite possible for a series of dreams to indicate one person stuck in stage two and never moving out of it. A second person in the same group might start at a third stage, leap to a peak performance, then plateau at some intermediate stage of relationship.

This phase differentiation can be caused by shifting between group dreaming and shared dreaming goals. Sometimes an individual may decide to relate to the task or goal specified by the leader or group. At other times he or she may choose to focus attention on relationship with other group members. Except for the first few stages, which are characterized by inward focus, shifting to deeper stages of development requires the cooperation of at least one other group member.

Stage One: Deciding to Join the Group

Even if folks decide to submit dreams to a shared dreaming project, their reports can reveal that they really aren't ready for the group experience. The "Loner" will distance himself from the group, taking an observer's stance while deciding to stay or leave the group. The "Drop-Out" will participate for a while, decide that shared dreaming is not for him or her, then depart. The "No Show" will demonstrate resistance to group involvement by consistently "forgetting" to recall dreams. The "Oblivious" will remain wrapped up in his or her own fantasies, never connecting with anyone else in the group.

The Loner

The Loner does send in a report, but his dreams give hints that he is in the process of withdrawing from the project. Dreams will have a "standoffish" tone. Dennis chose not to continue participation in Dreams[10] after submitting his one and only dream.

> **DENNIS:** *I am far above various groups of people, leaping out from trees and tall buildings and gliding in circles, gradually with outspread arms, down to the ground. I ask them to watch me as I descend, sort of showing off.*
>
> *At one point, I want to get down fast, so I plummet a long distance within feet of the ground, then "apply the brakes," gently landing. The feeling of exhilaration and personal power is enormously satisfying and a little scary.*

A "Loner" usually does not engage in interaction, but can be aware and watching the unfolding group drama. When Evelyn had her dream, she obviously didn't approve of what she saw. This was the first, last, and only dream she submitted to the Lucidity Project.

> **EVELYN:** *I don't like anyone in this dream. They all seem strange and coarse to me. Then I go away for a while and when I come back, C. is standing on the porch and she is dressed real extreme. She has large black plastic jewelry on and is wearing a pants and jacket suit in extremely bright colors and of a large print. I don't want to get near her. I talk to her from the street, and I know they think I am stuck up. They think that I think I am better than they are. I am intimidated because it is too noisy and there are too many people there for me to deal with.*

The Drop-Out and the No-Show

After a long period of participation, Greg was destined to leave the Shared Dreaming project. He signaled his intention to be a "Drop-out" to team members through a dream from his last report.

GREG: *I am traveling with a group of people by boat from one place to another. There are two large vessels.*

I am supposed to travel with one group, but I feel drawn to travel with another group on the other boat that is more interesting and lively. I don't know how to let the original group know that I would like to change boats for part of the voyage without hurting their feelings.

Like other Drop-outs, Greg's image continued to make guest appearances in the dreams of group members. In his case, however, Greg's supporting role lasted not only to the end of the Shared Dreaming project, but also in the first few dreams of people in the following project, Nexus. Members are curious about Drop-outs. Where did he go?

The "No-show" demonstrates passive resistance to group involvement, by consistently "forgetting" to remember his or her dreams. Sometimes virtually an entire team can be a no-show to a particular target goal. During the Dreams[10] project, one goal was "Discuss Senoi Shamanism." Hardly anyone responded to this suggestion, and either submitted no dreams or dreams about some other subject.

The Oblivious

Some dreamers regularly turn in dream sheets, but there is little if any correlation with the dreams of other group members. No symbols are shared. No events are held in common. The dreams do not give any indication of attempt to meet or mesh with others.

One dreamer in the Lucidity Project had a series of dreams in which she had trouble with her own vehicle. Felicia finally commented in exasperation, "Am I ever going to have a good car dream?" The "Oblivious" dreamer has a

personal problem on his or her mind that needs to be resolved or released before he or she can notice or relate to the
other members.

By far the greatest number of dreams in a mutual dreaming project report incidents separate from the group. This is
not surprising, given that personal dreaming is the default
mode for most dreamers. It is the style of dreaming to which
dreamers return naturally, if there is no outside stimulus or
intention to reach beyond personal concerns.

The Lucidity Project dreamers would at times resonate
with Felicia's personal problem by having car dreams of
their own, but their dream plots would be quite different. It
was as if their dreams were saying, "Oh, yes, that reminds
me of what happened when my car . . . ," and go off on a
tangent unrelated to the original narrative.

This level of group dynamic favors the "serial monologue." Team members are so intent on telling their own stories, they don't bother listening to anyone else. They use the
ideas of other people simply as an excuse to start rambling
off on their own. Serial monologue occurs when dreamers
are spouting images into the stratosphere, but not engaged
in the task of listening and emphathizing with one another.
Since much waking conversation goes on at this level of communication, it's not at all surprising that the serial monologue is reflected in so many dreams.

In this culture, learning to listen and empathize is an acquired art. Dreams, with their natural associative proclivity,
can be a helpful boon to this learning process, if they are but
considered for use in this way.

Stage Two: Wrapped Up in the Self

Like the "Oblivious," "Self-Involved" dreamers focus
primarily on themselves. But they do so in relation to the
group experience. Their dreams describe emotions of uncer-
tainty and struggle in the face of social activity.

At this stage of development, there can be initial concerns

of privacy, vulnerability, emotional overwhelm, performance, and loss of individuality, which it is feared might result from newfound intimacy. Jealously, nosiness, exposure,
and intrusion are strong concerns. But even when it seems
that problems are intensely personal, they can be found to
be shared by other team members.

On the very first Bay Area Dream Team date, dreamers
dreamt about all those individual concerns that come up in
any situation involving the sharing of personal space: Laura's "fear about being stuck inside," Wendy's fear about "the
interior is dark and possibly scary," Gwen's being
"shocked" when overhearing a conversation, and Karl's
being afraid of a stranger.

These similar symbols came up in the dreams: Laura's
and Karl's "backyard," Gwen's "back of an unknown
house," Henriette's "back of the house," and Wendy's "rear
end" of a house. Vulnerability was the issue, since the rear
was considered unprotected. The backyard, while being
one's own private space, was also seen as a place where
dreamers could overhear or be seen and heard by neighbors.

In the same project there were shared concerns about
male/female intimacy.

LISA: *He reaches to embrace me, but I sort of slide away.*

LAURA: *I rest my hand on his thigh at some point unconsciously, and when I become aware of it, I remove it, hoping
that I haven't embarrassed myself.*

TAMMY: *A friend of G's makes a pass at me. . . . I turn
him down, feeling embarrassed and uncomfortable to find myself in this situation.*

For two teammates during the Nexus project, the problem was intrusion.

LAURA: *I am living in a place which resembles my apartment. There are lots of other people living here. Some of*

them are expressing concern because the doors don't lock. I look at the front door, and its edges are as though eaten away by corrosion, so that even if the lock is set, it doesn't engage. Those who are concerned indicate that there is an intruder on the premises. But the only intruders I encounter are several little girls who keep popping in; they are delightful!

But somehow I get caught up in "escaping" this unsafe place. The getaway vehicle is a truck with wooden frames built up around the sides. A substance that looks like ice, but is not cold, and is solid like plastic, has partially filled the gaps in the frame. I try to climb through the frame into the truck bed, but the substance has made the openings too small for me to fit through.

SHARON: I see a young man robbing the church. . . . I run to lower levels—nowhere to hide, and then on to a smaller closet with double bolts that I shut from the inside. There is, however, a hole in the side where the robber can see me hiding, and when I see him coming—burst out the doors, surprising him and getting away to a still lower level, like a furnace room. . . . I hear the robber breaking through the two bolts of this door, and I know I must confront him.

This pair of dream comments shouts, "Performance anxiety!"

BONNIE: I am hiking in the mountains with a group of people—we have to climb rocks. The general impression is difficulty and danger.

BILL: I am with or involved with a friend I knew at school. I am working hard, but have a sense of failure.

In the Dreams[10] project, both Bonnie and Bill were intermittent dream sharers. Their dreams show they were aware of being with others, but had difficulties matching the pace that was being set by the group.

But there were those who were at least willing to try. On the first dream date, Craig dreamt, "I feel momentarily overwhelmed, like I won't be able to handle this job. . . . Then I realize it's my first few hours on the job and that I will work at my own pace." However, even this rate was problematical. By the second date, he was dreaming, "I feel frustrated because I can't get my car as fast as I want it."

By the sixth goal, Craig had responded to the majority of his teammates' dream perspectives and shifted his view of the project from military to recreational themes. But even then, he considered the experience strange and still believed it contained the potential for exposure.

> **CRAIG:** *I'm exploring a remote mountain range in a foreign and exotic land. My mother is with me. We are inside the top of the mountain peak. It is a solid glacier. It is beautiful inside, like being in some fantastic crystal palace. There are large oval portals opening to the outside. It is raining hard. I feel uneasy, knowing the rain will run inside. I feel trapped because the rain is making the surface of the glacier extremely slippery, and we can't climb out of the portals because we would slip down the mountain, which is very steep.*

Stage Three: Observation of Others

Even with actual hermits or self-absorbed people, sooner or later their shared-dreaming teammates will notice them standing in the corner. This observer mode results in one dream corresponding with another, but in the strictest sense this is not true mutuality. It's not a two-way dialogue, but

the active observation of a person engaged in one-way monologue, the lecture mode.

Craig's fearful, self-absorbed attitude did not go unno-
ticed by his teammate. Bill, who was a therapist by profes-
sion, took notice that Craig's dilemma echoed his own. Craig
had the meshing dream; Bill's was the dream meeting. Together their meshing and meeting dreams can be seen as a
diagram on page 225.

Most times, dreamers do not know exactly whom they
are observing. The evidence is found by comparing dream
reports for signs of meshing.

During the Nexus project, Henriette dreamt:

HENRIETTE: *All I remember is being in an unfamiliar
house. Weird neighbors that are being very secretive. . . .
My pockets are filled with all kinds of crystals. I empty
them out into a dish. A garnet and amber necklace falls out
of the dish on the pillow. A woman furtively picks it up and
takes it. It's fine with me that she has taken it, and I
wonder why she's being so sneaky.*

Who was the sneaky woman? Laura's report had the answer.

LAURA: *Various objects on the bed [including] a tin of blue
metal. Inside are tangles of strands of pale golden candy. I
eat some; it is merely sweet. I expected more colors, more
information. I also feel I am sneaking something that isn't
mine and I shouldn't be doing this.*

This is the stage when telepathic "hits" can occur as some
dreamers identify other group members by their surface appearance. On the very first Dreams[10] date, one member of
Team 2 was dreaming of "a man who is thirty-five to forty-
five, perhaps average height and build, medium-brown
rather straight hair, brown eyes. He seems to be glancing

MESHING AND MEETING

*I am walking down
the steps outside a house
leading to its basement. It is
typical of many houses which have
an area in front surrounded by iron
railings . . . . At the bottom of the steps . . .
a psychiatrist stands working, in a
therapeutic sense, with another man.
As I pass, I sense the man's
discomfort about exposing his
inner life in a public place.*

BD, ENGLAND

*I feel like I've been drafted,
because this is something I don't
particularly want to do. . . . I think that
part of the training must involve
not being allowed to wear clothes.
I think the purpose must be to be stripped
down so that nothing is hidden and one has
no sense of privacy and individuality.
I feel that I'm not going to like this experience,
I dislike military authority and the
loss of individuality it involves. . . .
I enter a building and look for the commander
in charge. . . . I go to the second floor.
At the top of the stairs,
there is a metal turnstile.*

CY, UNITED STATES

over someone's shoulder and smiling approval of how this
other person has depicted him in a written description." This
was very close to the appearance of teammate Warren,
whom the facilitator Kitra P. dreamt as "a slender man, perhaps about 5'9", in beige slacks and an off-white shirt . . . he
had medium-brown hair, straight and slightly long." She
also stated that in her dream he was "standing sort of outside the rest of the group, observing." This turned out to be
prophetic of Warren's contributions: few dreams shared, but
much "outside" analytical commentary in their stead.

When group members have met, they can identify one
another by waking appearance. Either they call the person
by name or describe obvious characteristics. On one Nexus
date, Kyla Houbolt appeared and was recognized in the
dreams of three team members. Nora talked about a woman
with "brownish light hair, cut like Kyla's" and Chad had "a
woman with light brown or dirty-blond hair" in his dream.
Charlene dreamt of standing "by the sinks [with] a ditsy
blonde in her early twenties," while Kyla herself was dreaming of a waitress "at the sink." The waitress was a frequent
dream character of Kyla's, "about my age and coloring but
with short curly hair."

At times, a dreamer's own family or friends seem to be
doing a "stand-in" for dreamers in the group. It's as if the
dreamers are reassuring themselves that it is okay to participate in a social setting because one or another team member
reminds them of a known quality. In the waking state, when
first meeting another, one can comment, "Oh, you look so
much like my uncle," or "You remind me of someone I
know." In the dream state this opinion is translated into visual images. In the Bay Area Dream Team project, Laura and
Lisa dreamt of their sisters instead of one another, yet the
remaining elements in their dreams were parallel.

LAURA: *I am with my sister B. and a friend tells me there
is an apartment vacant in her building. . . . At first I
think I do not want to live in this building; it is not as*

pretty as mine, and it has many units. The vacant one is on the ground floor. But I discover that there is a garden attached, much larger and nicer than mine.

I tour the apartment with my sister. We both want it, but this produces no tension. The stove and refrigerator are in terrible shape, and the stove has only two burners. I think of replacing them from what I will save on the rent. I never see the garden, but awareness of how nice it is pervades the dream.

LISA: I'm at my new apartment with D. (my present room-mate) who helped me move. . . . He's really trying to help me. Feels good. Inside is a very small room with lots of sunlight pouring in, a big white bedspreaded bed, a dresser, and a box full of books and albums (my two favorite things in the world). . . . I'm delighted by the room. . . . I go back to the living room. . . .

At some point, an Asian woman walks in and sits down. She hasn't noticed us. We wait patiently until she does. I figure she thinks she lives here. She finally looks up at us, and with a start gets up and leaves without a word.

Then I notice a white refrigerator. My sister has brought it for me. She found it somewhere. I open it. There's some half-eaten food in a dish. I figure it must be her dinner. She's there in the room now. I realize she's really trying to be helpful, too. I thank her. None of the furniture nor the refrigerator thrills me as far as their condition goes, but I think for now they're okay. I keep noticing the apart-ment has more space than I originally noticed. . . .

Laura told Lisa, "I think I'm the Asian woman in your dream. Sometimes I dream of myself as being Oriental. The

garden might compare to your room full of albums and
books—your 'favorite things'—because the garden is my favorite thing." Just as lab dreamer Eliot had alerted his partner Blanche to his Russian persona, so Laura could alert her
dreaming partner to an unaccustomed appearance by being
aware of the multiple aspects of her own personality.

Dreamers are very curious about one another. This is also
the stage when dreamers might peek into the waking lives
of their teammates and empathize with their dramas and
dilemmas.

During Nexus, Tammy vacationed at a hotel from which
she went skiing over spring break. Henriette dreamt of staying at a huge hotel where the outside area had "lots of
snow." She and Gwen "end up by sliding down a big hill on
our behinds." Gwen also dreamt of "hanging over a cliff,"
whereas Tammy actually fell off a cliff on her right wrist and
was still experiencing pain between wrist and elbow on the
target night.

In response, Bobbie carried things "in one hand" in her
dream. Sean found a grip as "very soft and cold and weak,"
and when Sharon reached out to squeeze a hand, "it hurts
so I cover it with both of mine intending healing."

On one mutual dream night during Nexus, four dream
reports mentioned dogs. For Chad and Sean, the dog was
specifically black in color. That night Bobbie commented on
her irritation with the dog down the hill yapping before she
went to sleep, and Sharon reported that her son's dog was
barking, keeping herself and the neighbors awake.

The waking stimulus does not have to occur on the same
night as the corresponding dreams. Dreams can be precognitive or retrocognitive of a correlating event.

On the third goal night of Dreams[10], a member of Team 2
dreamt:

EDWIN: *In an old house (on the second floor) . . . I hear
a noise in the front yard, after it has turned dark outside.
My grandfather asks what the noise is. I reply that the
others are on the porch below.*

For the next goal, not knowing the dreams of the other team, a member of Team 1 had this dream:

MALLORY: *I see two men, one light and one dark. . . . I am scared and force myself to wake up. I wake up (still part of the dream) in a very narrow bed against a wall. Get up and look out window to see if anyone could get in with a ladder. Too many bushes. Reassured, I go back to bed.*

What was the stimulus for these dreams? I nominate the waking state of a member of Team 2. In the commentary with her fourth dream, Thea reported, "The previous night I'd had a scare from the man downstairs. While playing my guitar in my bedroom, I heard noises at my window shade, gave a double take, and saw a hand at my window. I let out a frightened scream and ran upstairs to call my roommates for help. When I returned I saw an envelope on the windowsill from the man downstairs commenting on my playing (I was keeping him up apparently)." Thea's event occurred four nights after Mallory's dream.

Stage Four: Making Oneself Comfortable

Dreamers who are aware of their personal responsibilities to become functioning members of a group are willing to do some self-evaluation. They try to establish their own limits, and they clean up their acts.

On the fourth Nexus date, Bobbie dreamt of cleaning a dark woman's home; Wendy dreamt of a spot on the floor; while Gwen wiped up the floor; Tammy was cleaning out her car; and Chad's friends did repairs, cleanup, and re-arrangement of objects. Sharon had a dream in which she talked about the meaning of symbols "such as 'sweeping a road,' which might be like 'cleaning one's path.' "

Without cleansing, the problems of daily life can resonate

in one's own dream and the dreams of one's partners. With clear waters, the going is much smoother.

Whitney successfully handled her obstacles in-dream during the Dreams[10] project.

> **WHITNEY:** *I am repeating an experience of breaking through obstacles—physical—then relate a feeling—emotion—to it, then get a concept, and then trace that to my attitude. I keep going for it because the resistance I feel is so unpleasant and leads to being or doing nothing (!) I move in where I see an opening and am amazed that I feel "all is well." I can enjoy this process of riding through my resistance like the crest of a wave.*

Whitney's resolution resonated in the dreams of another member, Thea.

> **THEA:** *I'm near the shore when I hear lots of commotion—screaming and mention of a tidal wave. Taking no time to look, I run inland and uphill as far as possible. Am safe—have avoided the first wave. Remember my cats and call out to each of them. They come running—all are with me. There are a series of waves, so the trek inland and uphill continues, calling my cats as I do. They all respond in their own different times.*
>
> *Sit atop a hill on a rock on a mountain lake and look to the left below at the ocean and to the right below at the bay. See survivors at the ocean line—scurrying and wet. On the bay I see counterwaves formed by the originals striking the land and going backwards. See waves from the bay shore meeting mid-bay and forming a crest. Harmless wave. Sense all's clear now and prepare for downhill return with cats.*

Meet a woman who's invented pills to take to survive a tidal wave—absolutely no water content. They're especially for lifeguard type people—ones to survive and to help others. I don't see that the lack of water content is an advantage—all the salt water would make you thirsty. But she's so confident that I trust her word. She has a book coming out, too, about surviving a tidal wave. Wonder if it'd sell or not. People could just as easily write a book about surviving a hurricane and sell it on the East Coast. It seems, however, like an appropriate contribution, and after today may be just as needed (along with the pills). Her motives are pure.

These dreams describe the need to test the emotional water of the communal sea of consciousness in order to establish a sense of safety and to learn to survive emotional overwhelm, whether it be self-generated or the result of resonating with other dreamers' vibrations.

During this stage of the shared dreaming, people risk emotional meshing, even if the emotion is negative. They form stories about problematical content that nonetheless have positive outcomes. During Shared Dreaming, two members had parallel themes of flight and hiding.

WENDY: *I search for a way through to the "outside." I stop at an inner doorway and consider running through a room and taking off flying once I reach the outer doorway. That doorway is actually a double window/sliding glass door, so there's plenty of room for takeoff. But the room is the living room of some Indian couple's apartment. I couldn't just rush through when they weren't looking; I'd have to stop and open and close the door (or else crash through the window!) I'd have to stop and introduce and explain myself. Besides, this is their home—it'd be just plain rude!*

Since I still feel pursued, I go to another apartment, owned by an East Indian family. I eventually make a complete circle of it, ending up in the kitchen. The three young children spot me and follow me around, turning my furtiveness into a game of hide and seek. The father and mother join us in the kitchen, and we all talk in a spirit of friendly conviviality. By the end of the dream, the feeling of pursuit is gone, and I'm surrounded by playful friendliness instead.

EMILE: I go back to the house. . . . My stuff is on the second floor, my socks especially, and I know I can fly up there on my own, because I see myself in the air levitating to the second floor. But this is all in the realm of possibilities because I actually don't fly. I just see myself flying. . . .

I know now that the house is not mine and that someone else is living here. I then decide to look around the house, and I come across a box containing papers. I can't decide whether these papers are personal and important or just throwaway stuff. I take pleasure though, sneaking in as a spy. (The feeling is similar to what a child feels in an old attic.) The excitement has to stop because suddenly I can see a young girl running, through the window, and a small group of people is coming in the house. L., the lady who lives here, is among them.

As they get in, panic takes hold of me because 1) I'm half naked, I'm not wearing any pants, and 2) L. and the group don't know I'm here. I quickly grab my jeans and go in the toilet room for some privacy, but that is of no use because there are no doors. I then yell to L. that I'm in the apartment and that she shouldn't be afraid. Everyone then is gathered in the house.

On this same Shared Dreaming date, there were other reports of conflict. Charlene had two men fighting; Greg had a wrestling dream; Chad had a problem with a car.

However, there was also conflict resolution *in-dream*. Just as Emile prevented inner conflict by warning his female friend, and Wendy's chase turned into a game of hide-and-seek with children, so Charlene had a woman try to calm the fighting men, and Chad's problem was resolved with the help of the lights of another car. Only Greg was unable to resolve his conflict in this manner, and he would eventually drop out of the project.

Past the barriers of psychological conflict, dreamers feel more comfortable about being their persona-selves in company with each another. Nudity marks a shift from cognitive to emotional connection. As dreamers begin to go more scantily clad, those who are not usual "flashers" can feel quite nervous at first.

Exposure and intrusion was the concern of these members of Dreams[10].

KELLY: *I switch rooms in the dorm or camp, and wash out my underwear in another girl's room. I hope she won't think I am intruding.*

THEA: *I'm going to go swimming in a pool and choose between wearing a two-piece versus a one-piece bathing suit. Choose the latter, for it is more comfortable. The next time I'll wear a bikini. First be modest, and then reveal.*

But on the next target goal, Kelly resolved her exposure concerns in this way.

KELLY: *I am in the dorm with my roommate, Thea. We are both in bed, possibly the same bed. She is in bed also with her boyfriend. She is wearing something sexy. I am wondering if they will have sex—I am half hoping they will. They don't, and I wonder if I am in the way.*

My window curtain is flapping open, or I am opening it. I am thinking, "I'm not dressed, and all these people who are passing by outside the window can see me undressed, but I don't care—if being seen naked is bad, it's only a minor bad thing."

At the end of the Bay Area Dream Team project, there were reports of characters who clearly intended to strip down to the buff.

LAURA: *I see the [black woman's] butt is peeking out above her panties.*

GWEN: *There are two scantily clad girls . . . black and white . . . it's clear they will get nude. . . . The instructor makes a statement about me being lovely, though I'm not there to be a model.*

HENRIETTE: *[A gorgeous model] starts removing layers of clothes to show what's underneath. . . . The audience is a bit shocked.*

During Nexus, touching activities included Sean's hand shaking and Nora's soft hugs, as well as Wendy's breast sucking and Henriette's sensuous rubbing. Chad married his friend and imagined her naked. Sharon's friend "seems to get turned on and starts to get into my bed." Gwen's friend "mentions an affair with her therapist" and makes love. The same night Charlene dreamt of a friend having a tryst with a blonde. The bravest of souls are those who have the courage to include dreams with sexual metaphors.

CHAPTER 16

✦

DREAM CRAFT

Stage Five: Contest

O✦nce awareness of others in the dreamscape is established, dreamers begin to question where and why they might be coming together. To define the group task, project members first try to orient themselves in dream "space." If a particular waking spot is chosen, they may remote-view or go on a dream trip to that location. If the chosen spot is imaginary, they can dream using similar symbols. If no place is chosen, there can be journey themes in which the dreamer essentially asks, "Where am I going?"

This is the stage of the half-full/half-empty syndrome. Depending on their attitudes, dreamers can view dream space as a summer camp or a military camp; an operating room or a swimming pool; a bureaucracy or a school.

Almost every shared dreaming project defined the group task as some sort of "game." From Shared Dreaming come these two dreams:

FLYNN: *There is a large amount of confetti and loose change on the floor. I pick up the change and put it in a jar on the shelf.*

CHAD: *There's a carpet runner about two and a half to three feet wide. I find small change along the carpet: pennies, nickels, and dimes. There seems to be a young boy running along beside me or ahead of me also picking up change. I'm not sure if we're competing with each other or just playing together.*

The Dreams[10] project featured competition between the two different teams.

MALLORY: *A group separates. One part goes out; the part I'm in stays in the house. Then the other group returns. They've been drinking, are very exuberant.*

WENDY: *Friendly competition between two teams. . . . The other team is close to the water and so theoretically they should win a race to a pole in the water toward the west end of the bay. However, one of my female teammates runs down to the end of the roof and swings onto a rope, strung taut at a diagonal angle, and slides down it to the pier.*

THEA: *There's going to be a running race. . . . [The women] go fast and are really limber.*

EDWIN: *I continue running down the street, and it's as if I am a professional athlete in training for track competition.*

I feel very strong (much bulkier than I really am) and feel very much in control.

Whitney's first dream vividly describes the game as a martial arts event.

WHITNEY: *Team or teams of ten to twenty. A game of life is being played in a large modern gym. One side has more people, seems like more fun—they are talking, laughing, and obviously playing. Other group (way over on left end) is intense, wild, unpredictable. . . .*

At first I am with the larger group, then my attention is on the other. Some are carrying one from the first group to the second—looks like they're having fun. We are all wearing gees (martial arts "uniforms") with white belts (no distinguishing of rank—or, all beginners).

After one is carried to the second group, there seem to be only four. Most have dark hair. Even though this is the wild and intense and relatively serious group, this new guy and the others are freer to be and act how they wish in this group. So, it may appear he has been dragged here against his will, but now he'll discover his freedom and how much happier he will be.

Whitney also commented, "I sensed my being able to be a part of either team as a natural part of 'dream lucidity' that I seem to have automatically. . . . [I believe] the one team will grapple with this [second] level and discover something and bring it out into the open, something connected to freedom."

Facilitator Kitra P. responded to Whitney: "When we were choosing up the dream teams, much of it was done on feelings . . . of group connectiveness. When it came to you, there was a strong feeling that you were very comfortable on both teams, yet we finally decided you were on Team 1. Looks like a little ESP in the dream state!"

Whitney continued this theme throughout her dream reports. By the fifth target date, her dreams were reflecting her waking life, too: a rope training course she had taken.

WHITNEY: *I am being shown and told through my experience (as I do things): "You have done these tests of strength, ability, and courage." Several are involving leather straps with snaps for the wrists. I realize that I've done two tests involving the wrists and one other test. My fear and doubt about my ability are being transformed by my experience.*

The setting is outdoors where there's some excavation and construction. There are hills and chasms similar to the six-day ropes course (that I took last month). Those who are telling me what I've done, what I'm doing, and what I can do are like the trainers and assistants at the six-day.

So, I begin to take it in and feel good: I've done three tests—two involved my wrists, one my whole body. (At the six-day, there's the Rapelle, Lupine, and Tyrolean Traverse—they all involve the wrists and arms and whole body. The wrists don't have straps with snaps though.)

Contrast Whitney's view of the game as an increasingly successful test of strength with that of her teammate's dreams from the same target date. Bonnie was not a regular contributor of dreams. For her, the game degenerated from a children's contest into a serious war.

BONNIE: *We are going to fight a war, kind of make-believe war as kids do for play. The enemy army comes forward, in the bush, to the side, and hands me a sort of old rusty sword. The fight starts. The warriors are teenagers. No one has a great experience of wielding arms, so we look sort of embar-*

rassed and smile apologetically while fighting. And no one gets hurt.

In the second part of my dream I really worry because I am a pacifist at heart and I hate the idea of fighting and shedding blood—I find a way out. If I take my child along they won't make me fight—so I go and fetch him from a couple who has been taking care of him. He is a few months old. I put clothes on him and take him in my arms, ready to go.

I wake with an impeding sense of disaster and tragedy. War is unavoidable.

Half empty, half full. Who has the power and who feels helpless?

At first the game can be seen as a contest between "them" and "us" that calls for aggression and even violence. During the Shared Dreaming project, Charlene had this dream:

CHARLENE: We're all out together for a friendly stroll and shopping expedition, and we run into the bad guys. One of the men in our group, Chad, sets up a diversion by grabbing a bicycle from somewhere and whizzing past the bad guys, stiff-arming three of them in the process.

Was Charlene really dreaming about Chad? Yes, it would appear so. The same night, Chad recorded, "Part of the time it seems like we're riding a bicycle (both on one bike) on the left side of the street and part of the time we're walking."

But eventually aggression, anger, and entrapment can be handled with the calming of emotions. Also from the Shared Dreaming project are these two dreams:

EMILE: In between the two camps, a crazy woman suddenly appears; she is mad and throwing Molotov cocktails at each *side. I go after her, and there is a short pursuit that ends up when I finally corner her in the front alley of a commercial store. I have her trapped behind one of those retractable accordion iron gates very common in small shops. Although this last scene seems very action-packed, there is no big deal for me and I appear calm all the way through.*

CHARLENE: *But then I see one of the oldest ladies bearing down on me like a battleship under full steam, and I know I'm in for it. While the elderly lady spouts indignantly after me, I walk off with a small crystal, looking through [it] at the flowers and all the people from this interesting new perspective, feeling only very slightly guilty.*

Once the emotional concerns about the group task are resolved adequately, and dreamers demonstrate to themselves that they are, indeed, their own persons, the way is made open for rest, enjoyment, and relaxation in a group setting.

Stage Six: Recreation

Mutual dreamers seem to know when it's time to take a break from the effort of trying to struggle together. For example, the Shared Dreaming group's dreams made a very clear call for recess. On the seventh target date, about halfway through the project, comments from their dreams created this chain.

CHAD: *I don't know which way to go. . . .*
SHARON: *I feel weary. . . .*
BOBBIE: *Completely exasperated and quite out of my mind. . . .*

NORA: *We are discovering other people that are amongst us, also trapped.*

WENDY: *I'm going to cut down for shared dreaming. . . .*

FLYNN: *I know that spring and summer are the best times to make a change. . . .*

EMILE: *It is better to take our break now since we cannot continue. . . .*

CHARLENE: *We seem to have decided to take a vacation.*

The Shared Dreaming folks worked hard at their dreams and suffered from serious burnout. If they had all known about the approach of previous shared dreaming projects, they might have decided to relax together *in-dream*. This was the solution for certain members of Dreams[10] and the Lucidity Project. Five members of Bay Area Dream Team dreamt of going on vacation; three of them specifically mentioned Hawaii. Here are two of their dreams.

KARL: *I'm traveling with two couples, plus three other men, in a very large motor home on a vacation trip in Hawaii. We are coming close to the end of the day's travel and soon will be reaching the resort hotel where we'll spend the night. They've been drinking a lot and are beginning to act up obnoxiously. My "pal," who seems to own the motor home and has been driving most of the way, has promised the three men that each of them will have a chance to drive the motor home before we reach our destination, so he lets one of the men take the wheel. I think this is foolhardy for my pal to do, because the man is drunk enough to be unsteady on his feet, but I realize that "a promise is a promise."*

The next scene takes place in the resort's dining room, presumably the next morning, for we are walking from our cabins or rooms to get breakfast. I'm very hungry and am looking forward to eating breakfast. The dining room is already almost full, but we get seated right away; the room is all glassed in so we can look outside and see the trees and flowers, which are very luxuriant. When we walked over, the sky was clear and it was warm and sunny. Very quickly a heavy rain shower sweeps in, deluging the gardens and lawns with sheets of water, but still the temperature is warm, even tropical.

LAURA: In the restaurant with Tom. There is a feel of being on a journey—outside are highways, truck stops, motels, filling stations—automotive wandering American romance. A guy at the next table, bearded, someone Tom knows, asks him to pick up some Mateus. So I guess we're coming back. Tom agrees to do this. I think he's letting himself be used but keep my mouth shut. . . .

    This time the scene is clear; it is a beautiful little town overlooking the ocean. A road runs around the edge of the town and the ocean seems to flow on underneath the town. Everything is sunlit and brilliant. The man is with a woman, his wife. She is also on a scooter. They are tourists. They are riding slowly by, looking out over the ocean.

At this stage, the most successful mutual dreaming occurs with themes of recreation, especially involving water locations. Party celebration themes are also predominant, either to signal introduction to or closure of the social dreaming connection.

Nexus was successful in encouraging some of the ex-members of former projects to collaborate in creating a "round robin." Four participants provided their separate views of a shared dreaming event. When the jigsaw pieces were put together, they formed a communal pool in the larger sea of the unconscious.

The correlations may have been helped by the fact that the goal of this dream date was to "dream for Kyla," and some of the members of Nexus had actually met at Kyla Houbolt's apartment before the project began. However, two of the contributors to the jigsaw had not; they lived in locations too far away, but instead had sent along cassette audiotapes and photographs to introduce themselves to the group. Sharon and Nora lived at a distance; Henriette and Chad lived in the San Francisco Bay area; Henriette was an alumna of Bay Area Dream Team; the other three had been in Shared Dreaming. Yet these four managed to dream on the same theme. They had a **group meeting**.

Stage Seven: Collaboration

Once dreamers are comfortable with one another, they can turn their attention to the task they do together. This is the stage when communication and cooperation give way to collaboration. Collaboration means creating a shared space to play collectively with ideas and information. The group project task, to be in social relationship with one another, is described using network themes: creating a soup of many ingredients, sewing together pieces of material, or painting a huge communal mural.

Henriette, from the Bay Area Dream Team, dreamt of the task in this way:

HENRIETTE: *There's a group of people sitting around a table, working on a group project. We're all busy coloring in a huge rainbow on a large piece of paper. The colors are intense and vivid. I'm working on a magenta/plum segment. The color seems to have sparkle and glitter, so that it also shines silvery gold.*

GROUP MEETING

I'm on the back of a Harley-Davidson motorcycle, with someone else driving, roaring down a road. Suddenly the road kind of disappears and ends at a large swimming hole with lots of people in various stages of undress, bathing or sunning. Feels good.

HO

A father is entertaining some people by putting a large hollow head over his baby. He is a banker, and later I seem to become a guest in their house. Their home is beautiful with a pool with water slide where children are playing and an outdoor terrace.

SE

I am   surprised that someone   is in my car. She has brownish light hair, cut like Kyla's. She wants to know if I have a hot tub at the house. I say "Yes, please come in." She does so. In "my" house, I sense that this is a center for events, teachings, and community work. I lead her to the tub area. I remember that she comes in to the classroom area also. She talks about her husband and his work. I see him sitting in a large empty room, his back to the right wall. He is holding a young boy about thirteen years old in his lap.

NB

I'm at a house with a swimming pool in the backyard. I seem to go back and forth between the pool and the house. There's a woman with light brown or dirty blond hair. There are children in the backyard, many of them swimming in the pool. At one point a little girl of about two comes up and wants me to hold her. I sit on the ground at the end of the pool and hold her in my lap. She wants to kiss me, too. She opens her wet baby-mouth, but I kiss her several times on the forehead.

CU

Suddenly I look up and see two mandalas floating in a blue sky with white clouds. The mandalas seem to be like airline logos. I get the sense that one has to do with Mexico and the other, U.S. It's a pact of some sort that we're to incorporate in our rainbow project. The mandalas float down from the sky onto the top portion of our paper.

At the beginning of Nexus, Sharon dreamt a similar theme.

SHARON: I go into a room where the shared dreamers have gathered. I am fascinated by a work in progress. At one long rectangular table, a white canvas or cloth, the size of a bedsheet, has been spread over the table, and dreamers are painting on it, displaying the seaside things they saw in their shared dream experience at the beach. As I look closely, I can see that the entire canvas is softly painted and tinted, but the areas upon which the dreamers are working are actual pictures. For example, Chad has in front of him a lighted candle of a sort of Wedgwood or colonial blue— not bright sky blue but softer, perhaps some grayish toning down of bright blue—and elsewhere on the table is another lighted candle, both in candlesticks, the other being a different color, perhaps gold. In the process they are using, the candle is also used in the painting process, perhaps by dipping the brush in the wax somehow, although it is not the source of the colors, which are traditional watercolors or pastels or whatever each person is using. In front of Chad, and I don't know if it is his painting, is a picture of two or more sea creatures, dolphins, I think, dark-colored swimming in the water, facing each other as the water ripples around their turning bodies. *Very nice! The other drawings on the edges of the canvas or sheet are also interesting, and I realize they are the sum of the group's experience. I ask how they perform this painting technique since I wish to add my own.*

It doesn't take too much of a stretch of imagination to realize that these dreamers were equating their dream reports to paintings. This correspondence was especially evident during the July, 1984, target dreams from the Dreams[10] project.

PAT: *I have a large checked board in front of me. I am making some of the squares fly or float.*

CHARLENE: *I brush by a painting laid out on a table unformed, and some sand falls off it. I look and see that the painting is of rows of small squares, in each a tiny seashell, no two alike.*

KITRA: *An art show . . . like the Boardwalk Art show . . . down on the sand. [A woman] has several paintings. . . . They are thick oils, but there are lots of blues and greens in swirling colors and it is sort of an abstract design. . . . She paints a parrot on the bottom of one [box] and asks me whether he should be happy or sad. I say happy. . . .*

A lady is going to judge these ten small eight-by-ten watercolor drawings I have from these kids. . . . I think the woman might have been either Linda Magallón or Mallory, but I think Linda. We are discussing the pictures and how well they all did. All the pictures are wonderful.

The idea of judgment applies to those dreamers who are interested and involved in the process of comparing and contrasting the dreams of the group in the search for signs of mutuality. This requires a sensitivity to the patterns that mutual dream reports form as the dreams begin to mesh with and meet one another. Since both Pat and Kitra were team facilitators, they were engaged in such tasks. That's probably why Sharon used this same theme on me during Nexus.

SHARON: *Everyone is having a marvelous, low-key time, not a frantic party, but a gentle and warm intermingling of the guests as they get to know each other and compare pasts and present plans. Linda, for example, shows us some designs she has made on graph paper. There are symbols, and other natural objects, such as flowers and butterflies. She has colored in the first part of the pattern, but left uncolored those sections that will be "patterned repeats." The designs are to be transferred to fabric or tiles, possibly, and the neat thing about her work is that it is both creative and practical.*

Mutual dreamers seem to have a particular affinity for targets that involve some creative element. This Lucidity Project goal was to "Shop for a Christmas gift in the dream bazaar." Two members took this idea and ran with it.

SHARON: *In my dream bazaar, I wander among various merchandise on display and am especially interested in a small book with art prints. There are also art objects, jewelry, and other items for sale either displayed on the ground or on racks or shelves, although the place seems more indoors.*

I ask the price of several things, but since I don't understand the currency, have a problem with translating it into dollars. I select several items, including the art book I like, and am pleasantly surprised when the price in dollars is far less than I thought.

PAT: *I am in a large place—the section I am in is filled with tall bookcases which divide a large room into intimate areas. There are "creations" here—it's hard to describe— like one is a painting, but more than that it is living—like it is being created in the now. As part of the display there are library books and other material telling about that creation, like how to do it, history, etc., but these aren't to be taken out. The large bookcases are filled with books, comics, records—all kinds of things related to each creation—we can buy these things. I am very excited—the creativity seems so much fun. . . . The place is a kind of museum—like a living, current, creative museum where you can take part of it home.*

Individually, dreams seem to be unique creative endeavors that stand on their own, like paintings in separate frames, hung one after another down on a long wall. But unlike opaque media, dreams are translucent creations, akin to watercolor drawings on sheets of clear plastic. Place dream reports of mutual dreamers together and they begin to form a collage of information and imagery. Sections of dream reports can be woven together in those chains, jigsaws, and other sociometric patterns to form complete stories of communal events. But the dreams describe the potential for and process of the weaving by using creative imagery like a communal mural or a living museum.

Stage Eight: Magical Spirit

Up until now, the majority of mutual imagery has been of the mundane variety; that is, it is composed of motifs and activities consistent with waking events. However, it is quite possible for the dreaming mind to rise above the surface of physical reality into the archetypal zone.

When a dream is brought to them for processing, Jungian dreamworkers often use a technique called "amplification." This method involves inflating our usual dream symbols and correlating them with anthropological, religious, philosophical, and mythical symbolism drawn from the past. Contemporary dreamworkers will also include future-oriented symbols from high-tech and science fiction as well as from modern art, music, drama, and literature.

But dreams can do it for themselves! Just as competition leads to cooperation and communication precedes collaboration, so artistic imagery transforms into the archetypal. Group activities become rituals and performances. Terrestrial symbols rise up to become balloons, spaceships, and pageants in the sky. Normal skills shift to supernormal powers like astral projection, psychokinesis, flying, and transformation.

At this stage, group energy is flavored by the increasingly ethereal imagery of individual dreamers. These two dreamers from Shared Dreaming dreamt a ritual that one dreamer saw simply as passing a piece of wood. But the other pictured it as the psionic levitation of a steel bar.

EMILE: *I see that a shamanistic ritual is going on: people are passing to each other a little piece of wood (about 5 to 6 inches high) which is meant to be a power object. I'm somewhat reluctant to see this happening as I don't really know where I personally stand towards this ritual.*

LINDA: *I am seated with a group of people in a circle. We are practicing group telekinesis by levitating several different sized and shaped objects including a long notched steel bar. We first rotate it, then move it from side to side, like a helicopter blade.*

Bodies wrapped in bedsheets or bulky clothing are a symbolic representation of the astral experience of being "out-of-body." Usually, this theme is taken quite "lightly." From Dreams[10]:

CHARLENE: *I've been wearing a ragged pair of bloomer-like pants. And a man throws them over a high cliff. . . . The man laughs at me as I stand at the cliff edge looking down. . . . And then I hurl myself off the cliff edge into the air.*

KELLY: *I assist myself by imagining I have helium balloons under me and I am standing on them. . . . At one point I am flying so high it is beautiful. I am experimenting with having helium balloons above my head and wonder, how high can helium balloons go?*

GLORIA: *A man calls to me across the room. I walk towards him, folding to my knees in front of him. He asks me what's in my balloon. At first I don't get it, then say, "Oh! A balloon, like, what's in a word balloon going up and down in your head?" pointing to his head. He nods, "Yes, that's it. What's your greatest wish? Mine is to have the whole lot of us meet in the out-of-body!" We all say this is a great idea. I remark, "It's never quite like you think it'll be." He agrees . . . showing me how he floats awkwardly on his back. Another woman shows how she staggers around as if drunk; and a man demonstrates how one leg folds out from under him as he tries to walk. This break us up with laughter.*

At other times the "out-of-body" theme crescendos into a moving spiritual experience. These dreams are from the Lucidity Project:

CLARA: *I am in a church, and a pageant is taking place. I am standing at the pulpit waiting to sing a duet with a man. We start singing and intermittently use sign language. We both are wearing small dainty necklaces of an oil lamp. We hold the necklaces up in front of us and move them around using some kind of symbolic movements. The song we are singing is about symbols, and at one point we touch our hearts and imply a meaning the entire audience understands. There seem to be people everywhere.*

The pageant continues. Several men carry in long tables, and on the tables are rows of chairs with schoolchildren sitting on them, as if they are on a school bus. The announcer tells the children to go to the playground and play. All the children file off the tables and out of the room.

SYLVIA: *I am standing outside alone. I turn and notice hundreds of people emerging from my left. There are eight men; two on either side of two bright shiny new trucks. They each have one hand placed under the truck to lift it. To my amazement, the trucks and all the people are slowly rising in the air. I walk under these people as they rise higher and higher. At this point I become very emotional as I see them all dissolve into hot orange coals and fall back to earth.*

I know these people have "believed" so strongly that they do not have to die a physical death to merge with All That Is, that all they have to do is will themselves to God.

Now I notice another smaller group approaching. This time there are many children with the group. They are also rising in the air. I am crying hysterically by now, so moved by the beauty of the procession. I smile and wave.

Upbeat themes and levitation parallel a rise in awareness, a shift to positive imagery and increased activity. The magical plateau marks the beginning of yet another developmental phase in dreaming, one that requires the use of advanced dreaming skills like the increased consciousness of lucidity, the psychic ability to peer beyond surface façades, the tactile and visual awareness of bordering on another's dream, and the creative incubation of symbolic imagery. But the successful use of such skills for intentional mutual dreaming purposes is always dependent on the foundation of sociability that is built in the continued practice of reciprocal dreaming under the partnership model.

Part Five

◆

Results
of
Research

CHAPTER 17

◆

The Environmental Effect

The Men in Black

I am running, running, pushing, forcing, faster, faster. It's so hard to push myself! I am pursued by the Mafioso. The Men in Black are running, leering after me.

As I press my head and torso forward, my legs lift behind me. In time, I become airborne. I am spread flat on the air, trying to get ahead through the thick atmosphere. But it's like pushing through molasses. I can never get higher than the Mafiosos' outstretched arms.

They reach out and grab for my ankles. . . .

*E*ndlessly repeating itself, this tape loop dream was my main nightmare for over thirty-eight years. In some cases the Men in Black actually managed to grasp my feet. More often, the nightmare ended before they could do so, and I'd jerk awake in a sweat, my heart pounding.

I had just finished including the nightmare in a new piece of writing when my sister Cynthia came to visit. I handed her the manuscript to read and walked into the kitchen to get both of us something to drink.

"Oh, my god!" I heard her groan. I ran back into the living room.

"What's the matter?" I asked anxiously.

"I had the same dream!"

"Are you sure?" I couldn't believe it. Cynthia is fourteen years younger than me. I'd never told the nightmare to her, nor anyone else in my birth family, either. Sharing dreams just wasn't done.

I asked Cynthia to write down her version of the childhood dream and send it to me. This is what she had to say:

"The majority of my flying dreams I've had as a child or young adult. I don't recall any in recent years. My flying method was always to run as fast as I could and lean my upper torso forward. Then, using my arms as fins at my sides to guide and balance myself, I would take my feet off the ground and proceed upward. The longer I was in the air, the faster and higher I could fly. Unfortunately, if I didn't get up enough speed while running, I'd get a couple feet off the ground and drop back down again and have to run some more. Occasionally I was flying for the sheer pleasure of it, but more often I was being pursued.

"The most memorable dream occurred when I was no older than twelve."

It is daytime. I am in the garage peeking out the side door, looking down the street to see if all is clear. It is, so I make a run for it out into the street. I need a head start and a long takeoff strip to get into the air. Escape only comes from gaining altitude.

I have a head start, but they are coming after me. "They" are two or three men whose presence is always threatening. They are evil men, and I associate them with being spies (although in waking life I admire spies like James Bond and John Steed). Because of the spy image, perhaps, I recall trench coats and hats, which also prevent me from getting a good look at them. Their faces remain in shadow.

I don't know why they are after me, but they terrify me, and I know I can't let myself get caught. So I run and run. I want to fly so badly that I elevate myself before gaining enough speed, and, like a car running out of gas, I come coasting back down again. I remember gliding so close to the ground that I can see the street gravel and feel it brush my chest and legs as my horizontal body coasts mere inches above. I put my hands down to stop myself completely and then stand upright and begin running again.

By this time, the spies are right behind me. As I push and strain myself into the sky, they are on my heels, literally. For, as I become airborne, I can feel their hands grabbing at my feet. But I can fly faster than they can run, and I get away.

"On this occasion my dream ended in exhilaration, like swimming underwater and then bursting the surface as you come up for air. Other times I would awaken in anxiety just as the spies grabbed at my feet."

Neither Cynthia nor I have the recurring nightmare any longer, and the series terminated for Cynthia while she was

in her late twenties, a good ten years sooner than mine
ended. Perhaps each child in line gets better at resolving conflicts. I decided to write my other sister and brothers and ask
if they've had similar dreams, also.

I struck out with my brother Gerry. He remembered
hardly any dreams, and nothing that resonated with the Men
in Black nightmare. My brother Ken reported back that he
remembered trying to fly away from women!

"As a kid, I had a number of pursuit-type dreams, complete with molasses and dead ends," Ken wrote. "The
pursuers in those dreams were scary but usually unidentifiable; sometimes human and sometimes monsterlike. My
"flying" dreams have progressed slightly over my lifetime
from short glides and unsuccessful, limb-churning attempts,
to barely successful, limb-pumping flights of low altitude,
which always required constant or intermittent effort to sustain. The purpose of the flights was usually (or always) to
avoid an unidentifiable person, sometimes female."

But I hit the jackpot with my sister Debbie. She wrote
back:

"There are very few dreams that I can remember from
my childhood, but the one which you described is one of
those which I do recall. It went as follows:

*I am running through a forest, being chased by three or four
men in dark suits. I don't know who they are or why they
are chasing me, but I do know that they are "bad men." I
am well ahead of them, but I know the only way to keep
them from eventually catching me is to fly. As I attempt to
become airborne, my pace slows considerably. I push myself
to go higher, but it takes all my effort, and the men are
getting closer. They grab at my ankles, but I am just barely
beyond their reach. Then I wake up.*

"Although this dream left enough impression on me to
be remembered after all these years, I only had it once. I

believe I had a couple of dreams on a similar theme—attempting to fly to escape something and having trouble getting airborne. However, once I'd get high enough, flight would become easy and I would be able to circle back and soar high above whatever was chasing me."

After receiving my sister's letter, I paused to consider the irony of the situation. Here I was seeking the ultimate in positive mutual dreams, and it turned out that my own first mutual dreaming experience was that repeating nightmare!

The same nightmare in a single family—it had to be some powerful metaphor for what was really going on beneath our troubled waters. And a continuing problem, too, given the fourteen-year span between the oldest and youngest of us. Together, my sisters, brother and I had dreamt a perfect model of "criminal" family energy. A review of our mutual dreams added fresh insight to a traumatic time when our lives were under the arbitrary control of our parents. But now we were adults, and I was attempting to dream as an adult.

As the years of dream research passed, I noticed two special things about my dream life. My flying improved tremendously, and my dream content dropped from 100% negative to less than 10%. Part of this I attributed to dreamwork done by myself or in groups. Part of it was the increased awareness of lucid dreaming. But I was soon to discover that mutual dreaming made me a participant in a much bigger movement that is changing the dream environment from a shadow world to a world of wonder.

Spontaneous Negativity in Dreams

What's the most common theme in people's dreams? Fear and anxiety! It's as true for the general dream as it is for an important subset that is closely related to mutual dreaming: the psychic dream.

When it comes to spontaneous psychic dreams, researchers report that the majority fall under the term "crisis telepa-

thy." For example, over half of the 149 cases gathered by
Frederic W. H. Myers dwelled on the theme of death. The
second largest category were those in which the person
dreamed about was in danger or distress. Ian Stevenson discovered that the majority of spontaneous cases of precognitive dreams were premonitions of death, disaster, and
danger. In addition, successful dream telepathy experimentation both in and out of the lab highlights the category of
aggression.

Like most private and telepathic dreams, the majority of
spontaneous mutual dreams are likely to be either nightmares or contain some sort of blatant fear or implied conflict.
A full 49% of 84 published spontaneous mutual dreams were
negative. This certainly jibed with my own personal experience and that of my sisters and brother.

Dreams as Conflict Resolvers

When it comes to field projects, a goal to heal or problem
solve is virtually guaranteed to evoke negative emotions and
imagery in at least some of the dreamers. Specializing in con-
flict-driven dreams is unlikely to produce positive adventures for a group; concentrating on idea production rarely
reveals the people behind the material. It's more likely that
the healing motivation will set us off on a continual shadow
journey. Six or more goal dates of group problem solving is
too much work for the dreaming mind. The result is burnout
and the production of individual anxiety dreams, which
simply starts the cycle again. Nightmare activities "ground"
us in the underworld or the waking plane, but don't lift us
into the upper realms.

The reality of the cultural situation is that there are those
who come to shared dreaming projects with the best of intentions to act in a positive, upbeat way, but who nonetheless drag their own conflicts into the group unconscious.
Because dream study is so strongly associated with therapy,
a goodly number of folks think that shared dreaming is and

should be an open invitation to use the dream group as a dumping ground for their personal (and global) problems. So the dreams they share are episodes of pain and trauma. It's as if they stand in the middle of the field of dreams, screaming at the top of their lungs, eyes closed and oblivious to the rest of the group. Any member with the least proficiency in ESP is going to notice these self-absorbed "loud mouths" and sense their negative broadcasts.

If learning to resolve or go beyond such problems is seen as part of the journey, the group will emerge out of the valley of shadows and into the plateau of successful human interaction and understanding. But if conflict is considered to be an ongoing lifestyle, the partners will falter in their efforts to achieve such goals.

Team Attempts to Shift Attitudes Within the Dream

Group members can select several responses toward their errant members. They can choose to ignore them. They can recognize those dreamers in their dreams, but keep their distance. They can try to help their fellow members through their dreams or by way of written commentary or oral suggestion. Or they can concentrate their efforts on resonating with those who are not in conflict.

This is often the best response. The group then creates a new model of interaction. This model provides another option, a new way of being in the dream, for those who are caught in a squirrel cage of negative dreaming. The shared dreaming model encourages them to lay aside their problems for a time and get involved in a creative or recreative activity, instead. Patience and a sense of humor go a long way toward aiding this end.

Sometimes these troubled dreamers open their dream eyes and look around, realizing that most of the rest of the group is playing ball, instead. Good example helps change their complaining tone. Some respond to group "helping" dreams. But, unfortunately, others are just too immature to bother to learn good dream manners. The only solution I know is to set firm guidelines and keep emphasizing the co-operative aspects of positive mutuality. Those that don't play by the rules of the collaborative game eventually get bored and drop out on their own. Others finally "get it," and their dreams begin to show evidence of harmony. But it can take a while. The rest of the team members have to be good sports to put up with them in the meantime.

The Environmental Effect

When I reviewed those dreams incubated with the intention of being mutual productions, a whole new pattern emerged. In shared dreaming projects, no matter what the stated goals, deliberately incubated mutual dreams were most likely to be positive. *Seemingly* mutual dreams that contained implied or actual conflict were most apt to feature one-way monologues.

Only 17% of 40 published intentional mutual dreams were negative. During the shared dreaming projects, a similar percentage, 19% of 161 dream groups or pairs, began with negative themes. But not all of them stayed that way.

The pair of dreams by shared dreamers on page 263 shows a parallel shift from negative to positive emotions. The decrease in negative dream content as a result of intentional mutual dreaming is a very significant finding. I call it the **environmental effect.**

The bicycle symbology and the flying activity signal the ability to exercise mental and emotional balance, so necessary to achieve in order to successfully dream together in light of so many waves of potentially unsettling energy caused by the people around us. But it isn't just a static balance, like standing on one foot. This is balance caused by continually moving forward—toward the positive.

The mutual dream that lifts upward from mundane to magic is the antidote to the mutual nightmare. In the eighth

THE ENVIRONMENTAL EFFECT

I'm driving a big vehicle, awkward. Just learning foot pedal control. Drive into a street. Cop stops us and others. Must get out. Go off towards woods. Vehicles becomes a bicycle. You pedal forward to go and pedal backwards (at least one rotation) to stop. I'm getting great at it.

Am going downhill on woods path. Couldn't have done this before when I was just learning. I have to pull off now and then to allow others coming up to get through . . . .

There's a large beautiful bird that soars over the sea, dips under the water, and continues to fly underwater! I'm awed—absolutely beautiful! Watch more birds in an artificial closed environment. The space is more cramped and so the soaring is more like short flights. The wings look compressed. It's a large tank with transparent plastic walls elevated about twenty-five feet above water. It looks as if they could fly away, but they don't. It's very rhythmic and beautiful. See their intense and piercing eyes as they dive toward the water and as they ascend from the water. Very majestic and magical.

TT

I am peddling a bicycle up a rocky hill without shade. It is slow going. I see a shortcut and decide to take it despite a sign reading "No Trespassing." A cop comes chasing me. I try to elude him, first by running and then by hiding behind bushes. I have a feeling of dread, and I am angry with myself for being in such a hurry that I broke the rule. Other people are watching me, and I feel embarrassed as well. I realize that I can continue trying to evade the cop, or I can just act normal and he may decide to forget the whole thing. I begin mingling with the crowd, feeling okay about my situation, whether or not I get a ticket. I realize that I need to slow down, which was what I needed to understand . . . .

I am watching a diver practicing his dives for racing. He is a very handsome athlete, young, muscular, tan, and good-looking. His dives are perfect. He zooms straight as an arrow through the air for quite a ways, then he enters the water just a tiny bit, swims a couple of strokes, and reaches the other side. He is very fast and efficient. I am impressed, but I feel that his pool is too small to practice racing. Then I realize that he doesn't want to practice swimming but just his dives, so the pool is a perfect size. Such shallow quick dives!

BH

stage of social dreaming development, there is learning, growth of understanding, and resolution of conflict *in-dream*.

Our current astrological age of Pisces pictures us dreamers as fish in the vast sea of unconscious, swimming in dichotomistic circles, oblivious to our true heritage. When we're asleep we think we're fish, instead of human beings. And these days the sea of unconscious is likely to be both salty and polluted.

The partnership model of mutual dreaming is a container of cleansed dreams that we pour out onto the waking universe just like the Aquarian Water Carrier pours out her pure water as a stream that flows into the unconscious sea. The "Aquarian Age" ideals of cooperation, interdependence, and mutual responsibility are a perfect match with partnership dreaming. And they produce dream environmentalists.

A dream environmentalist has the same concern for the health of the environment of the dreamworld as an environmentalist has for waking physical reality. Both understand the need to achieve a level of social transformation to affect change in the way we live. Day residue is handled so well it becomes purified: a gift that is poured back into the land of dreams.

Most of my colleagues are dreamworkers. They still concentrate their efforts on cleaning up at the end of the stream, doing work on dream productions already completed by break of day. Some of them spend precious lucid dreaming time doing the cleanup work in-dream. What's intriguing about the environmental effect is that this same process is accomplished "automatically" in the midst of nonlucid dreams.

Can the waking self aid in this effort? Yes. I believe it's time to go upstream, back to the night before, and help clear the field of debris that can choke the emergence of positive dreams.

Learning to Encapsulate and Process Negative Day Residue

When I approach a mutual dreaming night in a bad mood, then anger, sadness, or depression can be projected toward my dreaming partners. If I spend the day at the computer, the mental activity of reading, writing, and moving words about can be incorporated into my dreams. If I'm in physical pain or ill health, that can influence my dreams as well.

When my mutual or telepathic project was just a one-on-one situation, I might be able to ask for a rain check. But when I committed to a group, then I had to go ahead with the experiment no matter what my physical, mental, or emotional state. I had to learn a way that would assure that the personal distraction be minimized.

After trying out several possibilities, I came upon a method I call **encapsulation.** Whereas the natural process of sleeping has the effect of decreasing or eliminating external sensory noise, encapsulation is a technique to cut down on internal physical, intellectual, or emotional noise. Such "noise reduction" allows us the opportunity to hear and send information on the intuitive-perceptive channel.

In turn, I shared this technique with other dreamers, including dreamworker friend Jill Gregory. Jill has this to say about the idea:

> "I see myself as a perceptive, sensitive, intuitive, intense, emotional, and socially oriented person. My life is extremely complex and interesting. For many years I have developed various dream skills including **incubation.** I knew that it was useful to process the day and clear an inner mental and emotional space for the incubation, but I thought that the better I became at incubating, the less I would need to do it. That was fairly true as long as I was just dealing with my own dreaming mind.
>
> "However, one time I was at a concert and the music moved me to grieve my first marriage in a new way. I figured that a feeling evoked by music, experienced fully and released, would not interfere with my role during the shared dreaming that night. But my dream partners picked up on the topic and feelings in their dreams of me anyway.
>
> "Now, if we were just trying to be telepathic, they

would be lauded for receiving something that I wasn't even aware of sending. However, shared dreaming has a different purpose. Most people do not appreciate experiencing the grief that resonates with similar emotions and thoughts in their own dreams. Maybe that is not how you want to relate to them in dreaming, either!

"So, we tried to notice in ourselves what thoughts, feelings, observations, and reflections, occurrences, etc. of the day, or past days, might be likely to be sent in a dream. If there was something major or long-term in our life, we would address that as well. The next method I tried was **repression.**

"I would say to myself, 'Hmm. This phone call from my stepson is pushing (or will probably push) a lot of buttons for me. But I do not want to send this stuff to my shared dreaming group tonight. So I will not deal with it at all today. I will not feel my emotions, think about the conversation or the situation, and I will not discuss it or process it alone or with my family. I will deal with it tomorrow when I can treat it properly and not mess up my shared dreaming project.' This way I thought I would be successful at delaying my inner experience of the event until the next day or two.

"But, lo and behold! My dream partners would be even *more* likely to pick it up on our shared dreaming night! Repression was a great way to send unpleasantries, intensities, and private matters! At this point, Linda tipped me off to **encapsulation.**

"The basic idea for encapsulation is to acknowledge the content that you do not wish to send while seeing it held within a sealed container which you are in charge of and which you keep connected to you.

"One way is to image it in some type of container that I see as being located in my mind. I find this works especially well for things that are primarily thoughts, beliefs, and mental images that engage or hook me through thinking. Other times, such as for a call from my stepson, the container will be located in my heart, because this is primarily an emotional connection. Emotion is the hook for my attention.

"I also imagine it, still in a sealed container, floating outside my body and connected to me by a cord as sturdy as the intensity of the imagery required. If I find I am starting to engage with it, I imagine it moving either away from me (as if I am unconsciously sending it off) or towards me (as if I am unconsciously receiving it). But I don't let it get too far away so others can pick it up when they target me.

"It's fun to be creative with the container because then the unconscious is more involved in the process and the chosen container will be more accurate. Balloons, boxes, drawers, safes, bags, and metal drums are some suggestions. The important thing is that they are sealed until I open them. And I do commit myself to opening them at an opportune moment after shared dreaming night.

"I found these ways of encapsulating imagery to be quite effective and soon discovered that they were easy to do. During daily experience, I would note, 'This is intense for me, and tonight will be shared dreaming night. I do not want to send this or have others pick this up when they try to tune in on me. What will I do with it?' And Boom! the answer would come from my subconscious, giving me the perfect and effective image to use.

"It is probably possible to do a generalized encapsulation for a specific time period. Like this: 'Anything that happens this week, up to a certain point (i.e., if my child has a high fever, to heck with shared dream clarity!) will be automatically sent to its appropriate compartment of a sturdy sealed container outside my body linked to me by a medium-length strong cord.'"

My own version of **encapsulation** is to picture a troublesome problem or intrusive imagery as a package that I place on an imaginary "holding shelf." This is only a temporary location, however. Like Jill, I make a commitment to my unconscious that I will retrieve the package as soon as I can— usually the next day. And I do honor that commitment!

Under the partnership model, I get best results when I play fair with both dream partners and my unconscious mind.

When I address the problem, I can use all those wonderful techniques of traditional dreamwork—interpretation, association, reentry, amplification, gestalt dialogue, and so forth. But I apply these to my waking-state problem. That's right, I do dreamwork on my waking life. Since I can do dreamwork on my waking life the day following the dream, it makes sense that I can do the same thing the previous night. Ideally, this is the preferred time to do dreamwork—before I go to sleep. Then there is no need to encapsulate. By doing "daywork" on "day residue," the way is made clear for the production of creative upbeat dreams.

A Shift in Spontaneous Dreams

Encapsulation, daywork, and in-dream conflict resolution may clear the sea of dreams from toxins and pollutants, but they don't add back the creative nutrients. To generate dream adventures requires fresh new incubation. Or perhaps it's the intention to act less like a worker bee and more like a playful being that does the trick.

I'm not sure which was most scary: to finally share my inner life with my siblings or to go flying in the waking state. Probably both. Shifting focus to positive dreams gave me the courage to try more daring waking-state events. Then I discovered my dream partners had resonance with my current life. So I wrote an article about it.

This article was then transcribed into a manuscript I entitled "Follow the Flying Heroes." Along with my inquiry about our childhood nightmares, I sent the following manuscript as a gift to my brother and sisters for taking the time and effort to respond.

Follow the Flying Heroes

Recall had been poor that month, so to energize new dreams, I retrieved an old, handwritten dream report from my journal and typed it into the computer. The dream featured two of my favorite dream activities, flying and sex. Soon I was captivated by the sensory feelings and uplifting imagery.

Down the building steps I come and stand where the Greatest American Hero is seated with his partner. The partner informs the light-haired Hero that I am going to work with him as his teacher.

"You have on your super suit?" I ask the Hero. He does; I can see the red collar peeking out from under his business outfit.

"Let's fly," I invite him, grabbing hold of his hand and lifting the both of us. Once in the air, he wobbles. I reach a leg underneath him to catch his feet and stabilize him. We are following a freeway route north when we see an alien spacecraft coming our way. So we duck underneath a freeway overpass with triangular girders that remind me of the Brooklyn Bridge. Although we're out of sight as they pass overhead, I sense the spaceships still know where we are.

"They're homing in on the suit!" I tell the Hero, "Let's go this way." We fly across a bay. In the water I see men in a tangle of arms and legs.

Then I'm with the Hero, floating above him in bed. I drift down to have sex with him. We stand, caressing one another. "I'm married," he whispers softly. "So am I," I say.

LINDA LANE MAGALLÓN, 8/15/84

The Greatest American Hero was a live-action TV science fiction series that ran from 1981–83, just during the time in which I became interested in dreams. According to the story line, aliens in a UFO give Ralph Hinkley a red super suit that

provides him with special abilities, including the power of
flight. Unfortunately, Ralph loses the instruction booklet for
the suit and can never quite attain aerodynamic stability.

I had told no one but my husband, Manny, about the
superhero dream. A couple of days after computer input of
this earlier dream, Jill Gregory called and related her own
dream of the previous night:

> I am flying with Eddie Arnold in his own personal two-
> or four-person airplane. We only fly above the streets and
> highways, quite low, maybe six to ten feet above the ground.
> He is happy and excited, showing his plane to me. It is red
> and white on the outside . . . very comfortable. . . .
>
> He starts to fondle me, putting his arm around me,
> getting close and beginning to feel my chest. I say, "You'd
> better keep looking where you are going!"
>
> He replies that the plane is on automatic pilot or cruise
> control. He and I resume friendly activities, getting more
> and more sexual.
>
> Suddenly I realize the plane has landed itself and is
> taxiing along a long driveway. Anticipating trouble but
> nothing too serious, I watch while he fondles me. Appar-
> ently I think he needs to learn a lesson. We crash into his
> farmhouse barn door. The plane and door are damaged but
> not hopelessly. We aren't hurt or even frightened.
>
> Eddie is mad for costing himself so much money. I know
> he'll concentrate on his piloting more in the future. Through-
> out all this, I am attracted to his dignified manner, his
> silvery hair, his twinkling eyes and air of success.
>
> JILL GREGORY, 4/30/90

I noticed that both Jill's dream and my own had sexy red
vehicles (the plane and super suit). In each dream, we had

flown, following the length of a highway. Plus we'd both enjoyed the company of a male who was not our spouse. Jill noted that although he looked like Eddie Albert from the old *Green Acres* show, she called her guy "Eddie Arnold."

Unknown to either of us, two days after Jill's dream, a second dreamworker friend, Melinda Nelson, had a dream flight with another Arnold. He wasn't her husband, either!

It's night and I find myself outside in an open rural setting. I begin to fly. I bounce off of the earth, and as if doing the backstroke, I fly at about a forty-five-degree angle upwards. I bend my knees, point my toes, and gracefully gesture with my arms, as if doing water ballet. I'm very pleased with the artistic feel of this flight. As I begin to soar upwards, I'm soon joined by Arnold Schwarzenegger.

We're flying through the air in a ballroom dancing style, weaving in and out of each other's path, sometimes touching, sometimes not, yet we are always within a very few inches of each other. The tone is sensual and erotic, and we talk together in a romantic way. I'm looking at his very muscular arms in a short-sleeved shirt, admiring him. He has a sweet, kindhearted playful manner which I enjoy.

I'm aware that this is a prefame stage of his life, and I somehow know that a very successful and famous future awaits him, yet this is at the back of my mind. I'm really just enjoying him in this moment. . . . He says something about not really having a job yet, or making much income, but I'm not bothered by this. I also realize he has a bright future ahead of him and am enjoying this youthful innocent stage that he's in right now. MELINDA NELSON, 5/2/90

Two flying Arnolds? The synchronicity was too delightful to pass up. I asked both Jill and Melinda to send copies of their dreams to me in the mail. The night after I received Jill's dream sheet and put it together with the others in order to write this article, I had a dream of flying next to a plane inside which a couple were busy fondling one another. It was as if I were peeking into Jill's dream, in much the same way as I had done while reading her report. Then the dreams bounded into the waking state.

The day after Melinda's dream, I started a new waking-state flying adventure. Hang gliding! During my first ground school lesson, at Mission Soaring Center in Milpitas, California, I hung from a practice frame in tandem, next to the flight instructor, Rob Engorn. There I learned to maneuver the triangular aluminum control bar (like a girder in my "Hero" dream). I was the only female among the men struggling to get in and out of the tangle of harness straps. As I wondered how much strength it would take to pick up a glider before getting airborne, I admired the muscle tone of my teacher's biceps, which were peeking out from underneath his short-sleeved shirt. I also noticed the streak of silver in his light-colored hair.

To stabilize and pilot a hang glider in tandem requires quite a bit of touching and holding on to one another in order to align two bodies in a parallel direction. On the inside I was having a giggle fit at all the synchronicities between dream and waking life, but outside I was as calm as a butterfly resting in a cocoon. Thank goodness for my instructor's friendly, professional manner, so necessary to reassure a neophyte in the risky sport of hang gliding.

A week later, at the first outdoor flying lesson, I told Rob my dream. But the rest of the dream didn't come true until our tandem flight.

With terrified excitement I stood at the edge of the mountain ridge. The glider promised resurrection, though. It was named the "Phoenix Dream"!

We balanced the wings of the "Dream" as they rippled in the gusts of wind. Our audience consisted of two glider students, Rob's girlfriend and a herd of cattle chomping the grassy acreage of a nearby hill. My husband, Manny, was fifty feet down the forty-five-degree slope, waiting to capture the event on video camera.

Ready, set, we began to stride forward. Rob and I took off, and I yelped in exultation. As we passed overhead, Manny panned backward and almost fell off the mountain from the displaced weight of the camera! The image on the film bounced and joggled just like my stomach. Rob and I were caught by strong crosswinds, producing a glide as wobbly as my dream flight with the Greatest American Hero. Three miles west from ridge to sea we flew, then turned to parallel the coastline. Rob gestured below: we were flying directly over and following Highway 1 northward. "It's just like my dream!" I exclaimed to him.

Then we stepped out of the air and into a lone prickly bush in the midst of the meadow by the sea. But we hardly noticed it. Another yell of triumph and a hug. We had landed! Climbing out of the harnesses, Rob pointed to the red collar peeking out of his blue overcoat. "See!" he said, "I have on my super shirt!"

Correspondences between the waking events and dreams of myself and my friends flew through the air like some playful night creature, bouncing from one person to another, and flitting back to me. As long as the three of us women were having telepathic dreams, I'd just as soon they be positive thrills, rather than the traumatic, dramatic variety. Sexual-flying dreams fit the bill just fine. And what a great way to incubate waking life!

Response from My Sister Debbie

I had sent my sister Debbie this "Flying Heroes" manuscript along with the Men in Black nightmare. She responded to both, with her version of our old nightmare dredged up from the past and then from the present. . . .

"After reading your letter, I was thinking that I hadn't had a flight dream since I was a preteen. But something was bothering me; then I remember that although I haven't had a "free flight" dream since that time, I did have a dream about flying the night before I received your letter. After reading your manuscript excerpt, I thought you might find it interesting.

> *I am standing on my front lawn as a red helicopter is coming toward me, flying low over my house. As it passes in front of me, I discover that I am holding on to a bar along with two other girls. The other girls are teenagers, and I realize that I am also in the body of a teenager. As the helicopter passes, it attaches to the bar and we are pulled through the air holding on it like a hang glider. I enjoy flying because we are close enough to the ground that I could jump down without much harm if I needed to. The pilot follows my street toward the west, then turns to follow it toward the east, but as he does I am worried he will start to climb too high. I wake up.*

"Well, my dream didn't have any sex in it, but I thought some of the elements in it were quite similar to those in your flying heroes manuscript."

Sibling resonance sure works well for both negative *and* positive dreams.

CHAPTER 18

✦

$\mathcal{V}$OTE OF THE $\mathcal{D}$REAMING $\mathcal{S}$ELVES

$\mathcal{U}$nderneath the covers, there's a revolution going on. A fresh wind is blowing across the sea of unconsciousness. It's a shift from negative to positive experience. The storm clouds of anxiety and nightmare are parting to admit the blue sky of sunshine, delight, and wonder.

We shared dreamers did pick the right vehicle, the partner-ship, to launch ourselves into into the Sea of Pisces. Like Columbus and his cronies, we were explorers of the unknown leading edge. We got together in a little flotilla of sailboats to set sail for the Age of Aquarius. And then the flotilla began to scatter.

"It's like trying to get a bunch of chickens to walk in the same direction," said Bill Stimson, first publisher of *Dream Network Bulletin*. That's how he described his frustration in trying to organize an international network of dream communities when interviewed by *Omni* magazine in 1983.

I know exactly how he feels, and it isn't just because I

also published *DNB* for three years, or served as a leader of Bay Area Dreamworkers Group, or any other waking-state communal commitment. It's because I've tried to get folks to dream together in the partnership paradigm. And I've discovered that we do have something in common: we're individualistic and independent. We want to interpret our own dreams. We want to do things our own way.

But we didn't realize we had other partners below decks whose opinions were helping to pilot our course. These unrecognized partners turned out to be my hidden allies. They were the ones who favored magic in mutual dreams.

Henry Reed's Entities

Henry Reed opened the door to these allies when he urged the prospective participants in his Dream Research Project to consult their dreams before committing themselves to the project.

He had two reasons for this suggestion. First, he felt that the unconscious was being given a chance to sense any unfortunate result from participating in the project.

"Second, since the project was to involve an attempt to interact with dreams and to engage them in dialogue, it seemed appropriate to start the project with such a petition, treating the dreams as if they were an entity unto themselves, and asking them for their reaction to the prospect of the project; asking them, in effect, if they wanted to join."[1]

Thus Henry was alerting the dreamers to consider the possibility that they had as a partner the *dream*.

Then the lucid dreamers walked right through the door and realized that they, themselves, were dreaming. But just who was actually doing this dreaming? They used terms like "dream ego" and "dream actor." And the "dreaming self." Not the physically oriented, waking ego.

There's a fellow dreamworker I know who, if she's lucid in her dream, can direct her flight. From a waking point of view, I consider her to be a fantastic flying dreamer. From the dreaming point of view, her dreaming self loves to fly and is very good at it.

When I showed her the videotape of my tandem hand gliding experience, she freaked. "Oh, my god, oh, my god!" she exclaimed. "I would never do that!" She was, of course, referring to her waking, physical self, not her dreaming self. The waking self and the dreaming self are not the same.

So, take Henry's idea that the dream should be consulted in the decision-making process and add it to the lucid dreamers' idea that there is a "self" in the dream state. Now, what do you get? Partnership with the *dreaming selves*.

The Hidden Partners

Consider this phrase: "I had a dream." It's so common; everybody uses it. "I had a lucid dream, I had a telepathic dream, I had a dolphin dream." I, I am the self, the waking ego self, the Whole Self. I possess this dream, this objective thing. It's like saying, "I have a brain."

If dreams are things, and we expect things to serve us, so we as "self" look for service from our dreams. We look for messages from the unconsciousness, we expect creative inspiration, we seek psychic information, healing, problem solving, and practice in expanding consciousness. These are the sorts of things taken into account whenever dreamers do dream incubation and dream interpretation.

So it that's the approach you use when you are in your private hermitage, why not bring it out and use it for the group? If one of us can learn to be lucid, why not use the group energy to become lucid? Let's gather to do a healing for John. Let's all of us dream up the winning number for the lottery. Let's all dream for World Peace. Those were the kinds of goals that were being suggested by the various members in response to the facilitator's question. "Why should we dream together?"

But what was the result? There were a quite a variety of opinions on just what constitutes a successful mutual dream.

Some of these expectations were met; some are still on the order of being "pipe dreams." At best the response was mixed; not everyone embodied an enthusiastic feeling of accomplishment.

We didn't become super psychics. We did not manage to "Save the World." And so we were disappointed. But then we're dreamers . . . we're idealists. It comes with the territory.

The thing about shared dreaming is that when you start talking about connecting via dreams, you begin using phrases like "Let's meet in the dream." The old term "dream" starts changing its connotation. Meet in a dream— that changes "dream" from a thing you possess into a place in which you dwell, as in "dream reality."

"Dream reality" has been considered to be somehow analogous to "waking reality." But if you do a cross-comparison, you will find they are not the same. In waking reality, a table is solid and can carry my weight. In a dream, I can put my hand right through it. And that's just one example of the difference between the realities.

If you continue along this line of reasoning, before you know it, you might begin to wonder: meet in a dream, well, who's doing the meeting? Certainly it's not my waking self. Even if I'm lucid, I don't bring my physical body into the dream. A lot more waking attributes get left behind at the gate of sleep, too. No, in the dream it's my **dreaming self.**

Again, you can do a cross-comparison and ask, "Well, is my dreaming self the same as my walking self?" Well, no, she seems to have different attitudes, different behaviors, and sometimes a different appearance. Definitely a different history: she has experiences that I, my waking self, do not have. My dream self is unique.

Now stick "dreaming self" into that old phrase, "I have a dream" and you get "I have a dreaming self." So, does the dreaming self serve me? Is the dreaming self a *servant* of me?

Remember: the shared dreamers were working with the partnership model. To say I will act as a partner to my waking companions but use my dreams, my dreaming self as a servant does not equate with that model.

The goals for mutual dreaming range from the base to the noble. But they all have one thing in common. They all spring from the value judgments of the waking selves, for the benefit of the waking selves.

Maybe the dreaming selves agree with those judgments. And maybe they don't.

Take the waking conscious decision to dream with strangers. What? say the dreaming selves. No way, José. I'm scared of intimacy with weirdos. So I'll go hang around my familiar folks first and peek over their shoulders at those strange people. Then, in time, maybe I'll edge closer to the new guys.

Let's dream about the Inner City, say the waking selves. Nope, we'd rather roam through the Inner Countryside, say the dreaming selves. And so go our dreams.

The Dreaming Selves and the Environmental Effect

If we waking egos consider dreams to be ours and only ours alone, it really doesn't matter to anyone else what kind of dream space we create. Our dreaming selves could live in a dream pigsty, if so desired. But when dreamers get together under the model of reciprocity, suddenly things like morals and manners, ethics and aesthetics take on new importance. Consciously or unconsciously, we take a look around our psyches with the eye of potential hosts to fellow dreamers. We consider taking our dirty socks down from the chandeliers. We start to clean up our acts. *Before* we go to sleep. And that makes all the difference.

This can involve a conscious effort, like the method of encapsulation, which helps us speed up the cleansing process. But it can merely involve a subconscious shift, rather like taking a deep breath before we dive into our dreams.

Then, the dreaming selves join in the effort. I've already mentioned that 19% of the dreams from the shared dreaming projects began with negative themes. They began that way. However, over half of the troubles were resolved *in-dream*, leaving only 9% negative at dreams' end. Most of these resolving incidents occurred in nonlucid dreams. This means that the dreaming selves are becoming more active and aware, even if they aren't becoming lucid. They are getting involved. They are making a difference, too.

I'm not at all surprised that the dreaming selves would want to contribute to this cleanup effort. We waking egos only visit the world of the dream at arms' length when we recall, record, or do imaginative work on our dreams. We visit on a more personal basis when we become increasingly lucid in the dream or wake still awash with dream imagery and emotions.

Now consider things from the dreaming selves' point of view. They live in the world of dreams all the time. Nightmares are troublesome enough for our waking selves. But for the dreaming selves, it must be like living in some kind of purgatory.

At any rate, psychic, mutual, or even regular dreaming has traditionally been associated with stormy weather in dreamland, the result of dumping waking-state emotional residue into the dreaming psyche. But when dreamers engage in toxic ego cleanup before they sleep and consciously decide to focus on a positive task instead, when dreaming selves help with the effort inside the dream, we all become dream reality environmentalists. We clean up the contaminants and provide a space for communal magic. Suddenly there's a break in the clouds. The sun shines, the birds sing, the sky turns brilliant blue. Now, that's cause for celebration!

I think our dreaming selves have the jump on our waking egos. They realize the serious nature of the environmental effect. The dreaming selves want to play the game of intentional mutual dreaming in a playground that is safe, healthy, and environmentally sound.

What do you think would happen if we gave the dreaming selves a break from working for the waking selves? And wouldn't it be a nice gesture of reciprocity if the waking egos intentionally served the needs of the dreaming selves for a change? Of course, we'd have to *ask* the dreaming selves what their desires are, not presume that we already know.

Consulting the Dreaming Self

Like other deliberate dreamers, I have often used my dreams as information sources through the practice of incubating questions for my dreams to answer. The "answers" that come are usually symbolic and have required a bit of interpretive dreamwork to decode.

The night I decided to ask my dreaming self what *she* wanted to do, I got a very unusual response. The answer was clearer, more literal than any I'd yet received in a nonlucid dream.

In this dream I, as my dreaming self, walk into a community center! There my dreaming self tells a man that I need some investment, some "venture capital." "The reason I want it," she says, "is so that I can teach people how to dream big."

To dream big? What did that mean? Well, I knew that "big dreams" are the archetypal dreams. They are the adventure-ous dreams. They are also the symbolic dreams. To dream big means to dream using fantastic rather than mundane imagery. Of course, my challenge, as a waking ego, would be to help gestate and decipher such big dreams. It was time for a detective upgrade.

Literalists and Symbolists

When J. B. Rhine collected ESP dreams at Duke University, he found that the most numerous where those most easily identified. That is, they were what he called "realistic" dreams. Louisa E. Rhine distinguishes between the two types of psychic dreams. She states, "In realistic ESP dreams [one] can picture a real scene almost as in a photograph."[2]

But other dreams are not photo-perfect copies. They paint symbolic pictures instead. ". . . The unrealistic ones," says Louisa, "can show quite clearly that some persons, whether or not they recognize it when they are awake, are inherent dramatists." She also says, "Fantasy is more likely to seem interesting, and therefore to excite comment, than a more realistic style of imagery. But the realistic style in ESP dreams is the much more striking. It also is more frequently reported."[3]

Psychic dreams can have symbolic resonance with another person's waking life. But mutual dreams can have resonance with another person's dream—which itself can be a "symbolic" event!

Symbolists and Literalists

When I taught elementary school, I once took a class of children outdoors so that they might all draw an oak tree. The kids brought their pens and pencils, crayons and pastel sticks. They all sat down on the grassy field in the same general vicinity of the tree and began to sketch.

Some were literalists. Their tree drawings were photographic renderings of the oak: same form, same colors, appropriate proportions, etc. But there were variants even among them. Some drew the entire tree, some concentrated on a single branch. Thus, their inner pictures of the oak tree were not equivalent, even when the literalists were looking directly *at* the tree.

Consider how varied their pictures would have been if they'd drawn the tree from memory, back in the classroom. But that's what we dreamers have to do. We don't draw our dreams from firsthand experience. Our dream reports are *memory* reports. And as law enforcement officers who interview witnesses at a crime scene will tell you, our memories vary widely.

And our attention wanders. Back in the grassy field, there were those who thought the oak tree was a very boring object. They were much more interested in other subject matter: their classmates. So they drew people, primarily, with the oak tree as a very vague background prop.

Still, they were literalists. The people in their drawings looked as much like their physical classmates as their drawing skills would allow.

But then, there were the symbolists. Their drawings did not look like a photo of an oak tree. They looked like paintings: impressionist, cubistic, primitive, rococo styles. Their oak trees were wiggly lines, weird shapes, and painted purple and puce! There was no way to "verify" from the drawings that any of these children had seen that particular physical oak tree. But I knew they had, because I was present at the time. It wasn't because they were "poor drawers." When I talked with them I realized that they were just picturing their emotional, intuitive reactions to the same primary stimulus.

And guess what? Our dreams most often react in the very same way!

What researcher Jan Ehrenwald says about psi could just as well apply to dreams: "It is a groping attempt to spawn ever new forms of adaptation, comparable to the nonrepresentational artist's quest for unprecedented shapes, spatial configurations, color combinations, and modes of experience. It is a rehearsal of things to come rather than a throwback; it is futuristic rather than archaic. Hence, it has a close connection with creative activity and artistic expression."[4]

If you are going to produce a realistic mimic of physical reality, then your inner pictorial production system has to have the sort of literal bent common to architects and engineers. But most of the people that have been attracted to the shared dreaming projects are symbolists. Their dreamselves equate dream reports not to photographs, but to *paintings*. As you may recall, in the shared dreaming projects, the group task is described using themes like painting a huge communal mural. Shared dreamers are also independent and individualistic. They have very definite opinions on what their dreams mean . . . and independently evolved data

banks of memories and associative linkages. So they tend to
be highly symbolic dreamers, not literalists.

This is a direct result of taking the hermit's journey, in
which you seek to discover what your own dream symbols
mean to you personally, and not to rely on the "dream dictionary" approach to interpretation. Independent individuals are concerned about expressing their unique selves and
not about goose-stepping to the same drummer. So how can
independent symbolists get past the objective standard for a
classic meeting dream?

Well, if their waking selves are committed to achieving
that standard, they've got a problem, because it goes against
the grain. They can try to get the dreaming selves to role-
play, acting like and perceiving like a waking self. Children
can be "educated." But that would certainly take a lot of
time and effort, and in the meantime be a perfect setup for
disappointment.

Now, the dreaming selves of the symbolists are willing to
try out the literal approach during the first few goal dates.
But remember I said that these dreamers shift through neutral lulls into another dreaming gear? After trying on waking
literal language for a while, their dreaming selves return to
their natural, symbolic dreaming languages. The "decline effect" sets in. Dreamers and researchers get less and less classic meetings, fewer and fewer literal psychic events.

At that point we waking egos can either object, reject, or
learn to go with the flow. We can give up the need to prove
that we are psychic, in the old terms. We concentrate on the
sociability factor, the exploratory factor, the artistic factor of
mutual dreams instead. For the foreseeable future, we must
be prepared to treat our symbolic differences as foreign languages that need to be translated, interpreted, and fit together.

Dreaming Language of the Symbolists

After doing all this mutual research, you can imagine that
I had quite a few pieces of paper—the dream reports—that I

had gathered from many sorts of people. I used to sit in my family room, surrounded by them. It was like trying to put together one of those gigantic jigsaw puzzles, but without any knowledge of the final picture and with a lot of the pieces missing. I'd think, "I know there's a pattern here, but what is it?" Then I'd get totally frustrated, give up, and go do some more research. I started with dreams but kept expanding on and on. By the time I'd finished, I felt as if I'd surveyed the entire field of liberal arts and a couple of sciences, besides. I was trying to make some sense out of what was going on. Mutual dreams do that: force you to go from the microview to the macroview. All this earnest effort rewarded me with this life lesson: for true connection, you must learn to speak the language of your dreaming partner. Of course, I'd thought that it meant my waking partners. Then one day, I had a breakthrough.

Have you have ever had the experience of learning a foreign language? When I first learned Spanish, I would open a book and see gobbledygook. After I learned a few words, some phrases, I'd open a book and try to make some sense out of them. I'd guess at what was going on—I was usually wrong, but I'd still try. Then one day I opened the book and I could read *everything* that was on the page. That's the sort of thing that happened to me with mutual dreams.

I realized that the reason I was having so much trouble is that I was bringing in an old assumption, the old method of interpretation of a single person's dream. Here in the U.S., latter twentieth century, we are basically monolingual. We speak English, period. When we go to interpret dreams, we take the information and try to funnel them down to a single language. So there is a built-in presumption that there's an equivalency, waking language to dream language, one to one.

But I'm here to tell you, that's not true. Our dreaming selves are multilingual. They speak the dreaming equivalent of Spanish, Swahili, sign language, and, yes, once in a while, literal English. And they can switch languages in the midst of the same dream. So if you get two dreamselves together, the chances of dreamself A speaking English at the same time as dreamself B is minimal. Which does *not* mean that they aren't all describing the same event. It's just they have a chance to express themselves emotionally, and they do. One dreamself can come into a room, look at what's on the table, and say "Yummy!" in Samoan, and someone else comes in and says "Yuck!" in German. They're still responding to the same event, but it gets translated into different symbols. And that's the kind of thing our dreamselves were doing all along.

Once I had this new view, I looked at the dream reports and realized that our dreamselves were meeting a lot more than we waking selves were giving them credit for. We'd been having dream "meetings" all along. We just didn't realize it because they didn't fit our waking conceptions of what a dream meeting should look like. They were dream reality events, conforming to dream reality rules. The dreaming selves were meeting . . . under their terms. So what kinds of "meetings" did they seem to prefer? Not the classic meetings. No. Group meetings. Meetings and meshing. Meshing dreams. Group meshing. Even missed meetings were a form of meshing.

Why so much meshing? It's because our dreaming psyches like to play the game of identification. They can role-play the abused child, the wounded warrior, the compassionate parent. They can conjure up the dream scenarios in which the dreaming selves think, act, and feel just like the waking egos. Whether literal or symbolic, these are the mundane dreams of drama and trauma that fertilize the field of dreamwork.

The dreaming self like to empathize with the waking ego! In fact, it does such a great job of empathizing, that we've barely been able to tell that there is any difference between us. First we assume that we are both the same. Then when lucid dreaming gives us a new perspective, we still assume what our waking egos want, so do our dreaming selves. But we are only the "same" when we mesh.

The Vote of the Dreaming Selves

As I looked at those classic and not so classic meeting and meshing dreams, I wondered, "Hmm. Under what circumstances do our dreamselves actually meet?" A bit of analysis and I discovered a nice new agenda that didn't line up with what we had expected beforehand. By having the results tell the story, I was asking, "Hey, dreamselves, what is your choice for mutual dreaming?" After all, they were the ones who were actually going to have to do the "meeting," so it made sense that they would cast the deciding vote.

In the arena of the shared dreaming project, the most common mutual dream themes included these:

1. *Sex (5%)*
   Explicit sex as well as all forms of intimacy between partners and friends including pregnancy and sharing a bed. With unfamiliar people, more muted versions: kissing, hugging, touching, rubbing, tickling, the wearing of scanty clothes.
2. *Communication and Observation (12%)*
   Dialogue, notices, books, movies, theater. Telephones, microphones, tape recorders. Trade, especially with money and jewelry.
3. *Exploration (13%)*
   Bedrooms, kitchens, elevators to different floors. Communes, caves, auditoriums, warehouses, large multistoried buildings. Cars, bicycles, boats, vacation tours.
4. *Creation (11%)*
   Sewing, cooking, drawing, painting. Excavation and construction of buildings.
5. *Fantastic Feats and Imagery (11%)*
   Out-of-body experiences, flying, floating, psychokinesis, telepathy, teleportation, mutability. Dragons and dinosaurs, aliens, angels, elves, witches, comic book heroes.

6. *Recreation (12%)*

Water places: swimming pools, lakes, rivers, oceans. Activities: hiking, running, karate, team sports like basketball, carnivals, processions. Parties: food, dancing, singing, music. Smiling, joking, laughter.

When all these ingredients for shared dreams were combined, our dreaming selves had cooked up this recipe:

First Have Fun!

So here we were, waking egos sailing out to Save the World. And who did we bring along below decks? Party people! What a revolting development! What a revolutionary development.

Are you familiar with the old hierarchy model of the self, like Freud's superego + ego + id? Or Eric Berne's parent + adult + child? The top, the middle, the underdog of ourselves? Of those options, whose voice would most likely be saying, "We want to have fun!"?

When we did the revolutionary shift from hierarchy to partnership, yes, the authority figures came down to join the group. Who sneaked upward and said they wanted to join the group, too? The k(id)s!

The id is that part of our psyche that is the source of instinctive energy and that favors the pleasure principle, impulse, and the fulfillment of desire. Because the psychic, creative self is the self most closely identified with the id, it makes perfect sense that the kids would want to engage in these sorts of activities.

Here we had sent out the invitation to dream together, half hoping that our Higher Wisdom selves would show up. But who accepted the invitation? Not whom we expected!

So what are we going to do now? Tell them to go home? Send your wise grandmommies and granddaddies instead? We could. Or we could take the other stance: Grow up and act like adults! We've got a serious mission, here. Come up on deck and do the really important work.

Maybe there are some other options. There's been a lot of talk about the "Inner Child" in the self-help books. Guess where the Inner Children have been living?

I'd like to suggest that there might be some useful, beneficial reasons why instead of having the kids balance on the ego-ball, we might pay attention to their natural state of being just as we're doing with all the flora and fauna out there in the waking wilds. And that it might be useful to take a look at them and see what gifts they have to bring to the group.

I can tell you one gift they bring. In all the shared dreaming projects, a full 24% of the mutual dreams focused on a single theme.

By far, the most favorite activity of our dreaming selves was flying.

The Flying Connection

When I went in search of the question, "What makes for a successful shared dreamer?" I considered many things: the usual demographics, other dream or psychic skills and experience, Jungian typology, astrological signs.

Lucidity was a strong contender. 79% of the 62 successful shared dreamers were capable of having a lucid dream, but not all of them used this skill in the shared dreaming projects. 50% of them were mutual lucid dreamers. My definition of a mutual lucid dreamer meant that the dreamer him or herself went lucid, whether his or her teammates did or not, and then had a cross-connective dream with at least one other dreamer. 42% were mutual lucid *flying* dreamers.

In the end, the flying factor was the strongest component among successful shared dreamers. At least 82% of the dreamers had the experience of flying in their dreams before they started the projects. These dreams had a flying or floating component, and most often the dreamers were involved in a firsthand experience, usually without any technological or winged support. In other words, their dreaming selves could fly like a superhero.

Most of the resultant themes of the shared dreaming projects correlated well with the stated goals to which the dreamers were incubating. The exception was that exploration (23% of stated goals) and fantastic feats (like an out-of-body experience: 18% of stated goals) would often produce flying dreams instead. So did lucidity (7% of stated goals). But even a "no goal" option (7% of stated goals) would result in flying dreams.

Now, there were almost an equal number of lucid dreamers as flying dreamers and about 94% overlap their populations. However, an even larger percentage of the total dreamers, 61%, achieved a mutual flying dream, which was much more than the mutual lucid dreams with or without a flying theme.

From my statistical analysis of mutual dreams overall, I've found the best bet for a positive mutual dream experience is one that is intentional and magical-symbolic, not a spontaneous mundane event.

The preferred approach would be to actively program a dream meeting with your dreaming partner, intending a goal with magical overtones. Since the most prominent magical-symbolic element in such dreams is flying, "Let's meet at my house and go flying together," would do very well.

So what's my best advice to one who wants to become a good mutual dreamer? Learn to fly!

I believe that the key to the new hero's journey is fair-weather flying dreams. They induce us to experience first-hand positive magic. When we dreamers incubate flying dreams, the result is increased awareness and activity among the dreaming selves. Flying activities release the super energy to resolve conflicts in-dream and to trigger mutual, out-of-body, psychic, and lucid dreams.

This example of lucid flight occurred in Shared Dreaming. The goal had been, "What do we enjoy doing in the dream state?'' The dreaming selves of Chad and Flynn re-plied:

CHAD: *I'm driving along a freeway in a Cadillac. . . . The setting changes and the road begins to narrow until it is obviously going to narrow down to no more than a footpath or nothing at all. On either side are jagged mountains, dark and volcanic-looking. Rather than slow down and stop be-fore the mountainsides come too close to the car, I keep on driving and have the car take off flying before the mountains close in. I must have become lucid at this point. After flying a short distance in the car, I leave and fly without it.*

I come down into a small town and land and begin walking along the sidewalk. I call to my Spirit Guide, but he doesn't respond.

FLYNN: *I drive in a car down a mountain road and sud-denly recall that I am supposed to go to the dream spot. I immediately open the door and fly out of it across a deep valley. The car continues until it goes off the side of the steep mountain road. I fly high and very fast above unpopulated evergreen forests, trying to reach the spot before I lose my lucid state.*

The scene changes and I am inside a friend's house in my hometown. I can see the bright sun shining at the edge of a cloud. It is so bright that I look away, unsure of whether I can be blinded in a dream. I feel myself becoming awake, and I desperately try to stay in the dream.

The voice of a wise master behind me says that I should breathe deeply. I answer that I have missed a rendezvous with my friends and need to go into the past or future to meet them. The wise old man says that I should pay more atten-tion to my breath to achieve this goal. I begin breathing deeply and steadily, but before I know it I am awake.

When the kids engage in mutual flying, it even attracts the attention of the Higher Wisdom figures!

The act of flying is a precursor and partner to all sorts of "big dreams," including the archetypal and spiritual ones. And extraordinary dreams and visions are the seedbed of mythic belief and cultural change.

It's possible to soar in a mundane world, like Superman does. In dreams, either the literal or symbolic dreamer can fly. But flying is a magical-archetypal feat just by itself. Thus the flying dreamer stands with one foot in the mundane dream world and one foot in the realm of archetypal magic. Flying is the first step toward extraordinary dreams.

CHAPTER 19

✦

*L*ITERAL AND *L*UCID

✦

*T*oday I am a recovering dreamworkaholic.

At the urging of my dreaming self, I began a new era of deliberate incubation. With groups, I used telepathic targets, mutual goals, and in-dream lucidity to induce flying dreams. The preliminary results were threefold. First, through intention, dreamland was more likely to shift to wonderland where the dreaming self could become a super self. And that's a very necessary talent for the deeper shadow work that was to come. Second, more flying in nonlucid dreams meant there was an increase in positive psychic, mutual, and lucid dreams. Third, the most fruitful approach to deliberate dreaming was that suggested by the dreaming selves. Have fun!

So in 1995, as the next step in my recovery program, I launched the Fly-By-Night Club. The Club has featured dreamplay and flying fun. Robert Waggoner helped provide me with the "venture capital" and agreed to serve as the first president.

But up until then I'd say that the major emotion that characterized my response to all the time and effort that had gone into my shared dreaming research was . . . disappointment. I had realized that I was a symbolic dreamer; that my family were symbolic dreamers; that most of my friends and colleagues were symbolic dreamers. But I still yearned for a classic meeting dream. A magical, lucid, **literal** meeting dream.

The Hidden Assumptions of Mutual Dreams

In the old model of mutual dreaming, there was an authority figure who told you what you were supposed to do, where you were supposed to go, and what it was supposed to look like when you got there. The route and destinations were predetermined. But in the partnership model, there wasn't anybody saying, "This is a mutual dream." Instead, there were those facilitators and coordinators who were explorers along with everybody else. They were just saying, "Let's dream together. We don't know what will happen. Let's just try."

Theoretically there were no pictures for anyone to judge with. But that didn't mean that individual members hadn't brought along their own pictures for the ride, just as I did with Joanne's painting. Oh, yes they did. They had two picture postcards stuck in their back pockets. Everytime they'd look out on the horizon and say, "Oh, I think I see a mutual dream," they'd drag their postcards out of their pockets, bring them up, and do a comparison.

If there was a good match, they were happy. And if there wasn't, they were deflated. One of the postcards is called "same dream." The other postcard is called "shared dreamscape."

At first "same dream" meant that my dream had to be a perfect copy of yours. But after the shared dreaming projects produced so many full meshing dreams, it became obvious that no one was in the business of cloning identical twin dreams. Rather, the meshing dream was found to have specific elements in common that could be selected and identified. So in the spirit of symbolic decoding and analysis, we shared dreamers took up our explorers' butterfly nets and began pursuing the "similar dream" instead. It wasn't such a stretch for those of us who had logged time working on dream interpretation techniques, either by outselves or in a group.

But "shared dreamscape" remained the elusive butterfly.

Now, the most frequently quoted meeting classic is that of Oliver Fox (Hugh G. Callaway). Lucid dreamers, especially, like to put themselves in his shoes:

> I am Oliver Fox at college in England. I have a lucid dream in which I'm on Southampton Common where I see my friend Elkington. Knowing I'm dreaming, I greet him, and he returns the greeting. We comment that our friend Slade is not with us. I awaken.
>
> The next day I go to Elkington. Before I have a chance to say anything to him, he tells me that last night he had a dream in which he realized he was dreaming. We were on Southampton Common. We greeted one another and commented on our absent friend Slade.

Assumptions: two dreamers, both lucid. Same event in the same place. Meeting in dreams is just like meeting in waking reality.

Classic Meeting Dream Reality Check

Since physical existence is supposed to be the standard by which we judge whether or not a dream is "real" or not, let's return here for a moment. Without going into depth, let me just ask you this question: does a meeting between two people in physical reality have the requirement of a "shared wakingscape"?

Think: letters, fax machines, video and audiotapes, two-way television broadcasts, and computer networks, and you'll begin to understand what I mean. Legal business is handled through telephone conference calls; our civilization wouldn't survive if we didn't conceive of these connections as legitimate. And just because I'm phoning from Tahiti to you in New York doesn't make our contact "unreal." Just because my "wakingscape" is a tropical beach and yours is a formal office doesn't negate our connection.

As I've tracked shared dreaming projects, I've observed that if a dream with the verification requirement of my dream = waking reality is going to occur, it "happens" at the beginning of the project. This is when you might get a dream that accurately pictures your partners, the house where they live, the events in their daily lives. It's a sort of "beginner's luck." Succeeding attempts to duplicate the successes of that first go-round never seem to live up to that standard.

What we've been doing is trying to get our dreamselves to play the game "Let's act just like you waking egos do in physical reality." And because it's a novel experience, the dreamselves are willing to try it out. But remember, the dreaming selves don't *have* to play this game.

If researchers are looking for this sort of verification, they need to seek out and persuade literal dreamers to dream together. This is the type of person you would need to be, or train yourself to be. And then hope that your dreaming self could be persuaded to go along for the boat ride without jumping ship when the scenery got boring.

Lab Dreaming

Telepathic and precognitive dreams have been induced in the laboratory. So have lucid dreams. Learning the real properties of psychic or lucid dreams is often secondary to this primary focus: to scientifically prove the existence of such dreams. But how can you prove their existence, if you leave out the hidden partners?

In fact, the laboratory experiment to scientifically demonstrate the existence of mutual lucid dreams has already been suggested. It goes something like this:

Two or more dreamers spend a night at the lab sleeping in separate rooms. Both become lucid. Both reach lucidity at the same time. They meet each other in their mutual lucid dream. Then they give eye movement signals in unison, either by counting together in dream or by having their dream eyes follow the moving dream finger of the person designated as leader.

Later, after waking and before leaving their rooms, each writes a report and puts it in a sealed envelope. Then the reports are reviewed by independent judges and checked for congruence with the eye-movement records of the electro-occulogram.

Sounds simple, doesn't it? So does singing barbershop harmony while standing on your heads and juggling a couple of plates and a microphone in front of a critical audience. Now, gather your dancing monkeys and walking chickens, get up, and actually try to do it.

I'm not saying it can't be done. Some folks have dreaming selves who like to try to achieve Guinness records. I am saying that, in the long run, after we develop a firsthand experience of and close relationship with our dreaming selves, we'll probably develop a hypothesis to demonstrate the nature of mutual lucid dreams other than the presumptions supporting this type of experiment.

Let's say we did want to produce mutual lucid dreams in a laboratory setting. Then we would have to deal with five distinct factors: (1) the ability to induce a lucid dream in a lab, (2) the ability to induce a psychic dream in a lab, (3) the ability to put the lucid and psychic together, (4) the ability to reach out for and connect with another dreamer (or more!), and (5) the ability to coordinate and harmonize with those other dreamers.

From my observations, lucid dream labs have had the most success with a select group of dreamers who are highly motivated, have no aversion to electronic gadgetry, can sleep easily in unfamiliar surroundings, and who can survive the constant waking and returning to sleep required by the experiments. Plus they have become acclimatized to the lab situation by sleeping there not just once, but often for several nights, maybe over a period of months or even years! Also, they have been accomplished lucid dreamers even *before* they set foot in the lab.

Psychic labs have also sought out dreamers who claimed consistent psychic dreaming ability prior to entry into the laboratory situation. Then they, too, had to acclimatize themselves to the laboratory situation. But psychic research has added factors to consider: the "sheep and goat effect"; the "experimenter effect"; "doctoral compliance"; not to mention mental contagion and cluster effects. To put it succinctly, psychic dreamers must consider whether the psychic climate of the laboratory created by the percipient, receiver, experimenter, and assorted aides is conducive to the fertile production of their psychic dreams.

To become lucid in a laboratory is a notable accomplishment. To have a psychic dream in a laboratory is an outstanding achievement. To have a lucid psychic dream is an even more amazing feat.

Now, lucid psychic laboratory experimentation has been successful in the labs of those folks interested in demonstrating the essence of the out-of-body experience. So why not assume that the same can be true for the lucid mutual dream?

Why? First, because we're talking about a lucid dream, not an OBE, and the differences between the two must be factored in. Second, because we're considering a mutual dream, not a psychic OBE, we have to involve more than one dreamer in the equation. More than one dreamer has to fit the criteria already mentioned, the most important of which is to be able to establish rapport with another human being with whom he or she shares the same literal-cultural dreaming language. And in this society, *that* requirement, when added to the others, shoots the probability factors into a logarithmic progression right off the "simple experiment" scale. I hope you can appreciate the complexity of the proposed task and the skill level of those mutual dreamers who do achieve the results they do, out in the field.

But do I consider such mutual dreamers to be the geniuses or prodigies of the dreamworld? No. I think just about anybody can have a lucid dream (especially if you are as open to the experience as children seem to be), and anyone can have a psychic dream (it helps if you look for it). Dreaming is like any other art or skill: there are those who have lots of natural talent, those who have less, but everyone can participate in the dreaming arts to some extent *if they practice.* The mutual lucid dreamers in this book I consider major league dreamers-in-training. But we've barely made it to the Little Leagues, and still play a lot of sandlot baseball.

Literal Lucid Meeting Dream

As contacts with the lucid dream community grew, I began collecting fine examples of spontaneous lucid meetings with friends and family by literal lucid dreamers. Most were single narratives. But I noticed that even some of the double dream reports showed influence by the narrator. The second dream report might say, "My dream was the same as Elaine's until . . ." or it might read, "When Omar told me his dream, I realized . . ."

There was a difference, though. Detail. I was discovering examples from more sophisticated dreamers whose advanced recall skills meant there was more material, including more raw data available for comparison.

As with the shared dreamers, this fact turns out to be detrimental to the generalizations that make for a smooth story. The more specific the record, the greater the likelihood for variance between dreams.

I found this example on the Internet. Serge posted a dream he'd had with his friend Niles. Serge had used an idea he took from Stephen LaBerge's MILD technique to induce a lucid dream.

"We started by playing the 'Are you dreaming?' game

every time we spoke to or saw each other," said Serge, "and, as you can imagine, we were soon asking each other during our lucid dreams, too. After comparing notes in the morning a few times, we had mutual dreams."

In their sixth month of experimentation, Serge had this lucid dream.

I come out of some store and spot my friend Niles standing by a large tree. As soon as we see each other, we ask, "Are you dreaming?" After looking around and doing a reality check, I decide that we are in fact dreaming. Niles finally agrees, and we try to decide what to do.

Just then a car with a very attractive woman pulls up. She gets out and walks by us. Niles stops her and starts up a conversation. Pretty soon they are getting into the woman's car to leave. Niles asks if I'm coming, and I say, "No, I promised my nephew I would take him out on the next lucid dream."

I create a really fast black sports car and jump in, racing ahead of my friend, pick up my nephew, and take him for the fastest car ride ever.

"The next morning I asked Niles if he had any interesting dreams the night before. At first he said, "Hmm, a strange dream about my cat. . . . Wait! I remember. Oh yeah, the girl, you and me by a tree . . ."

At this point, the Serge/Niles story was consistent with those antecdotes I'd heard before. But this time, I went one step further. I wrote an e-mail message to Serge to ask if he'd like to contribute his dream to *Mutual Dreaming*. And I asked for clarification.

"A book? Pretty cool!" he responded. "I was wondering when someone would be brave enough to research mutual dreaming. Well, to answer your question about my friend . . . I spoke to him about your letter last week, and he was pretty surprised and wanted to help, but the bad news is he does not keep a good a dream diary as I do.

"Niles remembers that he met me outside of a shopping center by a large tree and we both asked if we could be dreaming. He said the size of the tree or something about it was what made him lucid (when I thought it was the fact that we both did a reality check and argued that we could not be dreaming). He then remembered seeing the girl in the car, but no details about her. At this point his dream took on a sexual encounter of some sort and I left the picture."

"So not all details were exactly the same, but very similar, just like in real life when we compare our experiences."

Consistently, when I had the opportunity to ask for the specifics of the spontaneous and intentional lucid events, I began to get a picture that was similar to the results from the shared dreaming projects.

Time Shift

Lucid dreamer Gabe T. told me:

"Once I had a lucid dream (not on purpose) involving a woman with whom I was almost at the stage of sexual involvement. I had a very highly sexual dream where we merged into each other's bodies, extreme pleasure, etc.

"When I phoned her the next morning to talk with her about the dream, she was already upset with me. It seems that she had experienced the same dream, but for her, it had occurred twenty-four hours earlier than it had for me. Somewhat unfairly I think, she was angry that I had not called her the previous morning (forget about the fact that she did not feel required to phone me!). She assumed that I was lying, for some reason.

"I'm not sure what I would have said if she had called and told me about a dream that she had experienced, but which had not yet occurred for me. Would I still have had it the next night or not? Who knows?

"Anyway, when I told her that what this proved to me was that 'time works differently for different people,' she became exasperated with my nonrational conclusion and hung up the phone. What appeared to me to be a simple logical conclusion was, to her at least, an evasive answer and, more likely, a lie. Only she can know why she felt this way. I don't believe that I had given her reason to justify that kind of accusation. Maybe at some level she was frightened by the implications regarding the fluid nature of 'time' that this incident illuminated. This was the beginning of the end of my involvement with her. We never did become intimate outside of dreams."

Gabe and his friend engaged our old friend, **time shift.** Time shift is a variance on the same phenomena as the psychic researchers call "displacement." This is a descriptive term covering the tendency of some subjects to deviate from the target object and "hit" one next to the one intended. In this case, the target was a specific date. But which was the "correct" date? That's a matter of subjective judgment.

Dreams are not waking reality. They can mime the physical world. But they don't have to adhere to its laws of stability, space, and linear direction. Or time.

Neither do the dreaming selves.

Follow the Rabbit

Abracadabra! Nothing up my sleeve, folks. Now, before I pull the rabbit out of my hat, let me ask you a question.

Can we meet in our dreams?

Meet in our dreams? Does that make dreams as real as waking life? Do dreams act just like physical reality?

Let's say we try to meet in our dreams. And we think we succeed. Hooray! Yes, dreams are just like waking reality. Proof positive. Case closed. Send the rabbit home.

Or we try, and we try. And we try again. And each attempt to meet brings more energy into our dreams, energy that hops up and down, anxious to unlock the dreams' hidden potential—potential that allows our dreams to act less and less like our daily lives.

This rabbit has a waistcoat and a watch.

Follow the rabbit and our original criteria for a meeting dream begins to tumble down the rabbit hole. We fall downward and land with a thump! At this new level of realization, we rediscover an old truth. Dreams are a wonderland populated by some amazing creatures.

Like us.

Do the dreaming selves act like the waking selves? Yes, most of the time it seems they do. Given the job of handling the stress of daily life, they haven't had much opportunity to do anything but walk around and role-play our conflicts and problems. By focusing on our waking ego needs we discourage them to act any differently. But when the waking selves decide to let the dreaming selves "go native," guess what happens?

Give dreaming selves the opportunity and they don't walk at all. They levitate. They teleport through walls. They shift dimensions. Like elves and fairies and super heroes. They grow bigger or smaller. They talk to animals. They fall down rabbit holes and don't get hurt. Like Alice in Wonderland.

But they don't need to look like Alice.

X-Ray Vision

Here's another very hidden assumption from dreamworld legend and lore: our dream bodies look and act just like our physical bodies. That's how Fox and Elkington recognized one another when they met. That's how you will see me, and I will see you.

Verification requires that my dream body = my physical body.

Consider this very literal dream meeting by Jerimiah Molfese during a lucid dream in 1992.

JERIMIAH: *I close my eyes and visualize the series of boxes and circles from my previous lucid dream. I go into the last circle, but instead of waking up, I find myself in Jack's living room, and I realize I am dreaming! I see Jack walking toward his bedroom. I call to him and say, "Jack, you're dreaming!" He looks back at me, takes off his glasses, and says, "So I am." Then we split apart and I wake up.*

Jerimiah reported that the next morning he asked his friend Jack if he had had a lucid dream the previous night. Jack responded, "Only for a moment. I was in my living room when I heard somebody call me. I thought it was my brother."[1]

Now Jerimiah was able to recognize his contact as Jack. But Jack didn't identify the person calling him as Jerimiah. He guessed the caller was a family member instead.

Now why might Jack have made that *seeming* misidentification? Remember, in shared dreaming projects there's a stage we go through during which we substitute the literal person for someone else, especially someone we know and feel comfortable with. It's possible that Jack thought of Jerimiah as his "brother" and was using a bit of personal symbolism to characterize their relationship.

We can dream of people in terms of how familiar or alien they feel to us, how they project an alternate personality characteristic, like being blond instead of a brunette and male instead of female, or how they remind us of some animal, like a dog or cat.

Only the literalists were dreaming about me as the recognized Linda—female human being—and not that often. Instead, I was being seen as: a feline, a man, a sister, a friend, a sorceress, a monkey, a superhero, or Lily Tomlin! Sometimes the evidence was in meshing dreams, some in telepathic dreams. Sometimes I also had dreamt of myself as the same aspect. And sometimes the dreamer recognized me "underneath" in a sort of perceptual overlay.

Symbolic dreamers know it is possible to appear in the land of dreams as something other than our surface appearance. We can be younger or older, with a new tint or hair color. We can be another gender, a member of another ethic group, even of another species. So when dreams are psychic, wouldn't these alternate aspects be perceptible to other human beings?

Remember, it's not us, the waking egos with physical vision, that *see* the other person in the dream. It's the dreaming self's perceptual apparatus that does the seeing and manifests the imagery. And the dreaming selves have x-ray vision.

When I become aware that I am using the psychic abilities of **x-ray vision,** I can identify you with clues other than that of physical surface description. You may appear as an aspect—other than your waking self. Or I may not "see" you at all! Instead, I will get a "felt sense" of your presence or identity.

> **LINDA:** *In the midst of flickering hypnogogia, I seem to recognize Eric Snyder. This brings me to lucidity, and at the same time I "freeze" his facial image in order to start a dream. Even though his appearance is that of my brother Ken in his twenties, I address him as if he were Eric. He replies a mumble in which I catch only the name "Jeremy Taylor." The effort to hold on to the dream is too much, and I wake.*

Was I really in touch with Eric? I wondered. If so, why superimpose the image of my brother Ken atop his? I held off drawing conclusions until I received the next batch of dreams. Eric had included a dream about four dreamworkers. One was me. Two others were not members of the project; they were published authors and Eric knew them personally. They were *Ken* Kelzer and *Jeremy Taylor.*

The spoken words and the physical appearance of my brother was not "psi-missing." They alerted me to meshing elements that were actually found in my teammate's dream.

Sometimes the feeling tones of the team member may be so strange that other people can actually be characterized as "alien." During one Nexus goal, Chad had a couple who were "not human," I dreamt that "the humans turn into aliens," and Sean had "two very thin, very eerie-looking men with an odd aura—they don't seem human." In addition, three members dreamt of people in costume, including fairies or pixies and angels!

Contiguous Dreams

A very special way to become aware of the reality of mutuality is by the felt experience that your dream borders on another person's dream. **Contiguous dreaming** can occur in either meshing or meeting dreams. This sort of experience suggests an intriguing explanation for just why we lucid dreamers may not be experiencing the perfect "shared dreamscape." Maybe there's an innate problem in entering the same dreamscape and still being able to retain lucidity.

This type of dream can have the appearance of a doorway, portal, or other "edge." You can feel yourself being "pulled" into another person's dream. The sensation of being "pulled" in and out of a dream or toward another person's dream is a red flag for the reality of mutual dreaming, whether the encounter seems to be with a known human being or not.

Women of Power specialized in discovering our own alternate aspects. During that project, Natalie and I experienced mutual contiguous dreams. Natalie's initial dream was a nonlucid one.

My response dream was lucid.

I didn't feel myself becoming a bird in my dream. I simply went flying. But that's how Natalie saw me. She was perceiving a part of me that exists beyond my waking-state surface appearance. To her, I was a peacock.

CONTIGUOUS DREAMING

There are two realities happening at once. In addition, as my husband and I talk, and I see the notes, another reality intermixes, all at the same time. I'm watching a holographic movie, then get pulled in and out of it, occupying more than one dimension at once. Finally, I move into it entirely.

The scene is an exotic beach resort, sandy white beach, deep blue clear water, people playing in the surf, vacation yachts and luxurious hotel grounds nearby.

M and I are both now in the scene. We're walking on a grassy park area above the sand, adjacent to the hotel. Nearby is a

Just then, a huge odd peacock version walks out. It is massive! It has a long throat, flesh colored, and long knurled legs, then green iridescent wings. It starts to follow us around the picnic table and we go around, out of its way. It's a little intimidating. We find it awesome, and a mystically powerful being.

We begin to walk into the hotel lobby and I awaken.

NATALIE

I am outside and delighted to be airborne because I seem to have been swept up here by the air currents. "Look!" I exclaim happily, showing off. "I'm at the treetops!"

It's at this point that I realize the presence next to me is actually two women (one dark, one blond) in dresses who are also standing in the air, to my right.

"But you're here, too! That must mean you can fly," Or maybe my energy brought them here: not just them, but some of their imagery, too. The blonde, especially, seems to have brought her dream along with her.

I know that if I pay attention to it, I will be drawn into her dream. I can still feel the magnetic tug that these women are exerting on me, but I want to keep them in my dream. Yet, I know that I don't have the strength to keep us all up here for long. Nevertheless, I want to bring us all to my ground. "How can we get down?" I ask aloud, thinking that directing me, the two women and the attached imagery at once might be too much to handle.

There's the image of a **picnic table** off to one side.

"Oh, I know," I say. I reach out my left hand, and gazing at it, snap my fingers.

Instantly, we are all transported to the grassy ground. I'm tickled to have accomplished this teleporting trick.

I walk with the women down a slope to where we are joined by more women and talk together.

LINDA

Summary

I started this book by saying there's a good chance we're already having mutual dreams, much more often than we're aware, and that this awareness can be nurtured by sharing and comparing our dreams on a regular basis. That works as long as our dreams are essentially similar or we are involved in literal meeting dreams. But once we begin to cross over into the realm of archetypal magic, the rules change. There, we need new tools to discover evidence of each other's presence.

Let's review our findings about mutual dreams:

- Dreams can be social as well as private events.
- They are shared due both to psychic factors, like telepathy, and nonpsychic factors, like mutual day residue.
- We can dream with someone we have never met face to face, and it is possible to have a mutual dream with someone on the other side of the planet. But we don't have to dream together at exactly the same time.
- The dreams produced by dreaming together are not just what our imaginations have predetermined they should be. There are results other than the classic mutual dreams. Our dreaming selves can collaborate to create many kinds of artistic productions.
- We shared dreamers bring to a group many different degrees of experience and maturity. Our dreams describe several stages of development as we progress toward successful mutual dream connections.
- The goals of our dreaming selves and the goals of our waking egos are not necessarily the same. Most often, our waking selves want to do serious work. Given the opportunity, our dreaming selves like to play. In the end, the dream selves have the deciding vote.
- Shared dreaming results in the "environmental effect." Dream content shifts from negative to positive, creating the environment for play that our dreaming selves appreciate so highly.

- Despite the higher incidence of shared dreaming interest among lucid dreamers, the best indicator of success in producing intentional mutual dreams is not the ability to become awake in our dreams. It is the ability to fly.
- Both lucid and nonlucid magical-symbolic dreamers are finding clues that indicate we are meeting more often than we realize. Because of the essentially mutable nature of dream reality, our surface facade is only one possible way to present ourselves. We can appear to one another in alternate guises. There are auditory and visual leads to follow, but the tactile experience can be a prime indicator of mutuality.

Objective Reality

It's a big revelation to most lucid dreamers when I tell them that a mutual dream doesn't have to be psychic. They usually aren't very impressed. Why? They need psychic examples to help substantiate another hidden assumption. And this one is loaded: it's the motivation behind the desire to record evidence of the "shared dreamscape." These dreamers aren't looking to be social so much as they are seeking evidence of the existence of the dream-as-its-own-reality.

The assumption is that even if the "place" wherein the astral or dream body exists or travels does not mimic waking reality, it is nonetheless an objective reality of its own. Usually this non-earth domain has been considered to be the abode of the dead, of the ancestors. This is the presumption of innumerable religious and esoteric viewpoints, each with its own version of the map of the heavens and the underworld. Proof is usually not sought but existence taken on faith. That faith is bolstered when the stories of one experient support the stories of a second.

Verification requires my dreamworld picture = your dreamworld picture.

The belief in an objective, factual existence of a non-earth reality comes from parallel reports from more than one dreamer. So if one traveler reports dallying on the banks of the Styx, and another traveler reports crossing the underworld river with Charon the boatman, well, then, the Grecian underworld must exist. So goes the logical argument.

Those with a scientific bent would demand equal reports of the dreamscape from two or more dreamers in a laboratory setting. But such a thesis asks for proof of the objective existence of a *dreamworld*, not of the existence of mutual dreams.

But I hope by now that you have realized that just because we both happen to dream the same picture doesn't necessarily mean that we are psychic or traveling in the same dreamscape. It could mean that the residue of the day stimulated a like scene. Did we both see the same TV program, listen to the same tape, read the same book, experience the same events?

That we both dream of the River Styx does not prove that the River Styx exists anywhere but in our shared belief system, our tribal tales of the underworld that we've both tapped into this same night.

Just because we react to the same stimulus doesn't make the dreams any less mutual, however. If we are programmed by the same shamanic ritual, same picture target, same chant, and the result is a shared dreamscape, well, that's still a mutual dream. Not psychic. Mutual.

Mutual meeting dreams in a shared dreamscape are neutral to this hypothesis. They do not, taken by themselves, prove the existence of an objective reality. They don't disprove it either.

Objective? Subjective? So what is the actual nature of dream reality? *That's* a very different (and intriguing) journey. The mutual dreamers, social and psychic, have new insights to contribute to the discussion. This requires delving deeply into the nature of psychic perception and visual projection in an altered state of consciousness. It's a subject whose surface we have only begun to scratch in this chapter.

It deserves such a thorough investigation that I am prepared to take it up in another book.

Conclusion

In the partnership between the waking and dreaming selves, mutual dreaming flies beyond the classic assumptions of literal meeting and copycat meshing.

Meeting dreams occur because the dreaming selves gather together in a common cause or belief. They form a consensus, an arena of active agreement. But that agreement does not have to conform to the waking consensus! For the magical-archetypal dreaming selves, literal visioning is not enough. They use super action *and* super vision.

Mutual dreaming is about trekking into inner space aboard the same vehicle: the dream. It's about being open to the mundane responsibilities and to the magical surprises of the journey. It's about meeting challenges, solving problems, engaging in human drama, exploring new frontiers of consciousness, and going where no dreamers, no dreaming selves have gone before. Together.

Are you coming, too?

APPENDIX I

✦

$\mathcal{M}$UTUAL $\mathcal{D}$REAM $\mathcal{E}$XAMPLES

Mutual dream examples can be found in the following sources:

L Auerbach, L. *Psychic Dreaming* (New York: Warner Books, 1991), 179–180.

Bach, R. *The Bridge Across Forever* (New York: Morrow, 1984), 292–295; 299–303.

Bible (Douay-Challoner version: Daniel 2:1–2:49), 789–791.

Bruce, R. D. *Lacandon Dream Symbolism* (Mexico, D.F.: Ediciones Euroamericanas Klaus Thiele, 1979), 40.

Bynum, E. B. *Families and the Interpretation of Dreams: Awakening the Intimate Web* (Binghamton, NY: Harrington Park Press, 1993), 10, 17, 41–44, 50, 52–55, 85, 98–99, 101–104, 182.

Campbell, J. *Dreams Beyond Dreaming* (Norfolk, VA: Donning, 1980), 19–20; 98–100.

Crisp, T. *Dream Dictionary* (New York: Bantam Doubleday Dell, 1990), 152.

Crowe. *The Night Side of Nature.* As quoted in Joire, P., *Psychical and Supernormal Phenomena* (New York: Frederick A. Stokes 1916), 45–46.

de Becker, R. *The Understanding of Dreams* (New York: Hawthorn Books, 1968), 71–74; 76–78.

Dee, N. *The Dreamer's Workbook* (New York: Sterling, 1990), 174–176.

L Delaney, G. *Living Your Dreams* (San Francisco: Harper & Row, 1979), 155–6; 179–180, 181.

L Donahoe, J. J. *Dream Reality* (Oakland, CA: Bench Press, 1974), 52.

L Donahoe, J. J. *Enigma* (Oakland, CA: Bench Press, 1979), 54–61, 60

L Donahoe, J. J. "Shared Dreams," *Dream Network Bulletin,* 1/1, 1982, 1,6.

L = Involves at Least One Lucid Dream

L Faraday, A. *The Dream Game* (New York: Harper & Row, 1974), 331–336.

L Faraday, A. *Dream Power* (New York: Berkley, 1972), 303–305.

   FATE Magazine Editors. *Strange Fate* (New York: Paperback Library, 1965), 32–37.

   Fordor, N. *Between Two Worlds* (New York: PaperBack Library, 1964), 80.

   Fordor, N. *New Approaches to Dream Interpretation* (New Hyde Park, NY: University Books, 1951), 165–87.

L Fox, O. *Astral Projection* (New Hyde Park, NY: University Books, 1962), 47, 56–60.

L Fuller, C. and M. (Eds.). *The Strange and the Unknown* (New York: Coronet Communications, 1963), 9–12.

   Gaddis, V. H. "Romantic Dreams—Do They Ever Come True?" *Family Weekly*, 3/1/70, 14.

L Green, C. E. *Lucid Dreams* (Oxford, England: Institute of Psychophysical Research, 1968), 110.

   Hart, H., and E. B. "Visions and Apparitions Collectively and Reciprocally Perceived," Vol. 41, *Proceedings of the Society for Psychical Research* (New York: American Society for Psychical Research, 1932–1933), 234–240.

   Holzer, H. *The Psychic Side of Dreams* (St. Paul, MN: Llewellyn Pub., 1992), 190–191.

   Hunt, H. *The Multiplicity of Dreams* (New Haven: Yale University Press, 1989), 225.

   Jones, C. *From Parent to Child* (New York: Warner Books, 1989), 146, 155, 159, 162.

   Journal of the American Society for Psychical Research, 2, 39. As quoted in Stevens, W.O., *The Mystery of Dreams* (London: George Allen & Unwin, 1950), 225–228.

   Koch-Sheras, P. R., E. A. Hollier, and B. Jones. *Dream On* (Englewood Cliffs, NJ: Prentice-Hall, Inc., 1983), 143–144.

   Leek, S. *Telepathy, the "Respectable" Phenomenon* (New York: Macmillan, 1971), 85.

   Magallón, L. L. "Dear Dreamers," *American Psychic Magazine,* Summer 1992, 38–42.

   Magallón, L. L. "Dreams for the Family," *Dream Network Bulletin,* 5/5 (1985), 16.

   Magallón, L. L. "FATE Dream Telepathy Experiment Results," *FATE,* Jan. 1993, 82–85.

L Magallón, L. L. "Further Adventures with Willie," *The Coordinate Point,* III/3 (1987), 17–19.

L Magallón, L. L. "The Gift of Lucidity," *Dream Network Bulletin,* 5/2 (1985), 18.

L Magallón, L. L. "The Lucidity Project: An Experiment in Group Dreaming," *Dream Network Bulletin,* 4/5 (1985), 10–11.

L Magallón, L. L. "Mutual Lucid Dreaming," *Lucidity Letter,* 8/1 (1989), 74–76.

Magallón, L. L. "Report on the Lucidity Project Dream Telepathy Experiment," *Reality Change,* 6/2 (1986), 71–73.

Magallón, L. L. and Shor, B. "Shared Dreaming: Joining Together in Dreamtime," in Krippner, S. ed. *Dreamtime and Dreamwork* (Los Angeles: Tarcher, 1990), 252–253.

L Molfese, J. *My Adventures in Lucid Dreaming* (Ward, CO: Metaphysical Press, 1994), 11.

Mountainwing, H. I. "Dream Weekend," *Sundance Community Dream Journal,* 2/2, 266–272.

Payne, F. "Dream Walker," *Lucidity Letter,* 8/1 (1989), 31–33.

Perry, R. "Simultaneous Dreams that Influenced Our Lives," *DreamCraft,* 2/2 (1984), 8.

Proceedings of the Society for Psychical Research. As quoted in Stevens, W.O., *The Mystery of Dreams* (London: George Allen & Unwin, 1950), 221.

Quinn, A. and L. A. Selden. *Dreams, Secret Messages from Your Mind* (Tacoma, WA: Dream Research, 1981), 109.

Reed, H. "Dream America," *Sundance Community Dream Journal,* 1/1, 126–131.

Reed, H. "The A.R.E. Dream Research Project," *Sundance Community Dream Journal,* 1/1, 27–45.

Reed, H. "The Sundance Experiment, V: Subscribers' Dream About Sundance," *Sundance Community Dream Journal,* 3/1 (1979), 132–137.

Rhine, L. E. *The Invisible Picture* (Jefferson, NC: McFarland, 1981), 122; 124–125.

L Roberts, J. *Psychic Politics: An Aspect Psychology Book* (Englewood Cliffs, NJ: Prentice Hall, 1976), 209–221.

L Roberts, J. *Seth, Dreams, and Projection of Consciousness* (Walpole, NH: Stillpoint, 1986), 359–360.

L Russell, C. D. "Burt Reynolds Visits Three Members," *The Dream Explorer,* II/4, 11–14.

Russell, C. D. "Ruth's Dream," *The Dream Explorer,* II/3, 4–5.

Russell, C. D. "Tandem Group Explores the World of Dreams," *The Dream Explorer,* I/2, 1–2.

Ryback, D. *Dreams that Come True* (New York: Doubleday, 1988), 65–68; 70–71.

Schwarz, B. E. *A Psychiatrist Looks at ESP* (New York: New American Library, 1965), 124.

Shor, B. "The Promise of Shared Dreaming," *Gnosis*, 22 (1992), 39.

Sidgwick. "On the Evidence for Clairvoyance," *Proceedings of the Society for Psychical Research* 7, 41. As paraphrased in Joire, P. *Psychical and Supernormal Phenomena* (New York: Frederick A. Stokes, 1916), 147–148.

Sinclair, U. *Mental Radio* (Springfield, IL: Charles C. Thomas, 1930), 16. As paraphrased in Jones, C. *From Parent to Child* (New York: Warner Books, 1989), 162.

Smith, S. *Out of Body Experiences for the Millions* (New York: Dell, 1969), 51–2. As paraphrased in Jones, C. *From Parent to Child* (New York: Warner Books, 1989), 159.

Specht, P. "Dream Symbols," *DreamCraft*, 2/1 (1984), 6–7.

L Specht, P. "Shared Dreaming: Who Are We?," *Dream Network Bulletin*, 2/9 (1983), 6–7.

L Stevens, W. O. *The Mystery of Dreams* (London: George Allen & Unwin, 1950), 220–237.

Tart, C. T. *PSI Scientific Studies of the Psychic Realm* (New York: Dutton, 1977) 126–142.

Taub-Bynum, E. B. *The Family Unconscious* (Wheaton, IL: Theosophical Publishing House, 1984), 118.

Taub-Bynum, E. B. "PSI, the Shared Dreamscape, and the Family Unconscious," *Dream Network Bulletin*, 4/2, 1985, 2.

Taylor, J. *Dream Work* (Ramsey, NJ: Paulist Press, 1983), 92.

Time-Life Books, eds. *Dreams and Dreaming* (Alexandria, VA: Time-Life Books, 1990), 149–152.

Ullman, M., S. Krippner and A. Vaughan. *Dream Telepathy* (Jefferson, NC: McFarland, 1989), 12–14; 28–29, 225.

Ullman, M. "Psi Communication Through Dream Sharing," *Parapsychology Review*, 12/2, 5–7.

Ullman, M. and S. Krippner. *Dream Studies and Telepathy* (New York: Parapsychology Foundation, 1970), 12, 23–25.

Van de Castle, R. L. *Our Dreaming Mind* (New York: Ballantine Books, 1994), 411; 430–431.

Virtanen, L. *"That Must Have Been ESP!": An Examination of Psychic Experiences* (Bloomington, IN: Indiana University Press, 1990), 99, 103.

Von Grunebaum, G. E. and R. Caillois, *The Dream and Human Societies* (Berkeley, CA: University of California Press, 1966), 35.

Watkins, S. M. *Conversations with Seth, Vol. 2* (Englewood Cliffs, NJ: Prentice-Hall, 1981), 390–397.

Watkins, S. M. *Dreaming Myself, Dreaming a Town* (New York: Kendall Enterprises, 1989), 265–270.

Whitney, M. "Shared Dreams," *Night Vision*, III/2 (1992), 24–25.

Windsor, J. R. *Dreams and Healing* (New York: Berkley, 1987), 127, 130–133.

Woods, R. L. & H. B. Greenhouse. *The New World of Dreams* (New York: Macmillan, 1974), 97.

Yram. *Practical Astral Projection* (New York: Weiser, 1974).

APPENDIX II

❖

DREAM COMMUNITY RESOURCES

Association for the Study of Dreams
PO Box 1600
Vienna, VA 22183

Dream Network
1337 Powerhouse Lane #22
Moab, UT 84532

Dream Library and Archive
29 Truman Drive
Novato, CA 94947

NOTES

Chapter 2
Meeting: I'll See You in My Dreams

1. W. O. Stevens, *The Mystery of Dreams* (London: George Allen & Unwin, 1950), 230–231.
2. A. Faraday, *The Dream Game* (New York: Harper & Row, 1974), 331–332.
3. Time-Life Books, editors, *Dreams and Dreaming* (Alexandria, VA: Time-Life Books, 1990), 152.
4. P. Specht, "Shared Dreaming: Who Are We?," *Dream Network Bulletin*, 2/9 (1983), 6–7.
5. R. L. Woods, H. B. Greenhouse, *The New World of Dreams* (New York: MacMillan, 1974), 97.
6. L. Virtanen, *"That Must Have Been ESP!: An Examination of Psychic Experiences"* (Bloomington, IN: Indiana University Press, 1990), 103.
7. A. Faraday, *Dream Power* (New York: Berkley, 1972), 303–305.
8. C. E. Green, *Lucid Dreams* (Oxford, England: Institute of Psychophysical Research, 1968), 110.
9. S. M. Watkins, *Conversations with Seth, Vol. II* (Englewood Cliffs, NJ: Prentice-Hall, 1981), 390.

Chapter 3
Meshing: Take a Walk in My Moccasins

1. W. A. Salter, *Ghosts and Apparitions* (London, 1938). As quoted in R. de Becker, *The Understanding of Dreams* (New York: Hawthorn Books, 1968), 394–395.
2. J. Taylor, *Dream Work* (Ramsey, NJ: Paulist Press, 1983), 92.
3. B. E. Schwarz, *A Psychiatrist Looks at ESP* (New York: New American Library, 1965), 124.
4. C. Jones, *From Parent to Child* (New York: Warner Books, 1989), 162.
5. E. B. Bynum, *Families and the Interpretation of Dreams: Awakening the Intimate Web* (Binghamton, NY: Harrington Park Press, 1993), 98–99.

Chapter 4
Oh, the Stories I've Heard

1. D. Ryback, *Dreams that Come True* (New York: Doubleday, 1988), 66.

CHAPTER 5
Family Dreams

1. D. Ryback, *Dreams that Come True* (New York: Doubleday, 1988), 66–67.
2. Crowe, *The Night Side of Nature.* As quoted in P. Joire, *Psychical and Supernormal Phenomena* (New York: Frederick A. Stokes, 1916), 45–46.
3. D. Ryback, 65.
4. M. Whitney, "Shared Dreams," *Night Vision,* III/2, 24–25.

CHAPTER 6
Are We Psychic or Is It Memorex®?

1. S. Freud, *The Interpretation of Dreams* (London: George Allen & Unwin, 1961), 501.
2. My story also appeared in E. Bruce Bynam, *Families and the Interpretation of Dreams: Awakening the Intimate Web,* (Binghamton, NY: Harrington Park Press, 1993), 41–44.
3. J. Campbell, *The Portable Jung* (New York: Penguin Books, 1976), 505.

CHAPTER 7
Why Dream Together Deliberately?

1. J. Ehrenwald, *The ESP Experience* (New York: Basic Books, 1978), 281.
2. B. Shor, "Future Tech: Shared Dreaming," *Dream Network Bulletin,* 7/4, 19.
3. P. R. Koch-Sheras, E. A. Hollier, and B. Jones. *Dream On* (Englewood Cliffs, NJ: Prentice-Hall, 1983), 143–144.
4. L. Reneau, *The Waking Dreamer's Manual* (self-published, 1988), 162.
5. M. Ullman, "Psi Communication Through Dream Sharing," *Parapsychology Review,* 12/2, 5–6.
6. J. J. Donahoe, *Enigma* (Oakland, CA: Bench Press, 1979), 47.
7. S. LaBerge, *Lucid Dreaming* (Los Angeles: Jeremy P. Tarcher, 1985), 223.
8. P. Koch-Sheras, and E. A. Hollier, B. Jones. *Dream On* (Englewood Cliffs, NJ: Prentice-Hall, 1983), 143.
9. M. Mead, *Blackberry Winter: My Earlier Years* (New York: Morrow, 1972), 293.

CHAPTER 8
The Holistic Dream Universe

1. M. Talbot, *The Holographic Universe* (New York: HarperCollins, 1991), 285.

2. J. C. Pearce, *Exploring the Crack in the Cosmic Egg* (New York: Simon & Schuster, 1974), 123.

3. J. Mishlove, *Psi Development Systems* (New York: Ballantine Books, 1983), 332.

4. J. Mishlove, 330.

5. H. Reed, "Subscribers' Dreams," *Sundance Community Dream Journal*, 1/1, 139–140.

6. J. Campbell, *Dreams Beyond Dreaming* (Norfolk, VA: Donning, 1980), 97–100.

7. J. Mishlove, *Psi Development Systems* (New York: Ballantine Books, 1983), 325–326.

8. S. M. Watkins, *Conversations with Seth*, Vol. II (Englewood Cliffs, N.J.: Prentice-Hall, Inc., 1981), 396–397.

CHAPTER 9
Shared Dreaming: Intending to Meet

1. J. Campbell, "Beyond Dreaming," *Dream Craft*, 1/1, 2.

2. B. Shor, "The Promise of Shared Dreaming," *Gnosis*, No. 22 (Winter 1992), 39.

CHAPTER 12
Dreamwork and Decoding

1. S. LaBerge, and H. Rheingold. *Exploring the World of Lucid Dreaming* (New York: Ballantine Books, 1990), 238–239.

2. J. Morris. *The Dream Workbook* (Boston: Little, Brown, 1985), 158–160.

3. J. Morris, 81–89.

4. J. Morris, 160–165.

5. G. Delaney, *Living Your Dreams* (San Francisco: Harper & Row, 1979), 52–53.

6. R. Shohet, *Dream Sharing* (Wellingborough, England: Turnstone Press, 1985), 128–129.

7. W. Phillips, *Every Dreamer's Handbook* (New York: Kensington Publishing Group, 1996).

8. J. Morris, 45–46.

CHAPTER 18
Vote of the Dreaming Selves

1. H. Reed, "The A.R.E. Dream Research Project," *Sundance Community Dream Journal*, 1/1, 32.

2. L. E. Rhine, *PSI, What Is It?* (New York: Harper & Row, 1975), 151.
3. L. E. Rhine, 159.
4. J. Ehrenwald, *The ESP Experience* (New York: Basic Books, 1978), 282.

Chapter 19
Literal and Lucid

1. J. Molfese, *My Adventures in Lucid Dreaming* (Ward, CO: Metaphysical Press, 1994), 11.

BIBLIOGRAPHY

Bach, R. *The Bridge Across Forever*. New York: Morrow, 1984.

Barasch, M. "A Hitchhiker's Guide to Dreamland." *New Age Journal*. (Oct. 1983), 39–50.

Beebe, S. & J. T. Masterson. Communicating in Small Groups/Principles & Practice (Glenview, IL: Scott, Foresman & Co., 1986)

Bible. Douay-Challoner version: Daniel 2:1–2:49), 789–791.

Bruce, R. D. *Lacandon Dream Symbolism*. Mexico, D.F.: Ediciones Euroamericanas Klaus Thiele, 1979.

Buchman, D. D. *How to Make Your Dreams Work for You*. (New York: Scholastic, 1977.

Bynum, E. B. *Families and the Interpretation of Dreams: Awakening the Intimate Web*. Binghamton, NY: Harriton Park Press, 1993.

Campbell, J. "Beyond Dreaming." *Dream Craft*, 1/1, 1–2.

Campbell, J. *Dreams Beyond Dreaming*. Norfolk, VA: Donning, 1980.

Campbell, J. "Group Dreaming Research Report." *Dream Craft*, 2/2, 1, 3–4.

Campbell, J. *The Hero with a Thousand Faces*. Princeton, NJ: Princeton University Press, 1949.

Campbell, J. *The Portable Jung*. New York: Penguin Books, 1976.

Cardwell, M. "Dream Networking: Winter Solstice Dreaming Celebration." *Reality Change*, III/6, 1.

Cardwell, M. "The First World Dream." *Reality Change*, III/8, 1–2, 6.

Crisp, H. and T. Crisp. "Outline of a Nation." *Dream Network Bulletin*, 3/4, 8–10.

Crowe. *The Night Side of Nature*. As quoted in Joire, P. *Psychical and Supernormal Phenomena*. New York: Frederick A. Stokes, 1916.

de Becker, R. *The Understanding of Dreams*. New York: Hawthorn Books, 1968.

Dee, N. *The Dreamer's Workbook*. New York: Sterling, 1990.

Delaney, G. *Living Your Dreams*. San Francisco: Harper & Row, 1979.

Deutsh, M. and R. M. Krauss. *Theories in Social Psychology*. New York: Basic Books, 1965.

Donahoe, J. J. *Dream Reality*. Oakland, CA: Bench Press, 1974.

Donahoe, J. J. *Enigma*. Oakland, CA: Bench Press, 1979.

Eddins, A. W. "Anecdotes from the Brazos Bottoms." *Straight Texas*, XIII, Austin, TX: Texas Folk-Lore Society, 1937, 88–89. As quoted in Batkin, B., ed. *A Treasury of American Folklore*. New York: Crown, 1944.

Ehrenwald, J. *The ESP Experience.* New York: Basic Books, 1978.

Emery, M. R. "Programming the Precognitive Dream." *Dream Network Bulletin,* 8/3, 10.

Faraday, A. *The Dream Game.* New York: Harper & Row, 1974.

Faraday, A. *Dream Power.* New York: Berkley Publishing, 1972.

Fontana, D. *Dreamlife.* New York: Element Books, 1990.

Forbes, M. "Dream Teams: They rendezvous in their sleep as part of Poseidia experiment." *The Beacon,* August 25/26, 1982.

Fox, O. *Astral Projection.* New Hyde Park, NY: University Books, 1962.

Fregia, P. and J. Fregia. *Know Your Dreams, Know Your Self.* Brazoria, TX: OmniCenter, 1992.

Freud, S. *The Interpretation of Dreams.* London: George Allen & Unwin, 1961.

Gaddis, V. H. "Romantic Dreams—Do They Ever Come True?" *Family Weekly,* March 1, 1970, 14–15.

Garfield, P. *Creative Dreaming.* New York: Ballantine Books. 1974.

Garma, Á. *The Psychoanalysis of Dreams.* New York: Dell, 1966.

Geyer, N. "Dream Performance in Three Native American Rituals." *Sundance Community Dream Journal,* 2/1, 122–127.

Green, C. E. *Lucid Dreams.* Oxford, England: Institute of Psychophysical Research, 1968.

Hart, H. "Reciprocal Dreams." *Proceedings of the Society for Psychical Research,* 41, (1933), 234–240.

Hillman, D. J. "The Emergence of the Grassroots Dream Movement." In Krippner, S., ed. *Dreamtime and Dreamwork.* Los Angeles: Jeremy P. Tarcher, 1990.

Huyghe, P. "Group Dreaming." *Omni,* 6/3, 24.

Jung, C. G. *Dreams.* Princeton, NJ: Princeton University Press, 1974.

Keyes, S. "The Guild of Asaph." *Dream Craft,* 2/1, 1, 4–5.

Koch-Sheras, P. R., E. A. Hollier, and B. Jones. *Dream On.* Englewood Cliffs, NJ: Prentice-Hall, 1983.

Krajenke, R. W. "The Mt. Rushmore Full Moon Medicine Wheel Dream Quest." In Russo, R., ed. *Dreams Are Wiser than Men.* Berkeley, CA: North Atlantic Books, 1987.

LaBerge, S. and H. Rheingold. *Exploring the World of Lucid Dreaming.* New York: Ballantine Books, 1990.

LaBerge, S. *Lucid Dreaming.* Los Angeles: Jeremy P. Tarcher, 1985.

Levitan, L. and S. LaBerge. "The Stuff of Dreams." *Nightlight,* 6/1, 13.

Lindgren, H. C. *An Introduction to Social Psychology,* New York: Wiley, 1973.

Luce, G. G. and J. Segel. *Sleep.* New York: Lancer Books, 1967.

Magallón, L. L. "Back to Wonderland: Metamorphous of the Inner City." *Reality Change,* Fall 1994, 28–29.

Magallón, L. L. "Follow the Flying Heroes," self-published, 1990.

Magallón, L. L. "Interview with Henry Reed." *Dream Network Bulletin,* 8/ 4–6, 34–36.

Magallón, L. L. "The Lucidity Project: An Experiment in Group Dreaming." *Dream Network Bulletin,* 4/5, 10–11.

Magallón, L. L. "Mutual Dreaming." *Dream Network Bulletin,* 8/3, 14–15, 19.

Magallón, L. L. "Mutual Lucid Dreaming." *Lucidity Letter,* 8/1, 74–76.

Magallón, L. L. "Report on the Lucidity Project Dream Telepathy Experiment." *Reality Change,* 6/2, 71–73.

Magallón, L. L. "Sociometric Patterns of Shared Dreaming." Paper presented at 9th Annual ASD Conference, Santa Cruz, CA.

Magallón, L. L. "Telepathic and Group Dreaming: Some Considerations of Process and Analysis." Paper presented at 5th Annual ASD Conference, Santa Cruz, CA.

Magallón, L. L. and B. Shor. "Shared Dreaming: Joining Together in Dreamtime." In Krippner, S., ed. *Dreamtime and Dreamwork.* Los Angeles: Tarcher, 1990.

Mead, M. *Blackberry Winter: My Earlier Years.* New York: Morrow, 1972.

Mishlove, J. *Psi Development Systems.* New York: Ballantine Books, 1983.

Molfese, J. *My Adventures in Lucid Dreaming.* Ward, CO: Metaphysical Press, 1994.

Montagu, A. & F. W. Matson. *The Human Connection* (New York: McGraw-Hill, 1970).

Morris, J. *The Dream Workbook.* Boston: Little, Brown, 1985.

Morse, W. C. & G. M. Wingo. *Psychology and Teaching* (Scott, Foresman & Co., 1969).

Mountainwing, H. I. "Dream Weekend." *Sundance Community Dream Journal,* 2/2, 266–272.

Oricchio, M. "How to Win the Lottery." *San Jose Mercury News,* 10/25/88, 1D–2D.

Pearce, J. C. *Exploring the Crack in the Cosmic Egg.* New York: Simon & Schuster, 1974.

Phillips, W. *Every Dreamer's Handbook.* New York: Kensington Publishing Group, 1996.

Proceedings of the Society for Psychical Research. As quoted in Stevens, W. O. *The Mystery of Dreams.* London: George Allen & Unwin, 1950.

Quinn, A. and L. A. Sheldon. *Dreams, Secret Messages from Your Mind.* Tacoma, WA: Dream Research, 1981.

Reed, H. "The A.R.E. Dream Research Project." *Sundance Community Dream Journal,* 1/1, 32.

Reed, H. *Awakening Your Psychic Powers.* San Francisco: Harper & Row, 1988.

Reed, H. "Dream America." *Sundance Community Dream Journal,* 1/1, 126–131.

Reed, H. "Dreaming for Your Neighbor." *The Omni WholeMind Newsletter,* 1/11, 7.

Reed, H. "Learning to Meet in Dreams." *Venture Inward,* Nov.–Dec. 1988, 6–7.

Reed, H. "Subscribers' Dreams." *Sundance Community Dream Journal,* 1/1, 132–140.

Reed, H. "Subscribers' Dreams." *Sundance Community Dream Journal,* 1/2, 269–277.

Reed, H. "Subscribers' Dreams." *Sundance Community Dream Journal,* 2/1, 130–138.

Reed, H. "Subscribers' Dreams About Our Journal." *Sundance Community Dream Journal,* 2/2, 274–280.

Reed, H. "Subscribers' Dreams About *Sundance.*" *Sundance Community Dream Journal,* 3/2, 271–277.

Reed, H. "The Sundance Experiment." *Sundance Community Dream Journal,* 1/1, 108–123.

Reed, H. "The Sundance Experiment: II. Images of the Motif." *Sundance Community Dream Journal,* 1/2, 258–268.

Reed, H. "The Sundance Experiment: IV. Dreaming Together." *Sundance Community Dream Journal,* 2/2, 264.

Reed, H. "The Sundance Experiment: VI. Dreaming Together." *Sundance Community Dream Journal,* 3/2, 265–270.

Reed, H. and R. L. Van de Castle, with L.L. Magallón. "The Dream Helper Ceremony." *Dream Network Journal,* 11/3, 16–8; 25.

Reneau, L. *The Waking Dreamer's Manuel.* Self-published, 1988.

Rhine, L. E. *PSI, What Is It?* New York: Harper & Row, 1975.

Roberts. J., *Psychic Politics: An Aspect Psychology Book.* Englewood Cliffs, NJ: Prentice Hall, 1976.

Roberts, J. *Seth, Dreams, and Projection of Consciousness.* Walpole, NH: Stillpoint, 1986.

Roberts, J. *The Unknown Reality, Vol. 1.* Englewood Cliffs, NJ: Prentice-Hall, 1977.

Rogo, D. S. *Leaving the Body.* Englewood Cliffs, NJ: Prentice-Hall, 1983.

Ryback, D. *Dreams that Come True.* New York: Doubleday, 1988.

Salter, W. A. *Ghosts and Apparitions.* London, 1938. As quoted in de Becker, R. *The Understanding of Dreams.* New York: Hawthorn Books, 1968.

Schein, E. H. *Process Consultation: Its Role in Organization Development* (Reading, MA: Addison-Wesley Pub. Co., 1969).

Schmeidler, G. *Parapsychology and Psychology: Matches and Mistakes.* Jefferson, NC: McFarland, 1988.

Schrage, M. *Shared Minds.* New York: Random House, 1990.

Schwarz, B. E. *Parent-Child Telepathy.* New York: Garrett Publications, 1971.

Schwarz, B. E. *A Psychiatrist Looks at ESP.* New York: New American Library, 1965.

Shohet, R. *Dream Sharing.* Wellingborough, England: Turnstone Press, 1985.

Shor, B. "Dreaming Together." *The Omni WholeMind Newsletter,* 1/11, 7–8.

Shor, B. "Future Tech: Shared Dreaming." *Dream Network Bulletin,* 7/4, 19.

Shor, B. "The Promise of Shared Dreaming." *Gnosis,* No. 22, (Winter 1992), 36–42.

Shor, B. "Shared Dreaming." *Dream Network Bulletin,* 7/1, 14–15.

Shor, B. *Shared Dreaming.* Self-published, 1987.

Sidgwick, "On the Evidence for Clairvoyance." *Proceedings of the Society for Psychical Research,* 7, 41. As paraphrased in Joire. P. *Psychical and Supernormal Phenomena.* New York: Frederick A. Stokes, 1916.

Slate, J. H. *Psychic Phenomena.* Jefferson, NC: McFarland, 1988.

Smith, K. "Dream Consulting: A Pilot Project with a California Corporation." *Dream Network Bulletin,* 6/1, 14–17.

Soal, S. G. "The Present Status of Telepathy." In Gudas, F. ed. *Extrasensory Perception.* New York: Scribner, 1961.

Specht, P. "Dreaming with Peggy Specht." In Talvila, E., ed. *Inner Life & Toronto Dimensions.* 1987.

Specht, P. "Shared Dreaming: Who Are We?" *Dream Network Bulletin,* 2/9.

Stevens, W. O. *The Mystery of Dreams.* London: George Allen & Unwin, 1950.

Talbot. M. *The Holographic Universe.* New York: HarperCollins, 1991.

Targ, R. and K. Harary. *The Mind Race.* New York: Villard Books. 1984.

Tart, C. T. *Altered States of Consciousness.* San Francisco: HarperCollins, 1990.

Taub-Bynum, E. B. *The Family Unconscious.* Wheaton, IL: Theosophical Publishing House, 1984.

Taylor, J. *Dream Work.* Ramsey, NJ: Paulist Press, 1983.

Thurston, M. A. *An Investigation of Behavior and Personality Correlates of Psi Incorporating a Humanistic Research Approach.* Unpublished doctoral dissertation, 1978.

Thurston, M. A. *How to Interpret Your Dreams.* Virginia Beach, VA: ARE Press, 1978.

Ullman, M. "Dream, Metaphor, and PSI." In White, R. A. and R. S. Broughton, eds. *Research in Parapsychology.* Metuchen, NJ: Scarecrow Press, 1984.

Ullman, M. "Psi Communication Through Dream Sharing." *Parapsychology Review* New York: Parapsychology Foundation, 12, 2.

Ullman, M. "The World of Psychic Phenomena as I Came to Know It." In Piklington, R., ed. *Men and Women of Parapsychology: Personal Reflections.* Jefferson, NC: McFarland, 1987.

Ullman, M. and S. Krippner. *Dream Studies & Telepathy, An Experimental Approach.* New York: Parapsychology Foundation, 1970.

Ullman, M., S. Krippner, and A. Vaughan. *Dream Telepathy.* Jefferson, NC: McFarland, 1989.

Ullman M. and N. Zimmerman. *Working with Dreams.* New York: Dell, 1979.

Upton, C. "Dream Bridge Complete." *Dream Network Bulletin,* 7/6. 5.

Upton, C. *The Harmonic Convergence Book of Dreams.* Self-published, 1991.

Upton, C. "U.S.-Soviet Dream Bridge." *Dream Network Bulletin,* 7/3, 3.

Van de Castle, R. L. *Our Dreaming Mind.* New York: Ballantine Books, 1994.

Van de Castle, R. L. "Sleep and Dreams." In Wolman, B. ed. *Handbook of Parapsychology.* New York: Van Nostrand Reinhold, 1977.

Vaughan, A. *The Power of Positive Prophecy.* London: Aquarian Press, 1991.

Virtanen, L. *"That Must Have Been ESP!": An Examination of Psychic Experiences.* Bloomington, IN: Indiana University Press, 1990.

Von Grunebaum, G. E. & Caillois, R. *The Dream and Human Societies.* Berkeley, CA: University of California Press, 1966.

Watkins, S. M. *Conversations with Seth, Vol. 1.* Englewood Cliffs, NJ: Prentice-Hall, 1980.

Watkins, S. M. *Conversations with Seth, Vol. 2.* Englewood Cliffs, NJ: Prentice Hall, 1981.

Watkins, S. M. *Dreaming Myself, Dreaming a Town.* New York: Kendall Enterprises, 1989.

Whitney, M. "Shared Dreams." *Night Vision,* III/2, 24–25.

Windsor, J. R. *Dreams & Healing.* New York: Berkeley Publishing Group, 1987.

Woods, R. L. & H. B. Greenhouse. *The New World of Dreams.* New York: MacMillan, 1974.

Zweig, C. "See you in my dreams' test works/Senoi dreamwork now in question," *Brain/Mind Bulletin,* 10/1 (Oct. 1984), 3.

INDEX

second project, 117–19
third project, 119–21
Dream Train, 112
Dream Training Institute, 147–48
dreamwork
    defined, 169–70
    See also dream interpretation
drop-out, in shared dreaming
        group, 218–19
drugs, 141
drumming, 141

echo dreams, 191–92
Egyptians, 138, 169
Ehrenwald, Jan, 283
Eisenbud, Jule, 82, 83–84
Elrod, Mitch, 76
Emery, Marcia Rose, 82
emphatic viewpoint, 25
encapsulation, of day residue,
        264–68
energy shields, 142
Engorn, Rob, 272–73
environmental effect, 262–64,
        279–81
ESP
    ability, 100, 102
    creativity and, 283
    explanation for mutual dreams,
        72–76
    as field effect, 82
    See also holistic dream universe;
        psychic dreams
experimenter effect, 102
extrasensory perception. *See* ESP

facilitators, 146
falling, dreams of, 64–65
false awakening, 20, 209
family dreams, 46–58, 76–77, 108
    day residue and, 63–66, 74, 75
    discovering, 47–48, 61–62
    lucid, 65–66, 77

meeting dreams, 48–49
meshing dreams, 49–50
nightmares, 256–59
programmed dreaming, 68–69
psychic, 62–63, 72–76, 77
psychological history and,
        66–67
response dreaming, 69–71
sexual intimacy in, 50–58
in shared dreaming group,
        205–06
synchronicity and, 71–72
Faraday, Ann, 20, 178–79
fasting, 141
fiction, meeting dream in, 16–17
Firebird Rising, 212
flying dreams, 204, 256–59, 262,
        269–74, 276–77, 289–92
Fontana, David, 137
Fossey, Dian, 95
Fox, Oliver, 97, 295
Freud, Sigmund, on day residue,
        63–64
Full Moon Dream Conference, 89

Gate of Horn, 89, 147
Gates, 82
Goodall, Jane, 95
Greatest American Hero, The, 269–70
Greeks, 138, 140, 169
Green, Celia, 21
Gregory, Jill, 210, 211, 212, 265–67,
        270–72
Grosso, Michael, 102
group dreaming
    advantages of, 80–81
    conflict diagnosis and resolution
        in, 83–84, 260–61
    defined, 80
    field approach to, 94–95
    group issues and, 84–86
    information gathering in, 81–82